Underdeveloping the Amazon

Underdeveloping the Amazon

Extraction, Unequal Exchange,
and the Failure of the Modern State

Stephen G. Bunker

University of Illinois Press   *Urbana and Chicago*

Library of Congress Cataloging in Publication Data

Bunker, Stephen G., 1944-
  Underdeveloping the Amazon.

  Bibliography: p.
  Includes index.
  1. Amazon River Region—Economic conditions.
2. Amazon River Region—Economic policy.   3. Agricultural colonies—Amazon River Region.   4. Rural
development projects—Amazon River Region.   I. Title.
HC188.A5B86   1984   338.981′1   83-18197
ISBN 0-252-01121-X (alk. paper)

To the Great Cayman

Contents

Acknowledgments

More people than I can name here have helped me write this book. The contributions of peasants and government agents in the Amazon and of students and colleagues at the Núcleo de Altos Estudos Amazônicos in Bélem are, I hope, clear in the text. Students and colleagues at the University of Illinois have helped me enormously with their questions, criticisms, suggestions, and encouragement.

Many of the ideas in this book were first worked out in journal articles. I owe a great debt to the editors and anonymous reviewers of the *American Journal of Sociology* (1984), the *Latin American Research Review* (1983), the *Journal of Developing Areas* (1982), and *Human Organization* (1983) for insisting on greater clarity and for asking questions that were impossible to answer in article form. Harvey Choldin, Robert Schoen, Werner Baer, Charles Bergquist, Joe Foweraker, Marianne Schmink, Paul Drake, Joseph Love, and Donald Lathrap gave me valuable suggestions after reading these articles.

Jane Adams assisted me in numerous ways, most important by listening and talking as I tried to decide how I would organize and present different parts of the argument and as I geared up to start writing. My parents, Robert and Priscilla Bunker, read some of the early chapters and provided a haven with good company, sound criticism, and a fine view of northern New Mexico mountains while I pulled the final chapters together.

Joan Huber and Michael Gottfredson read the entire first draft. They, and anonymous reviewers for the University of Illinois Press, gave me valuable assistance in reworking it. Elizabeth Dulany, managing editor at the Press, helped me focus their suggestions for rewriting and answered my many nervous queries with great patience and good humor. Susan Patterson's skillful editorial work showed me numerous ways to tighten my writing. Sheila Welch and Margaret Quinn typed more drafts and fixed more mistakes than I care to admit. Their sympathy and cooperation have been extraordinary. Linna McDade helped us through the mysteries and quirks of electronic word processing and almost managed to convince me that the machines were not really malevolent.

Linda Seligmann listened, talked, read, edited, corrected, and read some more, and encouraged and helped me in many important ways as I did final revisions, and then more revisions. Her sharp critical sense and her fine feeling for words and ideas helped me make clearer in my head and on paper what I was trying to say. It is a tribute to her firm support through a difficult time that I was still enough of a person for her to be willing to marry me.

Chacon, New Mexico
November 1983

Glossary of Acronyms and Abbreviations

BASA Banco da Amazônia, S.A. (Bank of the Amazon).

BNCC Banco National de Crédito Cooperativo (National Bank for Cooperative Credit) makes loans to cooperative societies both for their own use and for secondary loans to members.

CFP Commissão de Financiamento de Producão (Commission for Financing Production), an "autarquia" under the Ministry of Agriculture, determines the minimum prices to be paid for particular crops and controls the funding for this program.

CIBRAZEM Companhia Brasileira de Armazenagem (Brazilian Warehouse Company), a public company subordinate to the Ministry of Agriculture, maintains a network of warehouses in areas where those provided by large enterprise are insufficient.

CIRA Cooperativa Integrada de Reforma Agrária (Integrared Cooperative for Agrarian Reform).

DNER Departmento Nacional de Estradas e Rodovias (The National Department of Roads and Highways).

EMATER Empresa de Assistência Técnica e Extensão Rural (Technical Assistance and Rural Extension Enterprise) is the state agency of a national public company, EMBRATER; its projects include technical assistance for agriculture, agricultural cooperatives, and the preparation of projects for crop loans.

FUNAI Fundação Nacional do Indio (The National Indian Foundation) has tutelary powers over all Indian groups and controls their reservations.

IBDF Instituto Brasileiro para a Defesa da Floresta (The Brazilian Institute for the Defense of the Forest) administers forest reserves and is supposed to supervise all forest clearance in areas of federal jurisdiction.

INCRA Instituto Nacional de Colonização e Reforma Agrária (National Institute for Colonization and Agrarian Reform) is the normative agency for surveying and titling land and for the registration and supervision of all agricultural cooperatives and for federal projects of colonization.

PDA   Plano de Desenvolvimento da Amazônia (Plan for the Development of Amazônia) I (1972) and II (1975).

PF   Projeto Fundiário (Land Project), the offices responsible for surveying and selling lands under INCRA jurisdiction.

PIC   Projeto Integrado de Colonização (Integrated Colonization Project).

PIN   Programa de Integração Nacional (National Program for Integration) included the highway building programs in the Amazon 1970-74.

POLAMAZONIA   A program aimed at developing sixteen "growth poles" in the Amazon. It replaced PIN.

RADAM   Radar na Amazônia (Radar in Amazônia).

SAGRI   The State's Secretaria de Agricultura (Secretariat of Agriculture) is involved in extension work and in colonization of state lands.

SUDAM   Superintendência do Desenvolvimento da Amazônia (Superintendency for the Development of Amazonia), the major planning, coordinating, and executing agency for the Amazon, provides limited resources for various of these programs. It is funded in turn by a variety of other federal projects. Its major concerns are with fiscal incentives for large industrial, mining, and agricultural enterprises.

Glossary of Words and Phrases in Portuguese Used in the Text

Aviador.   Literally, supplier. In the Amazon, an intermediary who supplies rural clients with basic production and subsistence goods at the beginning of a season and against eventual payment in kind.

Aviamento.   The system of exchange in which the aviador participates, typically involving multiple intermediaries and long chains of debt.

Caboclo.   General term for members of the rural lower class in the Amazon. They typically combine horticulture, extraction, hunting, and fishing in varying proportions.

Cartório de registro.   Land registry office that operates at the level of the município. Offices are owned by individuals who are licensed by the local states and who charge for each title registry.

Convênio.   A contractual arrangement between two or more public agencies, usually involving the transfer of funds to carry out particular programs.

Discriminatória.   A procedure that INCRA was required to follow to determine existing claims to and uses of land prior to surveying or deeding any area under its control.

Indústria da posse.   The practice of occupying land known to belong to a large enterprise or to a public agency to claim indemnification for improvements on the land.

Licença de ocupação.   An INCRA document that authorized and protected occupancy of land while a definitive title was pending.

Latifúndio.   A large tract of privately owned land, often including large unused areas.

Minifúndio.   A small tract of land used for agriculture but too small to sustain the family that owns it.

Minifundização.   Progressive fragmentation of small land holdings through inheritance and sale.

Município.   Subunits of the local states. In the Amazon most município seats were cities along the river banks, but the areas of each município extended back through miles of sparsely settled terra firme.

Seringal. Rubber-producing area owned, leased, or appropriated by a single individual; refers to both wild and cultivated stands of rubber trees.

Seringalista. Owner, lessee, or appropriator of a seringal.

Terra firme. Lowland forest not subject to annual flooding, characterized by rapid nutrient cycles which draw primarily on plant litter rather than on the generally poor soils.

Várzea. Flood plain characterized by highly fertile and friable soils renewed by annual flooding and sediment deposits.

Underdeveloping the Amazon

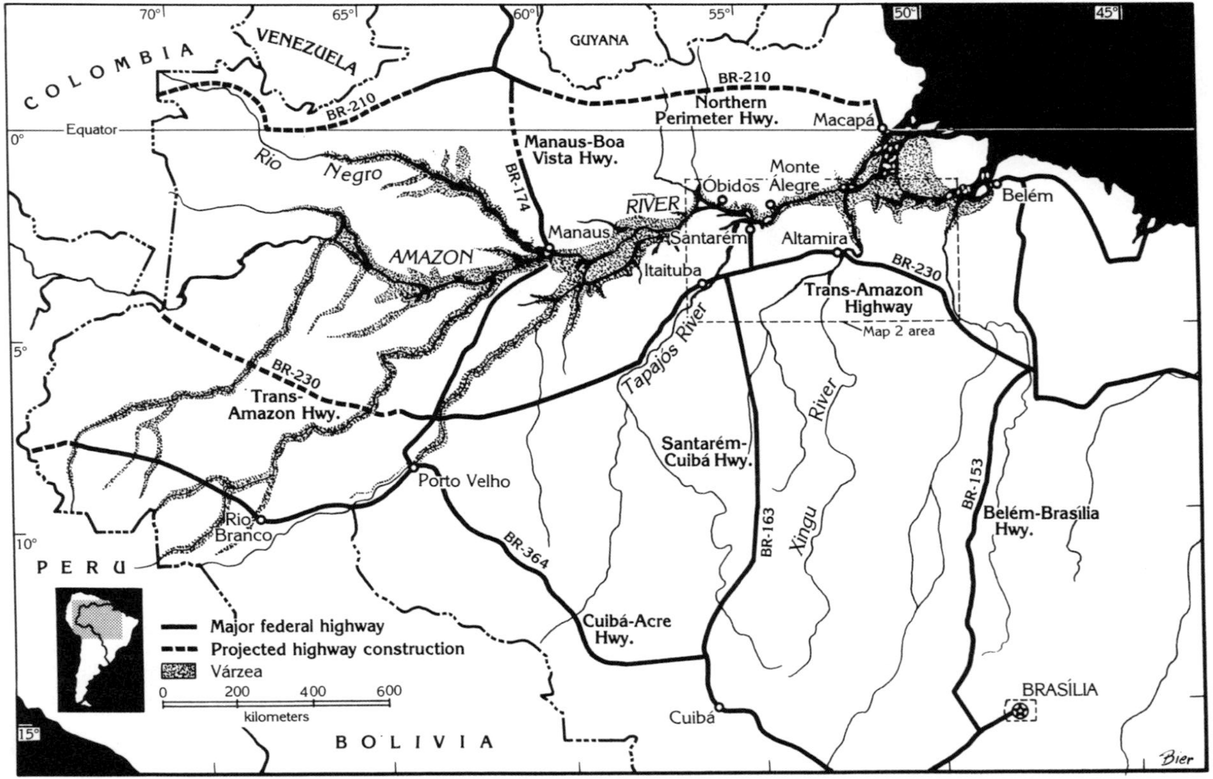

Map 1. AMAZÔNIA.

Introduction

Three months after arriving in Belém, Pará, the Amazon's largest and easternmost city, I took a trip around the entire Brazilian portion of that enormous river basin. What I saw on that trip struck me then as strange and wonderful. Seven years later, after writing most of this book about the ways that 350 years of different extractive economies had briefly enriched various dominant classes but progressively impoverished the entire region and about the incapacities of the modern national state to halt the disruption of human community and the natural environment there, I realized how much of what I saw in those eight days had foreshadowed what I was to learn about the region.

I had been sent with a Brazilian colleague, Paulo Cal, to interview candidates for the graduate program in regional planning in the university which had hired me. We flew north to Macapá directly across the Amazon's delta from Belém. Several great rivers converge here around the island of Marajó, but knowing this did not diminish the impact of having to fly for fifty minutes to get from one side of the delta to the other.

After completing our work in Macapá, we were driven twenty minutes to the Port of Santana, past the residential compounds of ICOMI, a company which had been mining and exporting bauxite in Amapá Territory for almost twenty years. The gleaming suburban homogeneity of the solidly maintained and obviously comfortable company town contrasted sharply with the hodgepodge of weather-beaten structures and dusty roads of Macapá. That Macapá is the territorial capital made the contrast even more striking. The single-purpose rail line which carried the ore from the inland mine to the port, the enormous machinery which loaded it, the great black slag heap which had built up over the years, and the fields and barns which the company had made for its cattle ranch all formed a strange and incongruous break in the tropical landscape. ICOMI's activities, however, were the sole basis for Amapá's rapid population growth and relative prosperity. I heard several people say that the bauxite would be finished soon, and the territory would be left with nothing except the hole.

From Macapá, we flew to Manaus in the state of Amazonas, much of the way along the main river and over the huge flood plains it forms. From the air I could see the multiple channels and levees which the river had formed in its meanders, discernible now in long lines of vegetation in the seasonal lakes. I watched the long stretches where clear water rivers, which drain the nutrient-poor soils to the south, and the black water rivers, which drain the even poorer soils to the north, flow into the brown waters with the heavier loads of Andean soils. Different colors of water run side by side for miles before finally mingling.

Though the city of Belém is both larger and politically more prominent, Manaus's ultramodern airport was far larger and much more efficient at handling passengers and baggage. Manaus had been declared a duty free zone eighteen years before in an attempt to stimulate industry and foreign investment there; Brazilian tourists flocked there to buy imported goods. The recently completed airport was but one of the ways the city was accommodating, and profiting from, the influx of travelers. The sophisticated design and expensive construction had not been sufficient, however, to prevent a large bull from wandering onto the runway and doing extensive damage to a jet which was taxiing in after a flight from Rio de Janeiro just before we arrived.

As in Macapá most of the people we saw, and most of the people we interviewed, worked in various government agencies for social or economic development. We conducted some of the interviews in the huge concrete headquarters of SUFRAMA, the Superintendency for the Free Zone of Manaus. I was told that the costs of this structure, as of the many others which the free trade boom had created, had been greatly increased by the need to import all cement from Belém, a thousand miles downriver. Various entrepreneurs were awaiting approval of their proposals to build a cement factory with government subsidies and tax credits.

Leaving Manaus was more difficult than arriving there. We had to go through a reverse customs search, designed to enforce the limits on the value of duty free goods which could be taken into the rest of Brazil. We finally set off for Pôrto Velho, this time in a prop-jet imported from Japan. I was told that the airline of the state of São Paulo had bought a number of these planes for their run between the two major Brazilian cities, but that they were not capable of the steep banking necessary to avoid the mountains behind Rio de Janeiro. After two had sideslipped into the Bay of Guanabara, the rest of the fleet was consigned to the much flatter Amazon.

Only one of the two propellers was still turning as we arrived in Pôrto Velho's small airport. We waited there for three hours while a mechanic was flown in from Manaus and then continued on to Guajará Mirím, a small town on the Bolivian border. Here we landed on the town's main road, kicking up a wall of mud high enough to obscure the houses from view. We waited again while the mechanic dismantled the propeller housings to clean out the mud and grass which the jets had sucked in. I asked why the airline didn't use a simple propeller plane for landing in these conditions. I was told that such primitive craft were not appropriate for regular runs by a major airline between the capital cities of Brazilian states and territories.

We finally flew on to Rio Branco, the capital of the new state of Acre. Acre was seized from the Bolivians by Brazilian immigrants at the height of the rubber boom in the last century and was connected to the rest of Brazil by road only in the 1970s. It was now suffering a second invasion, this time by wealthy entrepreneurs from the south of Brazil who were buying up or simply laying claim to the old rubber estates and turning them into cattle pastures. The small holders who tapped rubber for a cash supplement to their subsistence activities were resisting expulsion more tenaciously than were peasants in other areas of the Amazon, and the rural violence which I had already heard about around Belém was much more palpable in Acre.

We had flown thousands of miles over water and forest, with only the sparsest signs of human habitation between the major towns. At the farthest point in our journey, Rio Branco, we were 3,000 miles from Belém and the Amazon's delta, and only a few hundred from the Andes; but we were still in lowland jungle, only 600 feet above sea level. Acre's old river connections to Belém still weighed more heavily than the newer and shorter roads to the south. Discussions of politics centered on the nationally controlled regional development agencies headquartered in Belém and on the struggles between Pará's major political figures. Rio Branco sports fans were divided by their allegiances to different Belém soccer clubs. Many of the bureaucrats we met had been educated in Belém.

The predominance of government officials as fellow travelers, acquaintances, and graduate program candidates continued through our stop in Mato Grosso. I was fortunate to have Paulo as a traveling companion. He generously included me in meetings with his many friends and acquaintances. Their conversations gave me my first understanding of how dominant the public agencies were in the region's politics and of how closely acquainted their common origins and their extensive travel made the public agents. I also started to get some feeling for the ties of cooperation and hostility between the agencies of the increasingly powerful national state and the agencies of the increasingly dependent local states. I knew enough by the time we returned to Belém to recognize the acronyms of the government agencies which occupied so many of the buildings we passed on the way in from the airport, and I understood more of what SUDAM, the Superintendency for the Development of the Amazon, which occupied the largest and newest of the buildings we passed, was supposed to be accomplishing.

The predominance of government activities and expenditures and their extravagance in proportion to their results were first conveyed to me by our own very expensive trip. Several of the prospective candidates had not known we were coming, and several other candidates withdrew because they had not been able to arrange for scholarships to complement the full government salary they hoped to receive while studying. Of all the candidates we interviewed, two were finally admitted to the program. Most of the remaining students came from Belém, trained as undergraduates in its older, better university.

Manaus and the Japanese prop-jet meld into a single symbol as I remember them. Both represent incongruous and impractical modernities pushed into the Amazon by a distant, rapidly industrializing society in the central and southern regions of Brazil. Manaus, a decaying city which had blossomed during the ill-fated rubber boom, was intended by government fiat to become an industrial city. Tariff and tax holidays, however, could not abolish its dependence on air and river travel and its distance from other manufacturing centers. Its prosperity depended completely on the artificial effects of fiscal regulation. Its costs were magnified by the need to import even basic building materials and by the fuel spent in carrying Brazilian consumers so far into the jungle. The airplane, a sophisticated but badly designed instrument, totally inappropriate for flying in the jungle, was passed on to the Amazon by the same dominant industrial society which ran the airlines. Modern and very expensive, neither the airplane nor the Manaus free trade zone functioned very well. Both were reflexes of Brazil's commercial and technological dependence on foreign capital; the airplane, the industries, and the consumer goods were all imported from more industrialized countries, and all of them contributed to Brazil's rapidly growing foreign debt. The ephemeral prosperity which ICOMI brought to Amapá and the violence with which entrepreneurs from the south turned land which supported people in Acre into land which supported cattle were only symptoms of the ways that government support for large-scale and quickly profitable enterprise was making large portions of the Amazon uninhabitable.

Between Field and City

I took the job in Belém in 1975, after teaching and doing research on rural development programs in East Africa and Central America. In Uganda I had studied the interplay between the modern bureaucratic organizations of the state, a large coffee-marketing cooperative, and the lineage and political organizations of its members. As I analyzed those data, I increasingly felt that I would not really understand rural development politics in Uganda until I could compare them with rural development programs in a country where land tenure and the participation in export economies were far less evenly distributed. In Guatemala I headed a group research project on a variety of small holders' cooperatives promoted by the national government. I went on to Brazil three years later with some notions of how access to resources and degree of participation in national export economies affected the ability of peasants to bargain with the state in two small, poor, primarily agrarian countries. I was eager to look at some of the same processes in a larger, wealthier, and more industrial country.

The Núcleo de Altos Estudos Amazônicos (NAEA) of the Federal University of Pará provided an excellent base for this. NAEA's multidisciplinary faculty combined academic research with development planning and administration in government agencies. Visiting faculty with similar experience came from other parts of Brazil. Courses were geared to the needs of its primary clientele, students on paid leave from administrative and planning jobs in development agencies. Many of the faculty were also engaged in research and consulting commissioned by the various agencies of state and national governments. Teaching schedules were adjusted as much as possible to accommodate the requirements of their research.

NAEA's coordinator, José Marcelino Monteiro da Costa, gave me time and encouragement to develop a proposal to study a program of small farm cooperatives being organized by various agencies. This research was eventually funded by the Federal University, by IPEA/INPES in Rio de Janeiro, and by NAEA itself. In both the elaboration of the proposal and the early stages of the research, I was helped enormously by NAEA students who had worked in the agencies involved, by other employees of the various development agencies, and especially by the two cooperative technicians who had been recruited from the south of Brazil to coordinate the program. Access to their files and permission to accompany them in planning meetings and on field trips gave me information and contacts which were invaluable in later field work.

My original proposal had focused on the relations between modern bureaucratic organizations and the rural communities with which they worked. As my research progressed, however, I found it necessary to examine the complex and unbalanced relations between the various government agencies which participated in the cooperative development program. I found that these relations could only be understood by examining the other programs and activities, as well as the organization and funding, of the individual agencies. I returned to Belém to continue the courses I was teaching, and spent much of the time there following up clues from my field work about agency organization. NAEA's location and composition were extremely advantageous, as all of the agencies with which I was concerned had their regional headquarters in Belém.

During the first phase of field work I had seen how the riverine topography shaped agricultural, commercial, and transport sytems. The trade relations between the uplands and the more fertile annual flood plain and between the smaller flood plain towns and the larger cities of Santarém and Belém coordinated and complemented economic activities in several different ecological zones. The river systems, especially around Santarém, provided both resource bases and transport networks. Hierarchical chains of commercial intermediaries roughly approximated the hierarchy of the tributary rivers. The major trading centers on the main course of the Amazon supplied and were supplied by communities of descending size and economic importance as distance up the tributaries increased. Cooperatives there aimed at breaking the monopoly of this river-based trading network.

Two of the cooperatives included in the program, however, were far from the traditional riverine settlements. They were part of the official colonization projects established along the newly opened Transamazon Highway, which paralleled the main river some 100 miles inland. I had left these till last, as they were the least easily accessible.

I had been intrigued by the riverine communities, by their use of different ecological zones, and by the beauty and grandeur of the enormous river; but these upland colonization projects attracted me much more strongly. The audacity and raw courage of the landless peasants who had responded to the government's offer of land, the difficulties of clearing and cultivating in an environment completely unfamiliar to most of them, the stark contrast between the thin strip of cleared land along the highway, seen from the tops of long slopes and sharp breaks which the dense forest canopy hid from the air, and the towering forest behind it, all exhilirated and deeply troubled me. The impossible complexities which the various agencies assigned to establish modern agricultural communities in these remote areas faced so challenged explanation, and so excited me, that I knew these projects must be the primary focus of my study. The entire undertaking seemed preposterous and heroic. The tiny scale of the human energies moving machetes and small power saws to clear enough jungle for cropping both inspired and appalled me. The tall, valuable trees, standing dead and bleached after burning, confused me with the visual beauty of such waste and destruction. Soils were too poor, markets were too distant, the roads too difficult—a morass of mud or a choking cloud of dust—to allow for the coordination and communication which official plans called for. The government agents were too few, too little trained, and sadly lacking in equipment and vehicles. The peasant colonists were too poor to achieve what they were attempting. The government had already abandoned its original plans and was attempting to "emancipate" the colonization projects from direct supervision as soon as possible. Government agents and colonists alike talked of unending problems, but their very persistence seemed to bespeak an impossible optimism. Some, through luck, astute choices, hard work, or chicanery, had in fact become quite wealthy, but these were a small portion of the original colonists.

The two cooperatives were in terrible shape. Founded in lightning field visits by agents from Belém to satisfy legal requirements for agricultural colonization, both were in serious economic difficulties. New agencies had been contracted to deal with the problems but were hampered by bureaucratic competition and the disillusionment and contentions of the members. As before, in order to understand what was happening in the cooperatives, I had to examine the relations between the various agencies, though this time in their field offices. The managerial and financial difficulties of the cooperatives and the conflicts between different agencies over their supervision seemed to present, in crystallized form, the problems of the entire colonization project; the colonization projects appeared to present, in intensified form, the problems of rural development that I had seen in the rest of Pará.

I spent most of the remaining twenty months in Brazil working between the colonization and other rural development projects. I conducted interviews, direct observation, and archival research in the field, in Belém, and later in Brasília, the national capital. Alternating between the field, the agency headquarters, and the university was very useful. In addition to giving me a break from the physical rigors of river and forest and an opportunity to recover from the various diseases that abounded in the precarious settlements there, the transition allowed me to take questions from the field back to headquarters and vice versa. Discussion with colleagues and students helped make sense of much of what I saw. I was able to follow the process of decision making and negotiation between agencies, and the implementation of policy from the national to the regional and then to the local level. At the local level I focused on the interactions between bureaucratic functionaries of different agencies, on their interactions with the peasants and colonists, and on the effects of these interactions on subsistence strategies and outcomes for the peasants themselves. I was also able to follow problems, initiatives, and communications which originated in the field back up to the regional and national bureaucratic levels.

Seminars and discussions with faculty and students, many of whom had worked in or with the agencies which concerned me, helped immensely in understanding the internal politics of the agencies and their conflicts with each other. Roberto Santos and Amilcar Tupiassu, NAEA faculty members who had extensive research and administrative experience with government agencies, facilitated access to crucial information sources and provided valuable criticism and comments on my research. Many of NAEA's students had already attained fairly high administrative positions; I found that they were much more willing to discuss their agencies' problems in an academic setting than they, or their counterparts, were in interviews conducted in their official work setting. They, and I, were surprised to find how little they knew about the processes, requirements, and problems of the other agencies with which they had to coordinate their own agencies' work. In several different seminars, two of which went on six hours a day for a week, I simply listened and took notes as students started to explain the workings of their own agencies to their counterparts in other agencies, then to complain about the difficulties the other agencies created for them, and finally to discuss the possibility that the problems they encountered did not reside in the individual agencies but in the wider system into which they were supposed to fit. In each case I told the students that I was learning more about their agencies than anyone had yet been willing to tell me officially and offered to leave the room while they talked. They asked me to stay, but twice students acknowledged, laughing, that they had refused to see me while they were still working and asked me to come see them as soon as they returned to their jobs. Many of them, both while they were at NAEA and after they returned to their posts, arranged interviews which were much more productive than those I had managed when I began the research.

My contacts with bureaucrats in the field was of a different nature, but was also very useful and personally agreeable. As my research covered a very wide, recently settled, area, I was dependent on the bureaucrats I was studying for housing and transportation. The field agents tended to share houses, both for convenience and economy and because there were few houses available for them. I was invariably welcome to sling my hammock in some open space, to contribute to their communal meals, and to travel with them as they went about their work. Most of them were unfailingly generous about explaining to me what I saw. From them, and from the farmers we visited, I learned to read the jumbled landscape of fallen, half-burned trees in which the farmers planted. They taught me how to distinguish the different types of soil, the quality of the burn which cleared the ground and released nutrients from the cut forest, the extent of pest and plague invasion into the crops, and the extent to which the soil had deteriorated after clearing and cropping. They explained the problems of coordinating the planting and harvesting cycles with available manpower, with the state of the primitive dirt roads, and with access to transport and markets. Many of the government agents became good friends with whom I could talk easily about the frustrations and hardships of their work and about their growing skepticism of the agencies they worked for. As in Belém, the two modes of contact, formally in agency offices, and informally outside them, complemented each other very usefully.

From government agents I learned the complex rules, regulations, procedures, and accounting forms which governed their work, and the shortcuts and omissions they used to facilitate or avoid the most cumbersome bureaucratic requirements. By talking to the bureaucrats of all of the agencies involved, I came to understand that the modern bureaucratic rationality internal to each agency was not cumulative, but contradictory. I discovered, to my amazement, that even in the field the individual agents were not aware of the procedures in the other agencies with which they worked, and so could not understand the conflicting, and expensive, requirements for compliance with these accumulated bureaucratic procedures. Instead, they blamed peasant backwardness for their clients' difficulties and failures in finding their way through the modern bureaucratic maze.

It was from the peasants and colonists themselves, however, that I learned fully of the frustrations, delays, uncertainties, and time and money costs which the accumulated bureaucratic procedures imposed on them. Time and again, I met colonists who had made multiple trips to the land titling agency because no one had bothered to explain how to acquire all of the other documents required, or farmers who returned home empty-handed from long expensive trips to town because the banks' credit department was closed for audit, or men who had paid a trucker for up to eight days of waiting in line to sell rice at the government warehouses. Individual bureaucrats, confident in the rationality of their own procedures, expected peasants with no previous contact with such systems to learn and comply with these routines. It took me, with ease of travel and the leisure to talk endlessly, months to understand them, and I wasn't trying to raise crops to support a family.

I talked to widows whose husbands had been killed by falling branches before they could learn the complex art of felling huge trees bound in long series by jungle vines, been murdered by angry workers when the bank delayed the credit to pay for the harvest, or died of the various diseases which afflicted many of the colonists. Colonization plans called for families, so these women heads of households faced additional bureaucratic complications and economic difficulties. Unless they had mature sons, they had little chance of staying on their land.

I talked to colonists who had spent all of their available time and money to comply with the requirements for titling land and were still waiting, three or four years later, for the documents to arrive. Without the title, they could not get the long-term investment credit they needed for the more profitable crops. Many sold their rights to neighbors or newcomers and moved on.

I talked as well to the more recently arrived colonists who bought the rights to their predecessors' lots. Some came with capital and equipment to start the quest for land title anew. Others, believing free land was still available, arrived penniless to eke out a livelihood working for established colonists while trying to pay for and cultivate their own lots. Overworked and underfed, the adults of these families often seemed to age ten years in six months, while their children suffered from intestinal parasites, insect bites, and malnutrition. The dream of owning land kept some of them going long enough to succeed in at least that; others either left or continued in the servitude and poverty they had tried to escape. As occasional paid workers they helped solve the growing problems of recruiting labor faced by the small proportion of successful colonists.

By the time I left Brazil, in August 1978, I had a data base sufficient to explain the relations between the agencies in both the colonization and other rural development programs in Pará, the place of the rural development programs within the larger agencies, the kinds of political interference and opposition which had impeded the successful implementation of these programs, and a fair understanding of the organization and procedures of the various agencies themselves. I was able to satisfy myself that I knew why specific programs had failed or had arrived at the results they did.

I had increasingly been pushed, however, to examine the other governmental development programs for large-scale agricultural and industrial enterprise, to which the rural development and colonization programs were subordinated. I was fortunate in this to be in the Amazon at the same time as Joe Foweraker, Marianne Schmink, Susanna Hecht,

Charles Wood, and Dennis Mahar, all of whom were doing research related to mine. Conversations, suggestions, and arguments with them, as well as direct assistance in finding information in Brazil, and discussions and criticisms of papers and lectures since we left the Amazon for jobs in the United States and England were extremely important in my attempt to understand the wider processes which affected the rural development programs.

Paradoxically, many of these programs, which had contributed to the eclipse of the colonization and rural development programs, were clearly failing. As I left the field, I was faced with a question more interesting than the one I had spent three years researching—why and how did none of the government programs for the development of the Amazon appear to succeed, despite the massive financial and political commitment of the government?

The University of Illinois at Urbana-Champaign, with its superb library and its excellent Center for Latin American and Caribbean Studies, turned out to be a fine place to take this question. I taught courses on development for students from a wide range of disciplines. Don Lathrap and I organized a course on the social ecology of the Amazon in which scholars from various U.S. and Brazilian universities and from development agencies lectured on their own research there.[1] As I worked back and forth between my own analyses of Brazilian bureaucracies, the discussions with colleagues about the history, economies, and social ecology of the Amazon, the combative literature on opposed perspectives of development, and three more months of field work in 1980, I turned from looking to theory for explanations of the Amazon's continued underdevelopment to looking at the social, economic, and environmental history of the Amazon as a vehicle to integrate and synthesize the partial, and incorrectly opposed, major theories of development and underdevelopment. This book is the result of that process. In the rest of this introduction, I explain why the Amazon can show us the inadequacies of these theories and how we can correct them.

Energy, Value, and Models of Industrial Economics

The largest tropical forest in the world, an underdeveloped frontier of one of the most rapidly industrializing countries of the world, inhabited by a variety of indigenous and peasant groups with widely different relations to the national and international economies, extensively transformed over a long, varied history of participation in the world economy, and over the past fifteen years the object of major developmental initiatives, the Amazon Basin presents a macrocosm of the phenomena which have informed and inspired quite divergent interpretations of underdevelopment. The extraordinary complexity of its plant and animal life, the fragility of its soils, and the overriding importance of its hydrological systems dramatize the failure of most development theory to consider the impact of social and economic change on ecological systems.[2] That the Amazon's major export economies have been based on extraction of value from nature rather than on the creation of value by labor underscores the problems of using economic models based on the European and American experience of industrial production.

Economies like the Amazon's, based primarily on the extraction of value from nature, engender very different patterns of location, residence, accumulation, and environmental effects than do economies based on the appropriation of value from labor. Development theories based on Euro-American economic models therefore cannot work for them. Even though many theories of underdevelopment focus on the export of raw materials, none deals with the internal dynamics of extractive economies.[3]

Through a series of extractive exports, the Brazilian Amazon has formed an integral part of the world economy for over 350 years, providing first goods profitable to international commerce and, later, essential to industrial development. Nonetheless, it is still treated by government planners and by national and transnational firms as a frontier to be occupied and developed. "Frontier" expansion into the Amazon has recently provoked widespread concern that large-scale capitalist enterprises such as ranching, lumbering, and mining will irreparably destroy the complex and interdependent floral and faunal systems that have coevolved on the fragile soils and in the rivers of the world's largest tropical forest. The persistence of the Amazon as frontier and the paradox of development which destroys the environment on which it depends demand explanations which existing paradigms of development and underdevelopment cannot provide.

As I worked through the discrepancies between theories of development and the economic history of the Amazon, I saw that the differences between extractive and productive economies were more fully accounted for by the laws of thermodynamics than by theories of politically enforced unequal exchange. Production involves the transformation of matter and energy, neither of which can be humanly created. They must therefore be extracted from a physical environment. All such transformations involve the conversion of energy to humanly useless forms. The energy and matter which flow through production systems, however, are partially and temporarily conserved in useful forms which stimulate increasingly complex social organization and production-enhancing modifications of the physical environment. The extractive economy's loss of energy and matter and the consequent disruption of human and natural biotic systems, in contrast, increasingly simplify both social organization and the natural environment by reducing both energy flow-through and its useful retention. Once we understand the thermodynamics of the physical dependence of production on extraction and of the ways that complex social organization in extensively modified environments emerges from and intensifies human uses of nonhuman energy, we can extend Adams's (1975:126) sociological recasting of Alfred Lotka's principle that "in evolution, natural selection favors those populations that convert the greater amount of energy" to explain the uneven development of regions and the subordination of extractive economies to productive economies in a world economic system.[4] This, in turn, allows us to reintegrate sociological with economic explanations of development and underdevelopment.

This book examines and elaborates these ideas in a study of the predominantly extractive economies of the Amazon. Most social formations present variable mixes of extraction and production. If these ideas help to explain the extreme and progressive underdevelopment of the Amazon, they may also prove useful in our analysis of other societies whose economies are based on different combinations and proportions of extraction and production.

The economic history of the Amazon challenges Western notions about progress, man, and nature which form the bases of the economic models underlying most theories of development and underdevelopment. These models treat the environment as passive and plastic. Karl Marx's idea that humans create the means of their own existence through increasing control over and transformation of nature is typical of many Western explanations of human progress in which the natural environment is seen as the passive object of ever more elaborate technological and social arrangements of the energy used to exploit it. These ideas collide with others, equally stereotyped, of the inexorable power of the jungle over man. Notions of the tropics' power to crack the veneer of European civilization inspired novels like Joseph Conrad's *Heart of Darkness* and British colonial regulations requiring periodic home leave. Popular images of the Amazon maintain the myth of civilized man helpless against the horrors of the "green hell." A photograph of a bulldozer extending a reddish swath through the trees communicates the symbols of progress, while the diminute proportion of the bulldozer to its surroundings reaffirms the ultimate hopelessness of the undertaking. The clash of these two stereotypes results in a third; if human history is seen as the record of man's increased control over nature, then the Amazon is seen, not as having a history, but as having passed through a series of episodes—conquest and exploration, the rubber boom, present-day mining, lumbering, and cattle ranching, and colonization projects—with the entire basin continually lapsing into the ahistorical and uncivilized sameness in which each episode began and ended. Writers on the Amazon continue this notion by writing of cycles through which the Amazon has passed.

Nature is not passive in its relation to man, however, nor does the completion of cycles return the Amazon to an enduring "uncivilized" condition. Man can and does intervene powerfully in the Amazon's fragile ecosystem and has been doing so since long before the arrival of European conquerors and colonizers. Man's intervention, however, does not constitute the control supposed in the conventional historical myth, nor does his failure to control the environment end in the return of nature to its primeval state. Rather, each human intervention in the environment transforms it in ways which limit the possibilities of subsequent interventions. Human transformation of the environment at one historical moment thus establishes limits to the subsequent uses which man can make of his environment.

The environment which has both limited human intervention and been affected by it includes two related systems, the natural or ecological and the human or social. Both systems interact crucially, because human economic activity depends on social organization to direct and extend human energies in the transformation of natural resources extracted from the environment.

The power to exploit the natural environment and the power to exploit other humans are closely related. For Marx, it is by controlling access to nature transformed into "means of production" that one class can dominate and appropriate the surplus production of another. As the forces of production—which include the organization of a labor force—increase and become more complex, so, too, do the means of controlling men. Lenski (1966) has argued, more recently, that the growth of technological extensions of human energy in relation to the environment was a necessary condition for the increase of social inequality. Adams (1975) has carried this basic notion even further in his definition of social power as "the control that one party has over the environment of another party." For Adams, power is derived from control over energy flows, and those who hold power are those who can organize their environment, both physical and social, in such a way as to control energy by structuring the environments of others. While all of these ideas are essentially correct in their association of power over the environment and power over humans, they ignore a crucial aspect of the relationship between powerful groups and the

human and natural environment: While these groups, using and directing the energies generated or transformed by subordinate groups,
may transform their physical and social environments, they themselves
become dependent on the social and material organization they have
created. Humans become the prisoner of their own transformation of
nature and society. The history of the Amazon Basin provides numerous
cases of this process. Here, in different ways at different times, man's
transformation of nature and society in one historical moment has
limited his ability to exploit this environment in the next. In this book,
I attempt to trace these successive transformations and their effects
from pre-Columbian times to the present and to predict future trends.

The relation between man and nature in the Amazon since pre-
Columbian times can be seen as the result of the subordination of both
to progressively wider and more complex economic and political systems. The changing nature of this subordination reflected two related
processes. First, new technologies and new forms of the division of
labor within nations and between regions of the world brought about
increasingly complex transformations of energy beyond the Amazon.
Second these systems developed the capacity to penetrate ever deeper
into the Amazon itself. The history of this penetration, from the sporadic
and limited expeditions of exploration and attack by isolated groups
of adventurers, to the systematic conquest and attempts at control of
the rivers by competing European armies, to the enslavement and
transportation of Indians to work on plantations or in extractive expeditions, to the massive importation of indentured laborers to tap
rubber trees, and to the expulsion of the descendants of these laborers
by large companies interested in using the lands they occupy to cut
lumber, raise cattle, or extract minerals, has been a response to the
needs of changing productive and political relations outside of the
Amazon and the opportunities for enrichment which they offered. Each
of these penetrations has been effected and extended by locally dominant groups who have had power to transform the environment of
others. Each transformation, however, has created limits on the extent
to which organized energy can be used by dominant groups to exploit
the environment in their own interests. Powerful groups, rather than
controlling the environment, their own or others (see Adams, 1975),
have created the limits on the possible human uses of their environment.

Outline of Chapters

This book has two purposes, first, to explain the underdevelopment
of the Amazon, and second, to use the history of that underdevel-

opment to draw various theories of underdevelopment into a general ecological model which will resolve some of the debates between their proponents.

Much of the theoretical debate about national underdevelopment and development and about the effects of unequal exchange has revolved around the question of whether their causes are best understood by focusing on processes external to particular societies—i.e., imperialism, dependency, or the workings of a world capitalist system—or internal to particular societies—i.e., modernization or specific local modes of production. In Chapter 1 I review these various theories and argue that debate over internal-external focuses is essentially sterile. Rather, theory must articulate the interaction between internal and external processes. I propose that the problem of theoretical integration can be solved by analyzing the relations between world systems of exchange and the social, economic, and political organization of particular regions as an evolutionary series of ecosystemic transformations from the time of colonial contact until the present.

In Chapter 2 I analyze the ways that extractive economies degraded natural and human environments in the Amazon from 1600 to 1950. Indigenous populations in the Amazon, prior to colonial conquest, were characterized by elaborate, self-sustaining modes of production based on sophisticated understanding and utilization of the Amazonian ecosystem. However, world demand for specific extractive commodities after 1600 and the installation of locally dominant groups from the centers of imperial control led to the establishment of ecologically destructive modes of extraction. These new economies decimated native populations and limited the biological reproduction of the plant and animal species on which they depended and so ultimately impoverished themselves. The resulting degradation of the physical and social environments severely limited the capacity of locally dominant groups to respond to industrial demand for rubber at the end of the nineteenth century. The mode of extraction by which rubber was obtained, and its eventual collapse, set the stage for subsequent extractive systems which have been equally destructive of the human and natural environments.

In Chapter 3 I show how the relations between the national state and dominant capitalist groups introduced and accelerated new forms of extraction between 1950 and 1980. Government planners increasingly saw the Amazon as a resource pool that could be rapidly exploited to solve the balance-of-payments problems that followed from import substitution and rapid industrialization. Large-scale capitalist enterprises and government economic planners treated the Amazon as an empty frontier with little regard either for sustained economic participation by existing human social and economic organization or for the natural environment.

The disordered rush for land and other resources in the Amazon, and the collapse of local institutions controlling land tenure and social order impelled the state to embark on programs to control the expansion of capitalist enterprise and to channel it into the institutional framework that had emerged in the already capitalist center-south of Brazil. At the same time, growing pressures for land reform in other parts of Brazil stimulated the government to use the Amazon as a frontier on which it could settle displaced peasants and small farmers.

In Chapter 4 I explain how private capitalist interests were able to capture and redirect these programs away from the state's expressed goals. In this, and in the remaining chapters, I show how the social formations of the Amazon, disrupted and simplified by repeated extractive cycles, were so discrepant with the social formations which gave rise to the modern national state that this state's bureaucracy, though very powerful relative to Amazonian social organization, could not function rationally or effectively there.

Chapter 5 deals with the ways that power differentials and conflicts between agencies further distorted the state's development policies. The functional specificity and relative autonomy that characterized these agencies' organization in the center-south of Brazil were not appropriate to the tasks of major institutional and economic transformation that the national state's development plans for the Amazon required. A series of bargaining relations between agencies emerged, in which the different jurisdictions and funding levels of specific agencies overrode centrally established development policies. These bargaining relations and the fiscal transfers, delays, and conflicting authorities which they created impeded the effective operation of agents in the field.

The chapters in the second half of the book comprise case studies of the failure of modern economic and social forms imposed by government policy to function in an area whose social formations and ecological relations had been molded by 350 years of extractive export economies.

In Chapter 6 I show how inappropriate bureaucracy contributed to the failure of the colonization programs. The extension of bureaucratic agencies from the energy-intensive Brazilian center to the energy-losing Amazonian periphery required individual colonists to comply with a series of procedural requirements for which the necessary institutional structures did not exist. As the high costs of compliance were fixed, the wealthier petty entrepreneurs and salaried government functionaries were increasingly able to buy out the failed colonists and eventually to operate on a scale which permitted absorption of these institutional costs. The colonization programs thus failed in their original goal of settling landless peasants.

Chapter 7 deals with corruption in the colonization projects. The modern characteristics of the agencies provided numerous opportunities for corruption in the colonization areas, but the explanations of corruption derived from modernization theories do not sufficiently explain either the emergence or the maintenance of corrupt activities. I examine organizational variables to explain why this corruption was effectively checked in some projects and not others.

In Chapter 8 I show how competition between self-interested, expansive bureaucratic agencies crippled government-sponsored agricultural cooperatives. Government programs to establish small farmers' cooperatives in the Amazon were impeded not only by inappropriate bureaucratic requirements but also by jurisdictional and budgetary disputes between the agencies. Various agencies attempted to use the cooperatives to achieve their own functions at minimal cost. These attempts debased the cooperatives and resulted in impossibly high levels of debt for many of the farmer members.

In Chapter 9 I analyze the effects of programs to modernize land tenure. The state's programs to extend modern institutions of land surveying, titling, and registry have continued and expanded in the Amazon, despite the budget and staff reductions in rural development and colonization projects. The complex bureaucratic procedures of the land-registry agencies and the ideological preferences of modern bureaucrats, however, distort declared policy goals and accelerate the growing economic pressures on the subsistence strategies of local populations.

In the Conclusion I take up the theoretical issues addressed in Chapter 1, showing how a synthesis of internal and external perspectives with analysis of the environmental and demographic consequences of different export economies works to explain both underdevelopment and the constraints on national state attempts to overcome underdevelopment. This chapter concludes with a discussion of what forms of development might have been possible in the Amazon and what forms might still be viable.

NOTES

1. Lecturers included James R. Karr, Joseph L. Love, Richard Preto-Rodas, Norman E. Whitten, Jr., Reiner T. Zuidema, William Denevan, Susanna Hecht, Dennis Mahar, David Maybury-Lewis, Theodore Macdonald, Marianne

Schmink, Hilgard O'Reilly Sternberg, Charles Wood and Roberto da Matta. Karr and Whitten contributed greatly to the conceptualization of the course.

2. I do not attempt to present a full analysis of the climate, soils, flora, and fauna of the Amazon in this book. Readers seeking more detailed ecological information are urged to consider Sternberg's *The Amazon River of Brazil* (1975), the July/August 1978 volume of *Interciencia* (3, 4), and Hecht's (1981) article on deforestation as well as this book's citations to analyses of specific ecological problems.

3. Hechter (1971, 1972, 1976), for example, uses "resource extraction" as one of the mechanisms underlying internal colonialism, but he attributes the persistence of extractive economies in peripheral areas to active manipulation and cultural prejudice by center capitalists. He does not consider the effects of the extractive economy itself except as the absence of an industrial base, nor does he consider the internal, as opposed to the external (imposed), dynamics of extractive industries.

4. I should note here that Adams did not agree with my extension of his energetics model to the conservation of energy in efficiency-enhancing social organization when I proposed this to him. I greatly appreciate his patience in our long discussion, however, as his opposition helped me clarify my own ideas on this issue. I can only hope he finds these later written arguments more convincing than my initial and imprecise talking about them. (See also Adams, 1975:126-39.)

CHAPTER 1

Energy Values in Unequal Exchange and Uneven Development

The development or underdevelopment of any region results from the organization, coordination, and use of human and nonhuman energies and from the distribution of resources derived from and transformed in that environment or traded for resources derived from or transformed in other regions. Human uses of any regional environment depend on its ecosystemic characteristics; these are shaped in part by earlier uses and by deliberate human modifications. Social organization, which may enhance or limit access to, and the useful transformation of, natural resources, is both bounded by and further shapes these ecosystems.

Theories of development have focused on economic processes of material transformation, or production, but they have not recognized the absolute dependency of material production on resource extraction. Nor have they accounted for the ways that the extraction, transport, and use of natural resources and the social formations that emerge from these processes affect the subsequent developmental potential of the environments from which resources are extracted. Instead, most theories of development have been attempts to extend models derived from systems of industrial production to nonindustrial systems for which they have only limited relevance.

Recent theoretical literature on national development has compounded the distortions inherent in this bias to production models. Its primary focus has been a fruitless debate about whether the causes of underdevelopment occur in a global system of exchange dominated by industrial nations or within specific regional systems of production. Advocates of dependency perspectives criticize theories of modernization for their focus on the internal characteristics of particular economies; Marxist scholars counter world-system models of unequal exchange by insisting on the explanatory primacy of modes of production. In fact, a global system of exchange, made up of all importing and exporting regions, determines terms of trade which differentially affect all of these regions, but distinct regional social structures and political arrangements determine how the commodities on which the global system depends are actually extracted or produced.

Foster-Carter (1978) and Portes (1980) have pointed out convergencies and complementarities between these competing perspectives on national development. De Janvry's (1981) model of the relations between articulated and disarticulated economies brilliantly corrects many of the errors of modernization, dependency, and Marxist analyses of Latin American underdevelopment, but his emphasis on the economic logic of dependency and his exclusive focus on the labor incorporated into exchange values does not allow him to treat the internal dynamics of noncapitalist social formations, class relations, or the complex and costly bureaucratic organization of the modern peripheral state except as functional adjuncts of different accumulation processes. We still have no model which integrates these perspectives.

I do not believe we can adequately integrate these perspectives unless we recast and incorporate them into ecological and evolutionary models of social change that consider simultaneously the physical dependence of production on extraction and the interaction between regional and global systems. I reason that, regardless of the degree to which exchange systems have become global, commodities can emerge only out of locally based extraction and production systems. Models of regional and global systems must be complementary rather than competitive because these systems coevolve. I propose that different regional levels of development result from the interaction between changing demand in the world market for specific commodities and the local reorganization of modes of production and extraction in response. The cumulative ecological, demographic, and infrastructural effects of the sequence of modes of production and extraction in any region establish limits and potentials for the productive capacities and the living standards of regional populations. The flow of energy from extractive to productive economies reduces the complexity and power of the first and increases complexity and power in the second. The actions and characteristics of modern states and of their complex and costly bureaucracies accelerate these sequences. Modernization, as ideology, as bureaucratic structure and procedure, and as centralized control through complex regulatory organization, mediates and intensifies the socioeconomic consequences of the interaction between global and regional systems. Modern systems are themselves highly energy-intensive and can only emerge in regions where industrial modes of production derive large amounts of energy and matter from subordinate modes of extraction. The modern state is but one of the forms of social organization which draw on energy flows out of modes of extraction and which extend the dominance of energy-concentrating modes of production, both globally and within nations. I examine these propositions in a case study of the sequence of export economies in the Brazilian Amazon from the time of colonial conquest to the present.

Modes of Extraction and the Creation of Extreme Peripheries

The first essential step toward adequate analysis of the coevolution of regional social formations requires that we free ourselves from notions relevant only to industrial production systems. Concepts derived from the European experience of capital accumulation and technological innovations in industrial production still provide the basic metaphors for the analysis of nonindustrial economies. Economic models of industrial production neglect the extractive origins of the materials which industrial processes transform (Georgescu-Roegen, 1975). The internal dynamics of the extractive economies that have provided most of the exports from the least developed regions differ significantly from those of productive economies in their effects on the natural environment, the distribution of human populations, the growth of economic infrastructure (understood here as everything humanly constructed or organized which facilitates social and economic activity), and therefore on the subsequent developmental potential of the affected regions. I argue that production models cannot explain the internal dynamics of extractive economies because the exploitation of natural resources uses and destroys values in energy and material which cannot be calculated in terms of labor or capital. When natural resources are extracted from one regional ecosystem to be transformed and consumed in another, the resource-exporting region loses values that occur in its physical environment. These losses eventually decelerate the extractive region's economy, while the resource-consuming communities gain value and their economies accelerate. An adequate model of the interaction between global and regional economies must account for both the differences and the interdependence between the two systems.

The differences between the internal dynamics of modes of extraction and of modes of production create unequal exchange not only in terms of the labor value incorporated into products but also through the direct appropriation of rapidly depleted or nonrenewable natural resources. Extractive appropriation impoverishes the environment on which local populations depend both for their own reproduction and for the extraction of commodities for export.

Because this appropriation and its ecological results affect the class structures, the organization of labor, systems of exchange and property, the activities of the state, the distribution of populations, the development of physical infrastructure, and the kinds of information, beliefs, and ideologies which shape social organization and behavior, I introduce the idea, mode of extraction, to suggest the systemic connections between these phenomena. My usage thus parallels the more inclusive definitions of mode of production, which relate multiple aspects of social, legal, political, and commercial activities within unified frames of analysis (Anderson, 1974; Hindess and Hirst, 1975). I will argue, though, that both modes of extraction and modes of production can only be understood in terms of their integral interdependence and their impacts on natural ecosystemic processes. Orthodox Marxist notions of the reproduction of modes of production must be reformulated to account for these ecological interdependencies.

While the specific characteristics and dynamics of particular modes of extraction and of particular extractive commodity markets must be analyzed individually, it is possible to outline some general tendencies in extractive export economies. The characterization of extractive export economies which follows is elaborated from studies of specific extractive economies (Santos, 1980; Weinstein, 1980; Brockway, 1979; Blair, 1976; Cobbe, 1979) and from more general statements by Levin (1960), Furtado (1970), Daly (1977), Sternberg (1973), and Georgescu-Roegen (1970, 1971, 1975).

The extractive process frequently entails an extremely low ratio of both labor and capital to value, so it may initially produce rapid rises in regional incomes. These may be followed by equally rapid collapses when the depletion of easily accessible resources requires additional inputs of labor and capital without corresponding increases in volume. The rapidly rising cost of extraction usually stimulates a search for substitutes or new sources for the original good. Either alternative profoundly disrupts the economy of the exporting region. The ephemeral nature of extractive economies may lead to a series of demographic and infrastructural dislocations.

Productive enterprises typically are located in close proximity to each other. Transportation, communication, and energy transmission costs are thus shared by multiple enterprises. New enterprises can start without assuming the total costs of the infrastructure they require. Populations attracted to these locations provide a labor force which can move easily between enterprises with different rates and directions of growth. While individual enterprises may become obsolete, the infrastructure to which they contribute and the labor which they have employed remain for subsequent enterprise.

Extractive enterprises, on the other hand, must be located in close proximity to the natural resources they exploit. These resources are randomly distributed in relation to productive centers, so proximity to other enterprises occurs only by chance and becomes less likely as the most accessible resources are depleted. Extractive economies, therefore, seldom enjoy the continuities with earlier settlement patterns and infrastructural development which shared productive locations provide. Nor do they usually contribute to the labor and infrastructural requirements of subsequent economies. Instead, whatever changes they bring about in the distribution of population and in the physical environment serve little or no purpose when the specific resources to which they are geared are depleted or are no longer in demand.

Regions whose economic ties to the world system are based almost exclusively on the exchange of extracted commodities (that is, resources which occur in nature and in whose existence or continued reproduction there is no deliberate human intervention), can be characterized as extreme peripheries because of the low proportions of capital and labor incorporated in the total value of their exports and because of the low level of linkages to other economic activities and social organization in the same region. Even when depletion raises extraction costs, the additional capital and labor are most frequently required for exploration and transport rather than actual extraction. Even then, these costs constitute a relatively small proportion of eventual price, and an even smaller proportion of what their price would be if depletion rates were taken into account (Schumacher, 1973; Georgescu-Roegen, 1970; Schnaiberg, 1980). Examples of such commodities include not only petroleum and minerals, but also lumber from natural forest, the oils, meats, and hides of wild animals, nuts of undomesticated trees, most fish, and slaves. I will argue later that raising cattle on pastures formed by burning jungle is also essentially extractive. There is some human intervention in herd management and pasture clearing, but the pasture itself frequently depends on nutrients released from burning vegetation and usually does not last much beyond the rapid depletion of those resources (Hecht, 1981).

While processing and industrialization of most extractive commodities create additional value, extreme peripheries such as the Amazon tend to export them raw or unfinished so that the creation and realization of additional values occur in and benefit other economies. Moreover, even the limited contribution of extractive exports to regional economies tends to be unstable; if high demand and expanded scale increase unit costs of extraction by depleting the most accessible resources, entrepreneurs will attempt to domesticate or to synthesize agricultural or industrial substitutes and to transform the extractive economy into a productive one (Brockway, 1979). These new economies, once freed from the need to locate near natural resources, will tend to move to areas where land, labor, and infrastructure are more easily accessible.

The crucial difference between production and extraction is that the dynamics of scale in extractive economies function inversely to the dynamics of scale in the productive economies to which world trade connects them. The forces of production develop progressively in industrial systems because the unit cost of commodity production tends to fall as the scale of production increases. In extractive systems, on the contrary, unit costs tend to rise as the scale of extraction increases. Greater amounts of any extractive commodity can be obtained only by exploiting increasingly distant or difficult sources. Though technological innovation may reduce costs of some extractive processes in the short run, unit costs of extraction will continue to rise in the long run. Therefore, when extractive systems respond to increased external demand, they tend to impoverish themselves (1) by depleting non-self-renewing resources or (2) by exploiting self-renewing resources beyond their capacities for regeneration, thereby (3) forcing the unit cost of extracted materials to rise so high that the development of synthetic or cultivated alternatives in other regions becomes cost effective. These three results are likely to be aggravated by the disruption of the surrounding ecosystem and the consequent reduction of other useful resources whose existence or reproduction depends on biotic chains which include the extracted resource or which are disrupted by the process of extraction.

Successful plantation or industrial production of formerly extractive commodities completes the cycle of peripheral impoverishment by introducing progressive economies of scale in the new location. The competitive advantages of new locations eventually eliminate or seriously reduce the original and increasingly costly extractive economy. In many cases the economic activities and the settlement patterns which developed around the extractive economy either shrink or become useless. Falling unit costs accelerate production-consumption linkages and infrastructural concentration and accumulation in expanding articulated production systems. The rising unit costs, further dispersion of labor and investment, and intensified ecological disruption which accompany expanding extractive systems eventually decelerate these economies. The intensified energy flow to and through the socially articulated productive systems permits more rapid accumulation there of physical infrastructure, specialized technical and social organizational knowledge in an increased division of labor, and the coordination of research and development of new technologies. These both enhance productive systems' use of nonhuman energy and change the market prices for extracted resources. This capacity to change world markets through technological innovation frees the production systems from shortrun dependence on particular extractive commodities as they become depleted and heightens both their dominance over and periodic disruptions of the decelerating modes of extraction.

Production-dominated technological innovations may involve both plant transfers and synthetic substitutions. Brockway (1979) has shown how the development of the botanical and related sciences in the industrial core responded to and promoted the domestication and genetic adaptation of plants extracted in the extreme peripheries to other peripheral regions where center nations controlled both the land and the labor necessary to transform these cultigens into plantation crops. Successful transformation to a plantation system brought these cultigens—rubber, sisal, and cinchona—into a mode of production in which increased scale progressively reduced unit costs to levels at which extractive systems could no longer compete. (These plantation systems frequently aggravated the impoverishment of other extreme peripheries by requisitioning slave or indentured labor.) The incorporation of these extreme peripheries into the world economy, then, resulted not only in a transfer of value but also in a direct transfer of resources—both natural and human—to less peripheral regions. These plantation systems themselves were finally impoverished by industrial production of synthetic substitutes. Modern searches for oil substitutes—whether nuclear, solar, or agricultural—respond similarly to rising capital and labor costs as the most accessible oil sources are depleted.

Extractive economies tend to develop fewer lateral linkages than productive economies. The well-documented "enclave" nature of extractive economies (see Levin, 1960) results from several factors. First, the low proportion of capital and labor to market value concentrates profits in the exchange, rather than in the extractive, sector (Katzman, 1976). Second, extractive economies do not respond to the locational advantages that tend to foster the mutual proximity of productive enterprises. Extractive economies necessarily locate at the sources of raw materials, and these sources may be far removed from existing demographic and economic centers. Distance from existing demographic and economic centers increases the costs of labor recruitment, subsistence, shelter and infrastructural development. In extreme cases, labor is expeditionary, usually involving the temporary migration of males. The additional costs of migration are increased by a near total dependence on imported foodstuffs and other materials, which further reduce the possibility of local economic linkages. This situation in turn enhances control over the labor force, as the provision of subsistence needs is controlled by those who purchase labor. Distance from established communities further heightens the employers' control, as there are few alternative social organizations to provide support for laborers' resistance to exploitation.

The combination of (1) factors which lead to the eventual impoverishment or collapse of extractive economies in specific regions or subregions with (2) factors which limit the extent that extractive economies can share with other enterprises the locational advantages of population centers and infrastructure creates cycles in which costly infrastructure and human settlements are periodically abandoned or suffer a severe reduction in economic utility. Economic and social development based on extractive economies thus tends to be discontinuous in time and space. Production systems tend to build a social and physical environment shared by multiple enterprises. These enterprises suffer the effects of technological and demand changes at different times and rates, so a production system as a whole tends to be more stable and continuous than any extractive one. The locational advantages of shared labor pools and infrastructure which production systems usually enjoy are much more likely to allow adaptation to changing technologies and markets. That most of the infrastructure developed for extractive export economies is specific to the requirements of resource removal and transport exacerbates their loss of utility as the extracted resource is exhausted or substituted.

The concentration of capital in removal and transport infrastructure frequently creates especially severe technological dependencies on the industrial countries. Railroads, steamships, docks, drilling rigs, pipelines, and earth-moving machinery require techniques and capitals which extractive economies are unlikely to develop. The concentration of investment in export facilities further accentuates the concentrated control over exchange—and profit—which emerges from the absence of alternative economic and demographic linkages. (See especially Santos, 1980; Weinstein, 1980; Solberg, 1976; Blair, 1976; Cobbe, 1979; Levin, 1960.)

Another crucial distinction between extractive and productive modes is that they tend to engender highly distinct, and sometimes contradictory, regimes of land tenure and access to resources. (Distinctions between land ownership and mineral rights in the United States are an example of the different judicial status of production and extraction.) Because extractive location responds to different factors than does productive location, the discovery of valuable resources may well occur on land with no declared ownership, with little or no previous commercial value, and subject to public, rather than private, domain. For all of these reasons, access to resources is of greater import in extractive economies than is actual possession or ownership of land. Rapid increases in the commercial value of natural resources may severely dislocate prior social and economic relations governing possession and use of land, especially when these relations are only tenuously integrated into wider market systems (Bunker, 1979). The state, therefore, tends to participate directly in the regulation, authorization, and facilitation of extractive economies.

The tendency for state participation in and facilitation of extractive economies is in many cases enhanced as increasingly difficult access to valuable resources increases extraction costs. The increasing proportion of the Iranian national budget devoted to oil extraction (Fesharaki, 1976; Muzegar, 1977) or the recent decision of the government of Brazil to invest in the mineral deposits of Carajás (Pinto, 1982) may heighten national control of these economies, but they also reduce the state's fiscal capacity to provide social welfare and developmental services in other sectors.

The paucity of economic and political linkages and the demographic and infrastructural instability of extractive economies impede rational state participation and administration. The complex energy requirements of the modern state limit its effective capacity to operate in social formations which have progressively lost energy through extractive exports.

The modern state and its individual agencies coevolved with the progressive complexities, conflicts, and crises of industrial capitalism. Their operating procedures presuppose and depend on complex energy-intensive institutional and organizational forms in other sectors. Adams (1982) shows that the state and other parts of the regulatory sector absorbed increasing proportions of available human energy in Great Britain after 1850, with major growth starting after 1901. Human energy in the transformation sector started a steep decline as early at 1860 and was only slightly higher than in the regulatory sector by 1971, while nonhuman energy use had already begun its sharp and steady increase by 1840. Adams explains the lag in the growth of the regulatory sector as the time during which increased energy flow-through and complexity in the transformation sector created new problems for which new regulatory solutions had to be devised, organized, and implemented. While there was therefore no immediate correspondence between intensified (nonhuman) energy flow-through and regulatory growth, energy intensification and the liberation of human labor from transformation (i.e., material production) were both a stimulus to and a requirement for the increased flow of energy into the complex modern state.

In contrast to the productive articulated economy, the energy and matter taken from extractive regions do not flow through the extractive economy, do not enhance human productivity or social complexity there, do not engender local production-consumption accelerators, and do not remain embodied in physical infrastructure and complex social organization. The disarticulated extractive export economy can neither generate nor sustain the complex and costly organizational structures of the modern state or the institutions and organizations which the modern state presupposes and on which its functioning depends. The bureaucratic agencies of the modern state can only occur in extractive peripheries as an imposed, exogenous force and are therefore compelled to act without the corresponding civil organization which its own rationality and operating procedures require.[1] I will argue (in chapters 4-6) that theories of modernization and theories of the authoritarian developmental state provide concepts essential to analyses of these complex bureaucracies, but that these theories must be extensively refined to account for the irrationalities and failures of central state intervention in extractive peripheries.

The role of the state in extractive economies may also provide some insight into how predominantly productive economies can mitigate the disruptive effects of extractive economies when both occur in the same area. Current attempts to restrict off-shore oil drilling in California, for instance, gain impetus from the density, economic articulation, and political power of the affected populations. Attempts at environmental protection and social welfare in, for example, Wyoming, Alaska, or Appalachia are likely to be less successful (Gaventa, 1980; Throgmorton, 1983).

Workers in extractive processes within a predominantly productive economy will enjoy most of the legal and organizational protections available to production workers. Populations integrated into national productive systems may be far better prepared to protect their own environments than populations which are not. The state is most responsive to classes or groups whose actions most affect the economic activities from which it derives revenue or which can most directly threaten the public order on which its legitimacy depends (Block, 1977). Because the social formations of extractive regions seldom develop dense political and economic linkages, and because they lack viable, self-sustaining communities, local inhabitants cannot pressure the state to prohibit repeated disruption through extraction of whatever resources may offer profit to entrepreneurs from other regions. States where the extractive exports predominate in the entire national economy are likely to be more susceptible to pressures and interventions from production-based states, corporations, and cartels than states of nations whose economies are predominantly productive and autocentric.

The particular problem of regions where extractive export economies are predominant is that socioeconomic organization, which at one time responds to international demand for specific extractive commodities, is likely to lose its utility when the extractive source is depleted or when demand shifts away from it. Predominantly extractive economies disrupt human settlement patterns and the natural environment in ways which are adaptive only in the relatively short run and maladaptive in the long run. In the absence of self-sustaining and flexible productive systems, there is little or no economic basis for local opposition or resistance to entrepeneurs or to dependent national states that seek to organize the population and environment in such a way as to exploit the potential for quick profit. Thus, extractive economies tend toward eventual stagnation, broken only by new extractive cycles if new demands for new material resources available in the region emerge.

These factors may vary with the characteristics of the national environment, with the type and extent of the national resources extracted, and with the policies of the national state. In the Amazon the tendency for extractive economies at one time to leave the region susceptible to the establishment of subsequent extractive economies (whenever world markets create pressures or opportunities for easy and rapid profits) has led, not simply to underdevelopment relative to more rapid increases in productivity in other regions, but also to absolute impoverishment and progressive underdevelopment. Where there is little local population to disrupt, however, extractive economies may generate considerable benefits. Valuable minerals or fossil fuels exploited in desert areas with sparse populations may generate revenues which the state can tax or redirect to develop other, productive economies. (See, for example, Palmer and Parsons, 1977, on the very different results of extractive economies in South Africa and Katanga.) Even in these cases, however, the benefits are likely to flow to other areas of the nation where the raw materials are transformed and revenues are directed to more productive enterprise.

Theories of imperialism (Luxemburg, 1951; Lenin, 1939; Baran, 1957), world systems and dependency (see especially Galtung, 1971), unequal exchange based on wage or productivity differentials, and modernization have all acknowledged primary material export as a defining characteristic of most forms of underdevelopment, but they have not systematically explored the internal dynamics of extractive systems as a distinct socioeconomic type. Nor have they understood that the complex social organizational, demographic, and infrastructural forms that emerge as technological change and accumulation accelerate the flow of energy through the articulated productive systems ultimately depend on processes that progressively decelerate the economy, disrupt the ecosystem, and simplify social organization in extractive regions. None of these theories has accounted sufficiently for the ways in which the extraction and export of natural resources affect the subsequent developmental potential of the environments from which they are extracted.

The extraction of particular commodities from nature has measurable effects on the energy transformation processes in surrounding biotic systems and on the density and distribution of human populations. I expect that extractive economies tend to "build" the surrounding environment and to distribute human populations in ways which limit, rather than enhance, subsequent forces of production. If this is so, understanding the development and underdevelopment of these environments requires models which systematically take the historical sequence of these effects into account.

Such models are essential to any attempt to reverse or moderate the disruptive effects of extractive economies. It would be pointless to argue against extraction per se because human economic activity and social reproduction cannot occur without extraction. The problem then is to devise ways in which extractive economies can function in a world system of exchange without destroying the physical and human environments in which they occur. In order to do so, we must first revalue, theoretically and practically, the natural resources and processes on which economic activity ultimately depends. Theories of value which focus exclusively on labor and capital do not simply err conceptually. Rather, they reflect and legitimate a world view in which nature is subordinated to mankind and where natural resources are considered flow or income rather than part of a limited global stock or capital (Schumacher, 1973; Georgescu-Roegen, 1970). Theoretically and practically, nature, values in nature, and the economies which depend on values in nature have been systematically undervalued, while human labor, consumption, and reproduction in articulated societies have been correspondingly overvalued. Revaluing natural energy transformation on a global level would necessarily slow the rate of energy flow from periphery to core and, therefore, also slow rates of industrial production and consumption. I believe this is essential for the longterm reproduction of human society in both extractive and productive modes. Specifying the particular characteristics of and values in extractive economies is an essential first step in any attempt to reverse these economies' disruptive effects, but these characteristics and values must be integrated with more general theories of development and social evolution, both regional and global.

Energy Flows and Differential Social Complexity

Extractive export economies constitute an extreme case of what de Janvry (1981) has called dependent disarticulation. Socially articulated economies produce goods for internal consumption. The resulting acceleration of social and economic activity through linkages between wages, consumption capacity, and markets enhances return to capital and expands production of goods. This partially resolves the contradictions between wage costs and profits, making wage increases systemically rational. The disarticulated economy, in contrast, depends on external markets and therefore lacks any internal consumption-driven accelerator to rationalize high wages. De Janvry invokes the logic and contradictions of accumulation within each economy to explain the necessary relations and interdependencies between these economies. Crises of overproduction and falling rates of profit in the articulated core economies and the limited consumption capacity of internal markets in disarticulated peripheral economies create the necessity for each economy to establish external relations with the other; the necessity of each is the other's possibility. The relations between extractive and productive systems are more profound, however, than de Janvry implies.

Matter and energy, the essential components of production, cannot be created, only transformed, and every transformation increases entropy, that is, frees energy into humanly unusable forms (Georgescu-Roegen, 1970). Productive economies are all, finally, only the molecular, structural, and spatial reorganization of matter and energy extracted from nature. In the precise sense, humans can only produce ideas and symbols. The rest of what we call production is only our intervention in and redirection of natural processes of energy and material transformation. Production, or more properly transformation, cannot occur without some form of continued extraction from the natural environment. Extraction and production, though integrally related, usually occur in distinct geographical locations; this tendency is drastically enhanced as industrial production and the division of labor increase social complexity, population density, and urbanization. Typically, some economies specialize in particular extractive exports and depend on the importation of transformed commodities for their own consumption. Energy and matter are thus withdrawn from the natural environment of the extractive economies and flow toward and are concentrated in the social and physical environments of the productive economies, where they fuel the linked and mutually accelerating processes of production and consumption.

Matter stores energy and can be converted to energy. Adams (1982:17) argues that all life forms consume and dissipate energy and that "the process of dissipation constitutes [their] structure. . . . Society is composed of the energy it consumes, hence, it can be treated as a dissipative structure." This formulation provides a more adequate measure than de Janvry's exchange values for the flows which bind articulated to disarticulated, and extractive to productive, systems. Conventional economic measures can only capture the exchanges or flows between classes and systems in the monetary terms of wages, prices, and profits, or in the ultimately nonquantifiable notions of abstract labor value. Wages can be shown to create consumption capacity and thence the market demand which makes production and return to capital possible. By focusing on the flows and conversions of matter and energy, however, we can extend these measures directly to the accretion of humanly useful forms of knowledge and social organization, modifications of the physical environment, and the environmental costs of matter-energy transformations as well as to the production and exchange of commodities. We can also show that the relation between extractive and productive economies is not reducible to the accumulation strategies of regionally distinct dominant classes, but is a physical requirement of industrial production. Finally, we can show that the exhaustion of a series of modes of extraction must eventually extinguish modes of production which depend on them.

Accelerated energy flow to the world industrial core permits the social complexity which generates political and economic power there and permits the rapid technological changes which transform world market demands. It thus creates the conditions of the core's economic and political dominance over the world system to which the dominant classes of peripheral economies respond with their own accumulation strategies.

Adams, however, has not fully realized the sociological implications of his essentially physical formulation. The energy which organisms consume is dissipated at highly variable rates. Although all conversions of matter and energy heighten entropy, this rate is also highly variable. Human intervention in the conversion of energy and matter accelerates entropy, but it may also direct or embody energy and matter in forms which are both more durable and more useful. Genetic manipulation of plants, the storage of food products, or the treatment of wood are all possible examples. At a more abstract level, human memory and learning, and thus social organization, also involve the partial conserving of experiences which required the consumption of energy but which may make future uses of energy and matter more humanly efficient. Clearly, the capital plant and physical infrastructure of articulated production systems require and embody energy which has been consumed but which is being dissipated in ways and at rates which preserve its human utility. The socially and technologically complex organization of the articulated economy is finally only possible if vast amounts of energy are thus "embodied" or conserved in useful ways. Thus, if society is composed of the energy it consumes, articulated societies consume extractive economies and their natural environments and in the process become more complex and more powerful. As long as there are sufficient energy resources to consume, they also remain more flexible (unless the by-products of the energy and matter flow-through pollute their own environments to an impossible degree).

The extractive region, which loses energy and matter, becomes increasingly simplified, both ecologically and socially, and less adaptive or flexible both through its simplification and its loss of resources and through the disruption of the natural energy transformation processes related to or dependent on the extracted resource. Unable to embody energy in either durable physical infrastructure or in complex and adaptive social organization and technology, it becomes increasingly vulnerable to penetration by and subordination to the productive economies which can concentrate control over nonhuman energies and effectively coordinate much larger and more complex organizations of human energy.

The articulation and acceleration of the productive economy, then, does not only depend on nor is it adequately described by a wage-consumption-profit-production treadmill calculated in exchange values. It also requires the concentration and coordination of human and non-human energy flows and their embodiment in both complex social organization and durable infrastructure. This it achieves at the cost of the extractive economy and extracted environment.

Conventional economic models do not adequately explain the necessary relations between extraction and production. Nor, because of their derivation from production systems, can they adequately explain the internal dynamics of extractive economies. They limit their concepts of value to measures of labor and capital and so exclude multiple other values essential to human and social reproduction.

The imperfect fit between monetary measures such as wages and prices and theoretical notions of labor value severely distort the examination of unequal exchange between classes and between regionally bounded social formations (Emmanuel, 1972; Amin, 1978; de Janvry, 1981:15). The labor theory of value requires concepts of abstract labor that are theoretically coherent only within a fully capitalist economy (see de Janvry, 1981:79). Such economies do not exist, and the closest approximations to them are intimately bound to noncapitalist formations, both through exchange and through their necessary dependence on resource extraction. A labor theory of value excludes from consideration the usefulness to continued social reproduction of energy transformations in the natural environment. Nor can it take into account the value of the ideas, beliefs, and information which underlie human social organization. These and all other human experiences are formed out of previous dissipation of energy. They are all essential to humanly effective uses of natural energy and may make these uses more efficient in terms of their human energy costs. I believe that the unequal relations between articulated and disarticulated, and between extractive and productive, systems can ultimately be explained by the informational and organizational forms which energy-intensive economies foster in articulated productive systems and which simply cannot evolve in energy-losing extractive systems. The first generates more and more social power and the technology to extend this power over wider geographical areas. The second progressively loses social power.

Energy, Value, and Social Reproduction

The survival and reproduction of society itself must be the ultimate criterion of value, so our concept of value must include anything which affects this process and its outcomes. Labor value, or its imperfect monetary measures, cannot do this. Measures of energy and matter and of their conversion, however, touch everything which is humanly useful. Rather than separating human activity from other ecosystemic processes, these measures allow us to see the interdependencies between human energy use and energy transformation processes which proceed naturally, i.e., without human intervention.[2]

If value is defined only in terms of labor, we have no way to assess the costs which contemporary uses of the environment may impose on subsequent generations and social formations. Energy measures can provide us a calculus of costs and values—past, present, and future—for the multiple effects of human intervention in natural energy transformations. These effects include the disruption of the biotic chains which capture and store energy, the incorporation of energy into immediately consumable goods and services, and the partial conservation of energy and matter in more durable physical infrastructure and social organization.

To use these measures, however, we must reject the anthropocentric and temporally biased notions that value occurs only as a cognitive attribution to certain things or processes. We must also reject the idea that resources do not exist until they are discovered to be useful by humans. Humans may eat fish without knowing or understanding what the fish eat, but this ignorance does not diminish the value of the fish's sources of nutrients to the survival and reproduction of human society. Human activity at one period may destroy or reduce natural energy transformation processes whose usefulness can only be realized with future knowledge or technology; present ignorance does not reduce the cost, or loss of value, to future human generations.

Temporally and culturally bound attributions of value are both socially and epistemologically significant, however, because they affect the allocation and distribution of human labor and the forms of energy extracted from the environment. New technologies and new consumption patterns create new value attributions for the resources they require. The attribution of value to labor enormously influences human decisions about both social organization and uses of natural resources. The differential valuation of labor in different modes of production influences the flow of goods between different economies. Most important, labor is essential to the use value of most naturally occurring resources. All of these, however, constitute only part of the energy transformation processes which sustain human life and society. All of them finally depend on values which occur in nature as the result of energy flows largely independent of human intervention.

Pure extractive economies are the extreme case of human appropriation of these values, but many apparently productive processes include elements of extraction. Different agricultural and pastoral economies, for example, present a gradient of the proportions of human labor and natural values incorporated into the final product, ranging from the minimal modifications of the natural environment in ecologically complex swidden systems to the energy-intensive manipulations and simplifications of bounded ecosystems in large-scale monocropping systems. Forestry exhibits similar gradations.

Human societies depend on complex and variable combinations of natural and labor values. Energy as a measure can be applied to the creation of both kinds of value and allows us to relate them through a common currency. It also allows us to see the usefulness, and thus the value, of human learning and social organization. We can examine the ways that human societies reorganize matter to build their own environments as social inventions which extend the value of portions of the energy which society consumes and dissipates. Finally, it forces us to recognize that there is no possible unidimensional calculus of value because the long-term maintenance of human life depends on energy transformation processes of which we are not yet aware. We cannot measure yet all of the complex energy exchanges in the biotic chains which make up the ecosystems in which we participate. Nor can the value of human organization be directly measured. We know we can use both human and nonhuman energy more effectively because we have remembered past uses of energy and have stored and transmitted this knowledge through social organization, but we could only measure the value of this knowledge and organization by comparing its presence to its absence in the same society. Even without a unidimensional calculus of value, however, we can analyze the very different potentials for social organizational, infrastructural, and economic development in the societies which concentrate energy from outside and the societies which lose energy to them. We can then also explain how the dominance of productive systems accelerates extraction and ecological destruction.

Focusing our analysis on economies which are predominantly extractive highlights the particular internal dynamics of extraction processes and forces major revisions to theories of value. This is necessary to correct both the temporal and industrial biases of most theories of social and economic development. The ultimate goal of such an exercise, however, must be to reveal both the internal dynamics and the necessary external relations between different regional social formations. Only then can we understand either uneven development or the prospects for long-term, sustained human and social reproduction.

Most theorists of development and underdevelopment have erred in ignoring the special dynamics and sequences in extractive and other noncapitalist economies. Many have also become excessively engaged in increasingly sterile debates over the primacy of internal or external perspectives. They have, however, identified and analyzed crucial phenomena which contribute to development and underdevelopment, and their debates have helped them refine their concepts. I do not so much argue that they have been wrong in their own ideas as that their explanations have been too partial. Their ideas have helped my own attempts to understand the underdevelopment of a particular region and to develop a more general model of the interaction between regional and world economies. I believe that their explanations must finally be recast in ecological models of social evolution, but first it is useful to examine them on their own terms. I attempt to correct some of their errors and especially try to show where and how they may fit together. Finally, though, I return to the decisions and actions of local groups within their own total environment (physical, social, political, and commercial) as essential to the differences between development and underdevelopment of the regions which they inhabit. It is they, after all, who must balance local and global considerations; they who must live with the ecosystems they change; they who must synthesize what are otherwise abstractions of social scientists.

The Internal-External Debate and the Question
of Unequal Exchange

Though the rapid succession of competing models of national development since World War II created the impression of a series of
major paradigm shifts (Foster-Carter, 1976), the current debate between
proponents of world-system theories (Wallerstein, 1974a, 1974b, 1981;
Frank, 1979) and their Marxist critics (Laclau, 1971; Mandel, 1975;
Brenner, 1977; Weeks and Dore, 1979) about whether analysis should
proceed from a global system of unequal exchange or from specific
modes of production simply inverts the terms of an earlier debate.

In that earlier debate Frank (1969) and Wallerstein (1975) argued
that the modernization theorists' focus on systems of production and
exchange internal to particular underdeveloped countries obscured the
crucial effects of international trade systems. Modernization theories
(Smelser, 1963; Eisenstadt, 1964, 1966a, 1966b) had themselves emerged
as alternatives to the Marxist theories of imperialism (Lenin, 1939;
Luxemburg, 1951; Baran, 1957) and to the liberal theories of comparative advantage (see Ragin and Delacroix, 1979), which were based on
notions of international trade. Major differences in conceptual apparatus and theoretical elaboration have obscured the circular nature of
this alternation between global exchange and internal production as a
primary focus. The models proposed as alternatives in these debates
do not directly confront each other.

Theories which assign explanatory primacy either to global or to
regional systems ignore historical processes, continuities, and dynamics
in the other system. I believe that each system implies a distinct level
of analysis and that these levels of analysis must be articulated through
a selection of variables and through historical periodizations which
provide common referents for both levels of analysis.

Advocates of a global perspective have recently recognized that sociological explanations of underdevelopment must deal simultaneously
with two distinct levels of analysis: one appropriate to sequential changes
in the socioeconomic structures and processes in particular regionally
defined spaces, and the other appropriate to the dynamics of a global
system made up of many diverse parts (Frank, 1979:2-13; Wallerstein,
1981), but their attempts to do this finally founder on their insistence
on global levels of analysis. My own strategy is to elaborate a critical
synthesis of the externally focused theories of imperialism, dependency,
and world system with the internally focused theories of modernization
and modes of production. I do this in order to determine what parts
of existing explanations of development can be usefully incorporated

into a more comprehensive ecological model of social and economic change.

The internal-external debate, which has created so much controversy over the past fifteen years, has been influenced by state policy, by the outcome of development programs in the less developed nations, and by changes in the world economy (see de Janvry, 1981:7-20). As Asian and African colonies became formally independent nations and as Latin American governments sought to encourage "import-substitution" industrialization as an escape from the vicissitudes of fluctuating terms of trade (Furtado, 1970; Prebisch, 1963; Booth, 1975), theories of modernization responded to the sociological question of what forms of social organization and collective beliefs or attitudes might provide the necessary conditions for enhanced production and capital accumulation in industry and commercial agriculture (Smelser, 1963; Hunt, 1966; Eisenstadt, 1964; Lerner, 1968; Inkeles, 1971). Most of these theories were based on transfer or metaphoric extension of sociologists' beliefs about the social bases of production in their own already industrialized societies (Myrdal, 1970; de Janvry, 1981). This limited their prescriptive and predictive utility, but many of their basic concepts provide useful descriptions of developmental ideologies and programs of national states (Portes, 1980). Their ideological biases may vitiate their critical and theoretical validity (Frank, 1969), but this very bias closely conforms to the underlying assumptions of many development programs. These theories have directly informed official ideologies, and they can thus provide important sensitizing concepts for our analysis of the developmental state. They can also contribute to analysis of how complex modern bureaucracies, which evolved in capitalist industrial systems, operate when they are imposed on noncapitalist, nonindustrial social formations.

The size and complexity of modern bureaucratic organizations emerge from and rest on accelerated and intensified energy use in productive economies. Their organizational forms, ideologies, and behaviors, however, are not directly accessible through energy analysis. Rather, these phenomena require a type of sociological analysis which some modernization theories have most nearly achieved. The failures and other unintended results of modernization programs limit, but do not eliminate, the analytical utility of modernization theories.

Import substitution and institutional modernization bring about social, political, and economic dislocations by increasing income disparities, increasing foreign control of domestic production systems, displacing labor, and aggravating rural-urban and interregional inequalities. These dislocations stimulated a return to an external, or global, level of analysis focused again on international exchange (see Long, 1977).

Dependency and world-system perspectives were introduced into American sociological discourse with denunciations of the ideological obfuscations and theoretical distortions inherent in the internal focus of modernization theories (Frank, 1969; Wallerstein, 1975). These critiques centered on the underlying premise, shared by most modernizationists, that if internal obstacles to enhanced levels of production could be overcome then Third World nations could follow the same stages of development as had the central capitalist nations. The dependency theorists stressed instead the effects of politically enforced unequal exchange which accelerates capital accumulation in the industrial core at the expense of the nonindustrialized peripheral nations. They posed a complex set of processes, from primitive accumulation or direct appropriation of surplus from subject populations, to the repatriation of center capital through interest on credit, royalty payments, and transfer pricing, which channel surplus value from peripheral nations to the core, and thereby increase the relative underdevelopment of peripheral societies.

These external, or extranational, perspectives serve to explain the failure of modernization programs to eliminate poverty and inequality in most of the Third World and the social and political crises which occurred in countries which did experience rapid economic growth. They also allow much greater historical generality than the modernization theories. Early Latin American formulations of dependency theory (Cardoso and Faletto, 1969; Torres-Rivas, 1969) carefully examined the internal dynamics of class conflicts and alliances as they responded to external forces. The utility of this perspective has been severely flawed, however, by the polemical and conceptual excesses of other authors' tendency to treat internal, or regional, structures and processes as merely reflexes of the external, or global, processes on which they base their analysis. Wallerstein's and Frank's insistence that "the world-economy is capitalist through and through" (Wallerstein, 1981), no matter how carefully qualified, goes beyond its valid, intended point about the systemic relations which bind most of the world's economies in a single market. Frank (1967:7-8) absurdly reifies the abstract relations which comprise dependency when he extends his metropolis-satellite metaphor to the relationship between *hacendado* and *peon*. Wallerstein (1974a:400) homogenizes all regional class structures when he declares that slavery, coerced share-cropping, and wage labor are equivalent within a world capitalist mode of production because all three are organized to produce exchange values for profit. This extreme reductionism follows from his extrapolation of a single, global capitalist market to imply a single, global mode of production with a single division of labor (1974a:390-97).

This extrapolation is demonstrably invalid (Brenner, 1977). It is also unnecessary to Wallerstein's argument. I argue instead that the rapid accumulation of capital in the core, which is accelerated by unbalanced energy flows from the periphery, increases the rate of technological and consumption innovation and of consumption capacity in the core. The accelerated production-consumption-accumulation linkages allow the core to determine most global demand. Rapid innovation at the core subjects the periphery to a constantly changing market over which it has little control. If dominant classes in the peripheral areas reorganize modes of production and extraction in response to this externally dominated, frequently shifting market, the populations, social organization, and ecosystems of these areas are subject to repeated disruption. If the local modes of production are not so reorganized, the shifts in demand subject regional economies to falling terms of trade. Wallerstein's metaphorical extrapolations impede attention to these and other regional processes.

Similar problems emerge in Wallerstein's discussion of politically enforced unequal exchange. Consider Wallerstein's (1974a:401) statement, that "once we get a difference in the strength of the state machinery, we get the operation of 'unequal exchange' (Emmanuel, 1969) which is enforced on strong states by weak ones, by core states on peripheral areas. Thus, capitalism involves not only appropriation of the surplus value by an owner from a laborer, but an appropriation of surplus of the whole world-economy by core areas." Wallerstein is correct in asserting the systemic effects of uneven development on the relations between states. Systemically, these uneven relations enhance capital accumulation, and thus political or state power, in the core; he erroneously, however, treats the specific results of these relations as if they were themselves systemic (1974a, 1974b, 1976). In reality, the specific results of these uneven political strengths, such as the restrictions of certain manufacturing processes or exchange networks imposed by a particular colonizing state on a specific colonial economy, are not systemic. Rather, specific restrictions emerge from specific relations between two countries and vary according to colonial history, geography, and class structure, and according to the potential for effective colonial resistance or rebellion (see Bettelheim, 1972:319-20; Emmanuel, 1972:363-64, 380-83).

Frank and Wallerstein are similarly in error when they attempt to derive characteristics of component parts of the world system from their model of the system as a whole. Their tendencies to commit ecological fallacies have stimulated attempts to overcome the dependency model's naive determinism in its explanations of internal economic relations (dos Santos, 1973; Cardoso, 1972; Portes, 1976) and its simplistic treatment of class relations (Chilcote, 1974, 1978; Bath and James, 1976; Cardoso, 1977; de Janvry, 1981).

Various Marxist critics, however, have argued that the dependency model itself is invalid because of its emphasis on unequal international exchange as a primary explanatory variable. These analysts have insisted that development and underdevelopment can only be understood through a focus on specific modes of production. Unfortunately, in attempting to correct the fallacies Frank and Wallerstein commit by using a general world system of exchange to characterize particular modes of production, many of these Marxists commit the obverse logical error by trying to explain the entire world economic system in terms of the internal dynamics of particular modes of production. Capitalist expansion, as expressed in Mandel's (1975:47) notion that "capital presses outward from the center," is explained as an internal characteristic of capitalist modes of production which determines the stages of the articulation of capitalist, semicapitalist, and precapitalist relations of production. Palloix (1969:21, cited in Frank, 1979:4) categorically denies the autonomy of "external" exchange systems and maintains that "the external dynamic is nothing other than the external manifestation of the problems raised by the internal dynamic." Similarly, Bettelheim (1972:300) maintains that a country's "specific [class] structure—determines the way in which each social formation fits into international production relations."

Wallerstein and Frank see politically enforced unequal exchange as the root cause of an international division of labor which profoundly discriminates against the peripheral regions by syphoning off their capital and keeping their labor less productive. Their Marxist adversaries have inverted this formula by maintaining that the differential productivity in different modes of production is the root cause of unequal exchange. The ensuing debate has obscured the need to consider regional production as particular and international exchange as systemic. It has also perpetuated the error of using labor as a standard of value and as the basis of comparison for the exchange of all goods, even when these goods are extracted with relatively little labor or when the social relations of production do not involve wages.

Wage differentials provide the primary mechanism which these Marxist analysts employ to extend the internal concepts of modes of production to the external question of unequal exchange. Mandel (1975:53) maintains that large reserves of cheap labor and land resulted in a lower organic composition of capital and lower rates of primitive accumulation in the less developed countries and that these in turn reduced or restricted productivity increases. "The exchange of commodities produced in conditions of a higher productivity of labor against commodities produced in conditions of a lower productivity of labor was an unequal one; it was an exchange of less against more labor, which inevitably led to a drain, an outward flow of value and capital from these countries to the advantage of Western Europe." Emmanuel (1972:104-96) focuses even more specifically on wage differentials as the root of unequal exchange, arguing that goods produced for low wages are systemically undervalued (in market prices) in relation to goods produced for high wages, that the less developed countries all have low wage levels, and that development appears not as the cause but as the consequence of high wages. Amin (1976, 1977) extends these ideas to link high wages in the center to the expanded consumption necessary to autocentric industrial development and accelerated capital accumulation.

These Marxist authors maintain that the concepts of wage differentials, of the resulting unequal exchange of "more labor" for "less labor," and of the consequent restrictions on capital accumulation in less developed countries allow them to focus on the internal dynamics of specific modes of production, but they can only do this by confounding internal and external exchange. Exchange, in their formulation, is only one "moment" of a total mode of production which includes the social and technological organization and performance of production (Anderson, 1974; Hindess and Hirst, 1975; Terray, 1972). Bettelheim (1972:300), for example, argues that "relations of exploitation cannot be constituted at the 'level of exchange,' they necessarily have to be rooted at the level of production, or otherwise exchange could not be renewed." This extension of exchange within to exchange between specific modes of production does not, however, permit the systemic analysis of the world economy and of its operations aimed at by global-level analysts.

Exchange within modes of production is crucial to the dynamics of each mode of production, and exchange between specific geographical areas may be analyzed in terms of the articulation of these modes of production and transfer of value between them (Long, 1975; Bradby, 1975; Rey, 1973; see review by Foster-Carter, 1978). These notions work for analysis of internal processes, but their logic is based on binary wage and value differentials. These binary comparisons do not account for the world economy as a system of exchange made up of and responding to the totality of modes of production and exchange incorporated into it and changing through the reorganization of this system around new technologies and new commercial and political alignments whose origins and impacts are themselves determined by systemic, rather than binary, differences in rates of capital accumulation. It is precisely because the international market is systemic, i.e., the result of the combined production and demand of all of its component modes of production, that exchange in this market and the effects of such exchange on all participating economies must be analyzed as a totality. Actual production systems and their class structure, rates of exploitation, and wage differentials, on the other hand, can finally only be established by separate analysis of specific modes of production. Simply put, we must distinguish between two different levels of exchange. The first involves exchange which occurs between regionally articulated classes and is but one moment of a particular mode of production, or between specific groups in regionally articulated modes of production. The second establishes the global market situations of the various classes which control export and import, and the market-oriented production on which they depend, in all the multiple modes of production which participate in the world system.

Bettelheim's, Emmanuel's, Amin's, and Mandel's somewhat different formulations all presuppose a definition of labor and wages appropriate to a capitalist mode of production, that is, one in which labor as a commodity is used and recompensed for production for profit in a market.[3] Thus, they implicitly affirm the pervasive capitalist character of the production relations which concern them, even though they insist on the specificity of the various noncapitalist, less productive modes of production in the underdeveloped regions. Their focus on the labor incorporated in a product assumes, incorrectly, that this labor is always the primary determinant of value. While there is a clear basis for such a definition in parts of Marx's own work, Marx used this overly simple definition of value only in specific industrial contexts.[4] He extensively expanded and qualified the notion of value in his discussions of differential, absolute, and monopoly ground rent, all of which consider resource values, or values in nature, which occur on or in land. These latter concepts of value are of special significance in analyses of less developed economies which mostly export unfinished or raw materials, in which both labor and capital comprise a relatively small portion of the total value. The fundamental values in lumber, in minerals, oil, fish, etc., are predominantly in the good itself, rather than in the labor incorporated in it.

The use of labor as a standard of value for unequal exchange thus ignores the exchange inequalities inherent in extractive economies, where value in nature is appropriated in one region and labor value incorporated in another. Bettelheim (1972:300-307), for instance, restricts the concept of exploitation to the appropriation of surplus labor value in specific modes of production and thus excludes from consideration the international inequalities involved in the exploitation and export of natural resources. De Janvry (1981:20) extends Bettelheim's restriction in his criticism of dependency and world-system perspectives: "By focusing on the external factors, the underdevelopment school tends to replace the relations of exploitation between social classes with those between geographical areas."

Once we acknowledge, however, that not only the value in labor but also the values in nature can be appropriated, it becomes clear that we cannot counterpose the exploitation between social classes and between geographical areas. Instead, we must consider the effects of the exploitation of labor and the exploitation of entire ecosystems as separate but complementary phenomena which both affect the development of particular regions. We can therefore reject as well Amin's (1977) arguments that unequal exchange occurred only after center wages started to rise above subsistence levels as the result of imperialist strategies which opened world markets and world sources of raw materials for capitalist exploitation. The appropriation of values in nature, from the periphery, in fact initiated unequal exchange between regions, and between ecosystems, long before the rise of wages and the expansion of consumer demand in the core. Examination of the ecological effects of the ivory trade (Palmer and Parsons, 1977) and the demographic effects of the slave trade (Wallerstein, 1976) on large parts of Africa demonstrate the impact of exploitation between geographic areas as well as between classes on the evolution of unequal exchange.

Additional value is created when extracted materials are transformed by labor. The important point, however, is that this additional value is generally realized in the industrial center, rather than at the periphery. Thus, there are multiple inequalities in international exchange. One, certainly, results from the differential wages of labor. Another, however, is in the transfer of the natural value in the raw resources from periphery to center. Another is in the location of the full realization of value and of its accelerated consumption-production linkages in the center, rather than in the peripheral sources of the material commodities. The outward flows of energy and the absence of consumption-production linkages combine with the instability of external demand and with the depletion of site-specific natural resources to prevent the storage of energy in useful physical and social forms in the periphery, and leave it increasingly vulnerable to domination by energy-intensifying social formations at the core. Finally, if the resources do not renew themselves naturally, the inequality of the exchange is intensified by the loss of resources and by the disruption of associated natural energy flows in the periphery itself.

Bettelheim's and de Janvry's insistence that only classes and not regions can be exploited simply does not acknowledge that nationally or regionally dominant classes are themselves subject to different rates of exchange, both "downward" in their own modes of production and "outward" with international markets. These different rates affect their profits and their potential capital accumulations differently. The different regionally dominant classes themselves, therefore, are located in different market situations within the world system. Equally important, their own position within the world system depends on the viability of the local ecosystem. Locally dominant classes may be instrumental in depleting the natural resources within that ecosystem, but this does not mean that they are not themselves subject to the unequal exchange of natural values in the world market. Bettelheim's assertion that exploiters cannot also be exploited misses the important point that entire regions may be subject to unequal exchange, that this will limit both capital accumulation by dominant classes and production-enhancing social organization within those regions, and that this eventually impoverishes both dominant and subordinate classes.

Finally, there is a tendency in the modes of production approach to attribute "backwardness" (de Janvry, 1981) to specific modes of production and to specific class structures. The advantage of a world systemic approach is that "backwardness" is necessarily seen as relational, i.e., between connected economies, rather than inherent in a single economy. While it is clearly possible to compare technological and energy consumption levels between economies, societies may also be characterized in terms of their capacity to sustain long-term yields with minimal social inequality. World market participation has severely diminished this capacity in many noncapitalist societies, and the core economies have been able to reduce income inequalities only by intensifying energy flow-through from the periphery at rates which cannot be sustained over the long run (Georgescu-Roegen, 1970; Adams, 1975; Schnaiberg, 1980; de Janvry, 1981:17).

Wallerstein's attempt to systematize the totality of historical events which dependency theorists had analyzed separately and Frank's (1979) recent refinement and systematizations of his own concepts have been greatly enriched by their attempts to deal with criticisms from an internal modes of production perspective. I believe that adequate integration of these perspectives with each other and with explanations of how complex modern organizations operate is finally impossible, however, unless we recast our economic models to take into account (1) the absolute physical dependence of production on extraction, (2) the locational characteristics and regional inequalities which distinguish productive from extractive systems, (3) the very different ecological, demographic, and social structural evolutionary processes within each type of system, and (4) the longterm consequences of a net flow of matter and energy from extractive to productive economies. The necessary relations between production and extraction, the fact that they typically occur in different regions, and their different ecological results all fundamentally determine both their long-term and short-term potential for social production and reproduction.

Extraction and production may occur together in social formations bounded by a single regional ecosystem. In such cases the diversity of human needs may distribute extractive activity across such a wide range of species and minerals that biotic chains can reproduce themselves stably. Once the profit-maximizing logic of extraction for trade across regional ecosystems is introduced, however, price differentials between extractive commodities and the differential return to extractive labor stimulate concentrated exploitation of a limited number of resources at rates which disrupt both the regeneration of these resources and the biotic chains of coevolved species and associated geological and hydrological regimes. Once this stage of exploitation has been reached, the industrial modes of production inevitably undermine the resource bases on which they depend. Industrial modes of production have evolved the social organizational and the infrastructural capacity to change their own technologies and thereby to find substitutes for essential resources as they are depleted. This process is necessarily finite, however, as each new technology requires other resources from what is, ultimately, a limited stock.

Analysis of energy flows between regions and of different uses of energy in different regional social formations provides a much fuller explanation of uneven development than any drawn from conventional economic models. If energy and matter necessarily flow from extractive to productive economies, it follows that social and economic processes will be intensified and accelerated in the productive economy and will become more diffuse and eventually decelerate in the extractive economy. The flow of energy and matter to productive societies permits the increased substitution of nonhuman for human energies, allows for increased scale, complexity, and coordination of human activities, stimulates an increasing division of labor and expands the specialized fields of information which this entails, makes possible increasingly complex systems of transport and communication, and engenders the means of technological and administrative innovation by which the crises of resource scarcity are overcome. The mode of extraction, on the other hand, loses energy, and so becomes socially and economically simpler, less diversified, and subject to technologically determined changes in market demand which the modes of production generate. Once we understand this, we can understand as well that, while the actual flow of commodities between regions can be explained in terms of markets and labor costs, the consequent uneven development of different regions of the world can be fully understood only by considering the effects of uneven energy flows on both the physical and social environments of different social formations and on the progressive subordination of simplified, energy-losing societies to increasingly complex, energy-gaining societies.[5]

Our theories of unequal exchange and of uneven development have failed to integrate the internal dynamics of regional social formations with the external dynamic of a world market system because they have not accounted for the necessary relations between extraction and production or for their consequences on the evolution of different societies. These production-based theories can, however, provide essential components for an ecological model of regionally unequal development, because their basic assumptions closely match the central belief systems of modes of production which currently dominate the world system. Decisions about production, extraction, and exchange are in fact based on anthropocentric value systems which subordinate nature and nonhuman energy to human strategies for enhancing power and control over other humans and for increasing the effective productivity of human labor. These strategies tend to short-term maximization of return to labor and capital with little concern for long-term social reproduction. Conventional theories of development, if properly integrated, can provide us tools to explain the production and exchange decisions and the political and administrative strategies of dominant classes in different kinds of societies. We must go beyond these theories, however, if we wish to understand the consequence of these human decisions for either the short-term development of particular regional social formations or the long-term reproduction of society.

The Problem of Periodization

An adequate theory of development requires that we delineate the "chains of historical causation" (Gutkind and Wallerstein, 1976:7) in ways which permit simultaneous reference to both global and regional units of analysis as historically continuous systems. Analysis at the global level has achieved several effective "periodizations" of the world system, but these have all derived from sequential changes in the structure and composition of capital and in the relations of dominant classes to the state in the industrial core (Lenin, 1939; Frank, 1979; Baran, 1957; Amin, 1974; Preobazhensky, 1965; Mandel, 1975). While these periodizations make reference to the impact of these changes on the periphery, they do so by using different peripheral regions to exemplify the dynamics of the different periods (see, e.g., Wallerstein, 1976). They thus sacrifice historical continuity at the local level.

I propose that systematic consideration of the commodities exported from a region provides a useful way to periodize both the world and the regional economies and thus to relate the sequence of change in each. A focus on exported commodities allows analysis of the modes of production and extraction from which the commodity emerges at the regional and local levels and of the technological and market changes which determine demand for it at the global level. Analysis of the extraction or production and the exchange of particular commodities also allows specification of the power which domestic capital, international capital, the national state, and foreign states exert in these processes. Because specific export commodities provide points of common reference for both external exchange systems and internal production systems, they serve as a bridge between different levels of analysis. A focus on specific commodities also permits analysis of the ecological, social organizational, and demographic effects both in the region of extraction and in the region where its eventual transformation contributes to the acceleration of production and consumption.

Finally, a focus on specific commodities permits analysis of the ways that disruption, reduction, or depletion of natural resources may limit the subsequent developmental potential of the environment from which commodities are extracted.

Toward an Ecological Model of Uneven Development

A full account of the intersection between regional and global systems requires separate analysis of each system in terms which recognize the dynamics of each system as an integral unit while simultaneously permitting analysis of their effects on each other. I attempt to achieve this in a historical analysis of the underdevelopment of the Amazon Basin (1) by organizing this history into periods which correspond to the predominance of particular commodities in the Amazon's export trade; (2) by examining the extent to which the combination of political forces and the changes in world-system demand structured the relative composition of exports from the Amazon; (3) by describing how extraction and production of these commodities were organized, either through reorganization of prior modes of production and extraction or through organization of new modes; and (4) by analyzing how the demographic, organizational, infrastructural, and ecological effects of each of these modes of production and extraction established the potential for and the limits on later modes of production and extraction. This articulation of concepts across levels and across time requires precise attention to internal responses to opportunities and pressures generated in external systems. Both the world system and local modes of production and extraction constitute discrete units of analysis whose mutual effects can be seen in the ways that local actors—including those deriving power from organizations that operate beyond the local area—reorganize local modes of production and extraction in order to take advantage of exchange opportunities in the world system.

Treating each local mode of production and extraction as regionally discrete and historically continuous allows consideration of the internal dynamics by which societies may reproduce themselves independently of their participation in a world system and of the variation between societies and over time in participation in, response to, or occasional withdrawal from the world system. This avoids reifying dependency, unequal exchange, or capitalism as causal agents; rather, it permits development and underdevelopment of particular nations or regions to be understood as the ways that particular local classes reorganize modes of production and extraction in response to exchange opportunities and political actions in the world system.

This approach can be described as a model which specifies that a particular mode of production, or extraction, organized at one time (t_1 ... t_{n-1}) will set the parameters—ecological, demographic, organizational, and infrastructural—for subsequent modes of production or extraction (at t_2 ... t_n) in the same region. The world system as unit of analysis is essential to this model because it provides an explanation of the global processes and dynamics which create, and change, opportunities for exchange and profit for dominant classes from commodities produced in or extracted from specific regions. It becomes significant as a unit of analysis for a specific region (1) to the extent that actors, or groups of actors, derive sufficient power from beyond the local area to reorganize modes of production or extraction; (2) to the extent that local actors reorganize modes of production in response to exchange opportunities outside the local area; (3) in establishing and changing demand for goods which may be produced or extracted in the local area; and (4) in setting prices for goods exported from and imported to the local area. Levels of development and the potential for further development at t_2 ... t_n can thus be explained in terms of contemporary modes of production and extraction that are partially organized in response to world-system exchange opportunities, but are bounded in their response by the demographic, ecological, and infrastructural parameters set by previous modes of production or extraction and by present rates of exchange for their exports.

This model must also, however, include the effects of development programs initiated by modern national states and implemented by modern bureaucracies on both the natural and human environment. Modernization, as a set of prescriptive and predictive theories of development, has been extensively disproved. I argue in later chapters, however, that modernity, as a self-legitimating strategy of national states which facilitates the exploitation of peasants and workers, as a system of centralized control, as the administrative mode of the state's bureaucratic agencies, and as the predominant ideology of bureaucratic planners and functionaries, affects the ways that locally dominant groups — including bureaucrats — reorganize local modes of production and extraction. I argue that modernity, either as administrative procedure or as bureaucratic ideology, cannot simply be subsumed within the concept of capitalist mode of production and associated superstructure because of the frequency with which modern bureaucratic forms and ideologies are imposed on nonmodern, noncapitalist modes of production and extraction. Nor can we accept Wallerstein's dismissal of the national state (practically, he seems to mean only the peripheral national state) as an appropriate unit of analysis.

Rather, the organizational structure, the operating procedures and ideologies, and the political and economic activities of the modern state must be incorporated into any energetics model of the relations between particular regional and global systems. Just as the regional economy responds to and participates in a world system of exchange, the state participates in an international system of political relations. As much as the economy, national states have incorporated new technologies. Obligated to interact with other political and economic systems, peripheral modern states have imported structure, ideology, and procedure from core states and international organizations. Under "associated dependent development" (Cardoso, 1973; Evans, 1979), the state directly participates in and evolves in response to complex new forms of industrial organization.

Social and economic formations may be quite distinct in different regions of a large underdeveloped economy, but the state seeks to homogenize its political and administrative apparatus and its political control across widely diverse regional organization. The modern state, however, emerged out of energy-intensive industrial production systems. In its promotion of social welfare, in its attempts to maintain order, and in its regulation of economic activities, the modern state's complexity and size have corresponded to the high degree of economic differentiation, specialization, and complexity of the articulated industrial economy. As it has grown, its increased size and complexity have directly absorbed higher levels of human and nonhuman energy. It has indirectly absorbed further amounts of energy as the civil sectors of society have had to interact with and adapt to the demands of state regulation. Such forms of regulation are enormously costly, both in their own maintenance and in the requirements for adaptation and compliance with their procedures and regulations. They demand special training for those who run them and for those who must deal with them. Their very functioning presupposes complex legal and financial institutions. They can only be maintained and can only function, therefore, in energy-intensive systems where high proportions of nonhuman energy in production liberate human energy for other purposes. They are too costly to maintain or to achieve rational results in systems where the efficiency of human energy is not greatly enhanced by nonhuman energy.

Modern political systems, however, are expansive, dissipative structures. Modern bureaucracies are composed of specialized agencies which seek to extend their own resources and jurisdictions (Crozier, 1964). They simultaneously become more hypercoherent, i.e., excessively interconnected, as they become self-serving instead of system-serving (viz. Flannery, 1972). Thus, national states whose territories include both capitalist and noncapitalist social formations will tend to extend bureaucratic systems which may function relatively effectively in their own political and economic centers to the subordinate, nonindustrial or peripherial regions included in the national territory. This is especially likely to happen in a country like Brazil, where an authoritarian centralizing state defines and legitimates its functions as developmental. Such states participate directly in and attempt to stimulate, regulate, and direct rapid industrial development.

Analyses of dependent development (Cardoso, 1972, 1973; Evans, 1979) and of the corporatist or bureaucratic-authoritarian state (Malloy, 1977; Collier, 1979; O'Donnell, 1975, 1978) have shown how the dependent modern state may deepen and accelerate industrial development or may attempt to resolve its disjunctures and crises once it has reached certain levels. None of these theories of state intervention in the economy or of its enhanced control over the society, however, has recognized the developmental state's incapacity to transform economies which have neither the type of social organization nor the levels of surplus production and energy necessary to comply with and participate in the complex modern procedures which the state's own organizational logic and inherent expansiveness require. They have also ignored the ways that the extension of bureaucratic organization and procedures radically change the political, economic, and social relations between classes in noncapitalist social formations by favoring those groups with the capital, training, experience, and contacts necessary to comply with the requirements of central state bureaucracies. Nor have they realized the ways that the extension of modern bureaucracies into nonindustrial national peripheries and the breakdown of their operational rationality there leave the agencies of the state more susceptible to penetration and manipulation by private capitalist interests, further weakening and distorting the state's autonomy and administrative capacity.

Energy flows, the incorporation of energy into subsequently useful physical infrastructure, demographic distribution, and social organization, and the ecosystemic consequences of the different uses of energy clearly distinguish the varied modes of production and extraction which constitute a world system of exchange. Analysis of the extreme energy losses of extractive economies, and of their consequent incapacity to store parts of their energy flow-through in complex and flexible social infrastructure and organization, can inform a model for examining economies with different combinations and proportions of extraction and production. The activities and organization of the energy-concentrating and energy-directing modern national state can be incorporated into this model as a crucial instance of the dominance of energy-intensive organizations over social formations that cannot concentrate and preserve energy within their own structures.

Regions whose economies are largely extractive manifest extreme features of the disarticulated economy, but the articulated-disarticulated distinction is finally one of gradients, and the state provides a central mechanism in the articulation of the various regional economies, both with each other, with the national core, and with the world system. This approach to the state and to organizational complexity as a specifically modern characteristic both of articulated societies and of the centers which develop in "associated dependency" is a necessary complement to de Janvry's excessively economic model of the relations between these two types of social formation. Modern organizational forms are a crucial component of the means by which productive centers subordinate and attempt to control extractive peripheries. They may have unexpected and irrational effects, however, when they are imposed on less productive, less energy-intensive disarticulated societies. By incorporating the organizational and ideological aspects of the modern state into our model, and by attending to questions of its demands on energy and on production, we can more effectively deal with the complexities of internal-external relations. The reintroduction of the state also allows us to incorporate the special characteristics of regional inequalities within single nations into our analysis of world-system relations.

My ecological model also suggests that analysts of both world-system and modes of production theories have exaggerated the potential of capitalism as a mode of production and exchange to restructure other modes of production and extraction. Wallerstein's and Frank's affirmations that the entire system is capitalist, Bettelheim's (1972) assertion that capitalism partially destroys and partially preserves other modes of production in shaping these to its own ends, and Meillassoux's (1973:89) refusal to attribute any autonomous capacity for self-reproduction to noncapitalist modes of production when he claims that these are preserved because capitalism needs them all err first by attributing intention to capital itself but more fundamentally by ignoring that locally dominant groups enter into world market exchanges according to their own perceived opportunities, that they themselves may reorganize local modes of production and extraction, and that the opportunities to which they respond are frequently ephemeral, while the reorganization of local modes of production and extraction may have enduring local consequences (see, e.g., Palmer and Parsons, 1977; McCoy and de Jesus, 1982). Acknowledgment of the specific characteristics of extractive economies and of their differences from productive economies is crucial in this regard, as the geographical and temporal discontinuities of extractive economies are especially likely to lead to discontinuous participation in world systems of capitalist exchange. The human groups which enter and depart from this exchange network are responding to changing market opportunities (see Stavenhagen, 1966-67); they maintain themselves through other modes of production and extraction not because capitalism needs them, or because they themselves have become capitalist. Rather, they maintain themselves, as human groups always have, by adapting to their own environments, of which international exchange opportunities form a highly variable part, but which are also structured by the organization of earlier modes of production and extraction. If these adaptations reduce the long-term viability of the physical environment, they also reduce the life chances of the social groups which depend on it.

Georgescu-Roegen (1975) has shown how conventional economic models of production ignore crucial energy transformations which occur between the extraction of material from nature and its use in industry. By focusing only on production, i.e., the transformation of these materials by labor and capital, conventional economics ignores the environmental costs of extraction and energy transformation. We will only understand the inequalities inherent in the geographical separation of the different parts of the total processes by which materials in nature are finally transformed for human use and profit when we account for these differential costs to the various regions involved in the world system.

The Amazon: Extractive Exports and Underdevelopment

There are numerous regions of the world whose economic histories would provide relevant cases for a commodity-based model of underdevelopment.

The Amazon Basin in Brazil is one of the largest of these regions. The Amazon Basin has formed an integral part of the world economy for over 350 years. Soon after Portuguese colonization in the sixteenth century, it was supplying valued spices and animal oils to the European market. From 1860 until 1910 it supplied the bulk of the rubber for the automobiles and other machines which transformed American and European industry. In recent decades it has supplied increasing proportions of the components for the light metals required by modern transportation technology to reduce the effects of gravity and to reduce fuel consumption. Little of the energy extracted during the Amazon's long history of supplying valued commodities for world trade has been incorporated into enduring and useful social organization and physical infrastructure, however, nor is there much prospect that it will be in the future. On the contrary, the Amazon Basin is one of the poorest areas in the world, and the economic and social systems on which many of its inhabitants depend are seriously threatened by disruption or extinction. This impoverishment continues despite, and in many instances because of, major government development programs. I will examine the utility of my ecological model for explanations of the persistence of such poverty in this huge, resource-rich region.

Effective use and development of natural resources depend on human organization, and the possibilities for effective human organization are bounded by the effects of previous social organization and of previous uses of the environment. The cumulative effects of these sequences on a region's developmental capacities are dramatically illustrated in the case of the Amazon. The decimation of populations during colonial conquest and enslavement, the massive reimportation of human energy to satisfy international industry's needs for rubber in the late nineteenth and early twentieth centuries, and the present expulsion of both peasants and Indians from the lands on which they subsist, in addition to preventing effective and continuous human organization, have been accompanied by increasingly severe depredations of the natural environment. Each depredation, from the killing off of river fauna to the transformation of vast areas of forest into pasture of short economic usefulness and limited capacity for natural regeneration, has severely limited the potential for subsequent human settlement and economic use of the forest.

Sustained economic and social development is impossible when short-term economic and political interests can completely disrupt settlement patterns and the ecological systems on which they depend. In subsequent chapters I will show that the current exploitation of the Amazon, while lessening the impact of international capital flows and maintaining short-term economic growth for the Brazilian national industrial center, promises to perpetuate the demographic void which previous modes of extraction created in the Amazon's rural areas and thus to restrict its usefulness in the international and national economies of the future. I will also show how the energy-intensive and energy-absorbing nature of the national state's bureaucracy accelerated the extractive enterprise and the associated disruption of energy flows in the Amazon even when it attempted to reverse these processes. By irrationally extending energy-expensive structures and operating procedures into the energy-poor social formations of Amazonia, the state undermined existing but fragile human communities, devastated the ecosystem in which they subsisted, and severely distorted its own developmental projects. Instead of allowing environmentally balanced strategies for long-term sustained yields, modes of extraction conditioned by politically determined relations of unequal exchange continue to limit the possibilities of social and economic development in the Amazon.

The export economies of the Amazon Basin have been primarily extractive since the colonial period, but the commodities extracted have varied considerably. I expect that both the historical sequence and the internal characteristics of these extractive economies account in large part both for the continued poverty of the region and for the fact that it remains, still, an extractive frontier. In the following chapters I examine the interactions between the ways that specific modes of extraction affected subsequent developmental potential and the ways that world-system pressures and opportunities affected the establishment of each of these modes of extraction.

NOTES

1. The disjuncture between complex modern bureaucratic forms and the simpler institutional forms which emerge in an extractive periphery may be so great that the state abdicates administrative control to the military (see Martins, 1982; Schmink, 1981, 1982).

2. In purely physical terms, the distinctions between human and nonhuman energy and even between energy and matter are arbitrary, but they are necessary and useful if we are specifically interested in human society. The energy-matter distinction of the laws of thermodynamics does presuppose a physically

stable environment (Adams, 1982:13), but in fact the temperature of the environment in which human societies have evolved has been relatively stable, so this distinction is also useful.

3. Ragin and Delacroix (1979) classify these authors' theories somewhat differently than I do. I believe their distinctions between these authors are correct. There are, however, important shared charcteristics in these authors' approaches to modes of production and unequal exchange.

4. Marx and Engels did, however, steadfastly refuse to consider an energy calculus of value. See Martinez-Alier and Naredo (1982) for an intriguing discussion of their reasoning and of the difficulties it has caused for subsequent Marxist analysis.

5. The concepts of regions, of regionally defined social formations, and of regional ecosystems are crucial to analysis of extraction-production relations. Modes of extraction may emerge within nations dominated by modes of production; Appalachian mining and northwestern forestry in the United States are easy examples; Amazonian extraction and the growing industrial plant of south-central Brazil provide another. Inclusion of extractive regions under the authority of modern industrial states requires us to pay close attention to the different boundaries of overlapping political, legal, economic, social, and ecological systems.

CHAPTER 2

Extractive Economies and the Degradation of Natural and Human Environments

The failure of Western temperate zone agricultural technologies in the Amazon and ignorance of the utility of a wide range of protein sources not commonly used by European populations have fostered considerable debate about the density of human population in the Amazon prior to European conquest. The exuberant vegetation characteristic of much of the upland jungle, which comprises over 90 percent of the area, in fact occurs on extremely poor soils and depends on extremely rapid, tight nutrient cycles that deposit little organic matter on the soil. The soils, once the forest is cleared, are subject to rapid leaching and deterioration; monocrops planted on them are subject to pest and plague invasion. The inability to maintain dense monocropping in the Amazon has led numerous authors to assume that precolonial indigenous populations had to be very sparse. Recent research on contemporary indigenous adaptations through shifting agriculture, diversified cropping, and the use of a wide range of food sources, together with archaeological and historical research, however, increasingly has indicated that indigenous social organization and technology were capable of sustaining large, stable societies without disrupting the regenerative cycles of plant and animal reproduction. Evidence of dense, long-term human settlement provides a baseline against which the effects of colonial commodity extraction and exchange can be measured.[1]

When Denevan (1976) attempted systematic analyses of some of the historical records and extrapolated from existing knowledge of different ecological zones, he arrived at a tentative, and deliberately conservative, estimate of 6.8 million as the total precolonial population of what he defines as greater Amazonia. Denevan omitted some areas of high carrying capacity from his calculations, however (N. Whitten, personal communication). Isaacson (1980), using RADAM data (Brasil, 1976) published since Denevan's analysis, has shown that Denevan's estimates of twenty-eight people per square kilometer for the carrying capacity of the *várzea* (floodplain), the area of densest pre-Columbian settlement, should be revised upward to at least thirty-three people per square kilometer and possibly higher.

All the new evidence tends to confirm the early chroniclers' extensive, and mutually consistent, reports of high population density (Medina, 1934; Heriarte, 1874; Batista, 1976). These explorers reported that large indigenous settlements along the rivers maintained stores of maize, manioc, sweet potatoes, dried fish, live turtles, and fowl, together with plantations of pineapples, avocados, guavas, and other fruits. One early account claims that a single society, the Tapajó, was capable of fielding an army of 60,000 men (Heriarte, 1874; Palmatary, 1960). Food supplies were sufficiently large to sustain the inhabitants and a Spanish expedition of 900 men for over a month in a single village (Sweet, 1974). Lathrap (1968a, 1968b, 1977) has shown that these riverine societies could maintain dense populations and complex social organization by coordinating hunting, fishing, and agriculture with the yearly rise and fall in the river's height. Beckerman (1978) has pointed out a wide array of nuts and grubs which could have provided additional rich protein sources.

These large populations could only be maintained by technological and social organizational adaptations to seasonal fluctuations in water levels. Access to fish, turtles, and mammals varied with the floods. Annual floods deposit sediment from the Andes across a wide floodplain (*várzea*), thus renewing its fertility and permitting intensive and highly productive agriculture. Cultivation had to follow flood cycles as well. Indigenous societies combined *várzea* cultivation with cultivation and extraction on the *terra firme* (uplands). The water's rise and fall imposed a marked seasonal cycle on subsistence strategies but simultaneously amplified the resource base. Adaptation to seasonal cycles and diversified exploitation of a wide range of energy sources maintained ecological balance. Though most of the *terra firme* was sparsely populated, the *várzea* and the bordering *terra firme* together supported large, dense populations on a stable basis. Indigenous societies also maintained dense populations by adapting their technologies and social organization to other favorable ecological zones, such as the rich ecotone between savannah and upland gallery forest (Nimuendaju, 1946, 1967) or by modifying less favorable environments with canals, causeways, and various forms of raised fields (Denevan, 1970.)

Lathrap (1974:149-51) suggests that the *várzeas* around the mouthbays of tributaries to the Amazon maintained dense settlements with relatively complex social organizations. These groups dominated trade with more sparsely settled, politically weaker groups, which population pressures on the *várzea* had pushed up along the tributary rivers and into the less productive *terra firme*. Thus various indigenous groups were hierarchically ordered up from the *várzea* hearths, along tributaries and into the *terra firme*. These *várzea*-based hierarchies formed a series of separate alliance and trade systems along the main river channel. The mouthbay-dominated trading and political systems and the articulation of economies adapted to different ecological zones which they fostered allowed greater population density than would have been possible if isolated groups had depended exclusively on the ecological zones they themselves inhabited.

These populations could sustain themselves only through finely balanced and complex relations with the natural environment and with each other. They were, therefore, enormously vulnerable to the distortions and dislocations of European penetration, which brought virulent new diseases such as influenza, smallpox, and measles and imposed the requirements of world trade, with its demands for excessive and ultimately destructive exploitation of a narrow range of natural resources and its devastating use of slave labor.

Neither the immediate nor the long-term results of this penetration can be adequately characterized in the way Bettelheim (1972) suggests—as the restructuring or partial dissolution of a prior mode of production with an imposed or predominant one. Rather, the following sections will show that this penetration established a locally dominant class which created a mode of extraction and so exploited both labor and nature that neither could fully reproduce itself. This class organized various modes of extraction in response to international market opportunities, but the rates of exchange for their exports were so unequal that the cycles of extraction and trade ultimately impoverished not only the physical and human environments but also the dominant classes that depended on them.

Commodity Extraction and Environmental Destruction

The progressive underdevelopment of an extractive periphery organized in response to world market demands is dramatically illustrated by the decimation of indigenous societies and the devastation of key plant and animal resources resulting from colonial exploitation of the Amazon. Where indigenous societies had exploited a wide range of natural energy sources at rates which allowed for their natural regeneration, colonial extraction responded to international demand by exploiting a few highly marketable resources beyond their capacity for natural regeneration, in many cases leading to environmental impoverishments, with widespread ramifications.

The rivers provided a major share of the resource base for dense aboriginal population, but they also provided the avenues for direct European penetration of the most heavily populated areas. As early as the sixteenth century, the Dutch, English, French, Spanish, and Portuguese were struggling to control the Atlantic coast of what is now northern Brazil. Chief among the prizes each sought was control over the sugar producing areas which extended 2,000 miles south of the Amazon delta. Secure tenure of these areas depended on control of the river. The earliest permanent penetration started in 1616, when the Portuguese started to build forts to protect national claims to the river basin (Tambs, 1974).

Portugal was economically incapable and politically indisposed to finance this military presence in a backwater of a minor colony (Sweet, 1974). Both civil and military posts were therefore filled by offering prebendal rights over land and labor (*donatários*). The spectacular success of sugar plantations on Brazil's Atlantic coast stimulated attempts to implant a similar economy in the Amazon, and the enthusiastic reception in Europe of native spices (*drogas do sertão*) inspired the organization of extractive expeditions upriver and inland from Belém (Reis, 1945; Sweet, 1974; Batista, 1976). Sugar and spices both required large amounts of manpower. Clearing jungle for monocrops, and planting, harvesting, and processing sugar cane are all extremely labor intensive. The average spice-gathering expedition lasted eight months and required large numbers of Indians as rowers, bearers, hunters, and gatherers (Maclachlan, 1973).

Though the Portuguese crown had evidently not intended to repeat its unsuccessful use of Indian labor on sugar plantations (Maclachlan, 1973), its practices of granting prebends to its functionaries in the Amazon and drastically limiting the supply of currency there (Sweet, 1974) led to extensive enslavement of Indian populations. Colonial production in the Amazon was never profitable enough to support either the purchase of expensive African slaves or the immigration of a European labor force. Slaving expeditions were conducted under a number of pretexts, the most common being that enslaved Indians had been captured in "just wars" or had been ransomed from other Indians who had enslaved them. The threat of slave raids led many Indians to submit to the agricultural-extractive labor regimen of the missions, where they were at least afforded a modicum of protection against such raids (Ross, 1978). Even the missions, however, which nominally controlled access to Indian labor, were obliged to make 20 percent of their labor force available for settlers' use, and their ability to enforce restrictions on civil use of Indian labor steadily eroded under political pressure from local government and settlers (Kiemen, 1954; Maclachlan, 1973; Sweet, 1974).

There is evidence that some slavery was practiced among the Amazon tribes prior to the European conquest, but the European demand for "red gold" increased and deepened this practice to the point of severe depopulation. Tribes such as the Tapajó, close to forts and susceptible to constant attack, were held for ransom until they provided slaves of other tribes (Nimuendaju, 1952; Sweet, 1974; Hemming, 1978). There are accounts of the Tapajó turning over their own children when they could not satisfy the European demand through their slave raids on other groups (Nimuendaju, 1952). The violence of the slaving raids and the flight of indigenous populations from the fertile river banks, which exposed them to attack, initiated the first, great reduction of native populations (Heriarte, 1874).

The demand for Indian slaves and mission labor and the resulting decimation of native populations accelerated as the colonial economy declined. Amazonian sugar could not compete with the sugar plantations on the Atlantic coast in either quality or cost of production. Depletion of the native spices near colonial settlements meant that collecting expeditions had to go farther inland, expanding their need for Indian labor even as European prices fell and local costs rose (Sweet, 1974). The slaving expeditions became more and more wasteful of Indian life as the drastic reduction of Indian populations along the rivers increased the time, distance, and expense of slaving expeditions (Reis, 1949; Ross, 1978). As early as 1693 there were complaints from slavers that it was necessary to go upriver as far as the present boundaries of Peru to find slaves (Hemming, 1978). As slaving expeditions had to go farther, they used more Indian rowers and provisions. Due to declining sugar and spice economies, insufficient capital was available to provision the slaving expeditions, so that numerous Indians died from malnutrition on the homebound trip (Sweet, 1974). The progressive impoverishment of the colony's natural resource base thus accelerated its decimation of the Indian labor force on which it depended.

The failure of export agriculture heightened the colony's dependence on extraction, and this in turn intensified secular opposition to missionary control of Indian labor. The missions were secularized in 1755; in 1757 the crown stopped encouraging the export of sugar and tobacco, and in 1759 the Jesuits were expelled (Kiemen, 1954; Maclachlan, 1973). All of this coincided with the establishment and growing power of Companhia Geral do Grão Pará e Maranhão, directed by Governor Mendonça Furtado, brother of the marquis de Pombal. The Companhia's main business was exporting cacao, which grew wild and required the prolonged extractive expeditions which the missions' ability to restrict access to Indian labor would have impeded (Herndon, 1853; Maclachlan, 1973; Alden, 1976; Ross, 1978; Dias, 1970). The Companhia also exported considerable amounts of lumber, for which it also depended on Indian labor (Dias, 1970; Alden, 1976).

Infectious diseases brought in by the Europeans may have reduced native population even more than slavery did. The dense riverine populations would have been enormously susceptible to the rapid transmission of new diseases, even ahead of direct contact with Europeans (see Denevan, 1976). The combination of crowding, excessive work, and poor nutrition made urban slaves particularly vulnerable to disease. Belém suffered a series of devastating epidemics which ravaged the Indian populations there (Maclachlan, 1973; Sweet, 1974; Batista, 1976). Trade with the missions would also have spread epidemics.

Competition with Dutch and Spanish colonies for territorial and economic control further reduced native populations. Struggles with the Spaniards at the headwaters of the Amazon stimulated conflict between different indigenous groups as well as punitive military expeditions by both colonies (Sweet, 1974; Hemming, 1978). Dutch manufactured goods were transported up from the Guyana coast and down as far as the middle Amazon in trade between indigenous groups. The Portuguese, worried by this challenge to their monopoly, mounted an extended military compaign against the groups which controlled this trade along the Rio Negro. This campaign culminated in the hunting down, capture, and death of this group's chief, Ajuricaba, and the dispersion of what remained of his group in remote areas of *terra firme* (Sweet, 1974).

In addition to direct reduction of native populations, European demand for animal oils eliminated natural resources crucial to the subsistence of dense populations. The manatee, a large aquatic mammal, and the turtle had provided rich supplies of oil and protein for indigenous groups. Smith (1974) has shown that cultural checks and the regionally bounded exchange system maintained a harmonious relation between turtle and aboriginal populations. Turtles were kept in captivity to balance seasonal fluctuations in other protein sources. They flourished sufficiently in the Amazonian waters to allow their extensive use for meat and oil without population reduction. Pressure from missionaries and early Spanish and Portuguese traders led to massive exploitation of turtle eggs for oil to be sold on local and international markets and of meat for sale as a delicacy much prized by the Europeans.[2] The manatee was intensely hunted both for local consumption and to supply both oil and meat for ships involved in the West Indies sugar trade.

The rapid reduction of the turtles and the manatees directly deprived the indigenous populations of important sources of oil and meat. It reduced the region's carrying capacity indirectly as well by seriously disrupting critical links in the riverine ecosystem, thus reducing the other riverine resources on which these human populations depended. Turtlings form part of the food chain maintaining the larger fishes, and the manatee's water-surface grazing is crucial in keeping the lakes and channels adjacent to the main river sufficiently free of vegetation to allow the passage of canoes and to permit the entry of light required for the storage of energy in the form of complex organic molecules. Turtles and manatees also stabilize nutrient-cycles on which fish depend (Fittkau, 1973). As the richest fishing occurs in the quieter waters that are removed from the rivers' main flow, the reduction of the manatee and the turtle greatly diminished the protein resources available to riverine societies.

Finally, the establishment of cattle raising in areas of natural pasture, especially on the *várzea*, the extension of the communities around the various forts, and the later rush for precious minerals pushed the remaining Indians farther away from the more fertile river's edge into the forest where they could only subsist in dispersed and shifting settlements (Palmatary, 1960; Bastos, 1975).

By the end of the eighteenth century, the twin assaults on native populations and natural resources had created a demographic and economic vacuum, broken only by a few small and impoverished cities. "The existing labor pool had been so overtaxed that no sector, public or private, was able to meet its labor needs" (Maclachlan, 1973), even in a depressed economy. The *várzeas* had been almost completely depopulated; much of the technology necessary for their effective exploitation had disappeared with the indigenous societies which had used them (Ross, 1978). Europeans had conquered the Amazon, turning those portions of it which had commercial value—Indian labor, turtle and manatee oils and meat, wild spices, and grass—to their own short-term profit in ways which precluded sustained economic exploitation.

The Europeans' rapacity, and their stubborn belief that as members of a master race they should not engage in productive work (Sweet, 1974), rapidly exhausted the resources on which their dreams of great wealth were founded. The Amazonian colony sank into unrelieved poverty and stagnation aggravated by political intrigue, frequent epidemics, and the tumult of the years following Brazil's independence from Portugal, when struggles between various ethnic, political, and economic factions eliminated about 20 percent of the total population

(Raiol, 1970) and devastated the already limited productive capacity which had been developed on the surviving sugar plantations and cattle ranches (Weinstein, 1980).

With the exception of sugar and tobacco, little had been produced during two centuries of Portuguese colonization. A great deal, however, had been extracted and sold. The technology used in this extraction was primarily indigenous (Maclachlan, 1973), but the core of indigenous productive technology had been lost. Locally dominant classes had established new modes of extraction in response to international exchange opportunities and had used these modes of extraction in ways which decimated local forces of production. The exchange relations in which this class attempted to transform its control over labor and resources into profits were extremely unequal, but conventional calculation of unequal exchange rates based on a labor theory of value or on transfer of surplus to the center is clearly inadequate to analysis of this case. The extraction costs of what was being exchanged included not only human labor but also human life, social organization and technology, and the ecological viability of various interdependent plant and animal systems on which human communities had depended. The effects of this unequal exchange and of the mode of extraction which sustained it directly limited the capacity for local response to and benefit from subsequent exchange opportunities created by industrial development and technological advances in the world system.

Trade strategies designed initially to finance military goals had eliminated effective human occupation and use of most of the Amazon, thus annihilating a previously self-reproducing and sustaining mode of production. When in the mid-nineteenth century Europeans turned to industrial use what many Amazonian Indians had long known— that rubber could be molded into various forms which were both pliant and durable—lack of an adequate labor force retarded the response to a booming new market and was eventually a major factor in the inability of locally dominant classes to organize modes of production adequate to supply and to keep this market.

Labor Consumption in a Boom Economy: Rubber

Goodyear's discovery of rubber vulcanization in 1839 and the subsequent technological refinements which made vulcanized rubber sufficiently heat resistant for use in internal combustion motors coincided with a major new development in industrial capitalism—the production of machines for general consumer purchase and use. The bicycle craze created an enormous demand for rubber, which the later development of the automobile greatly increased.

Though rubber could be found in various forms throughout the humid tropics, only in the Amazon Basin did various types of trees provide the quantity and quality of the raw material necessary for its industrialization. Most of these trees, which grow widely dispersed through vast areas of *terra firme* jungle, will yield indefinitely if properly scarred and tapped, but they yield in slow drippings which must be collected daily. The distance from tree to tree—up to 100 meters (Batista, 1976)—and the requirement of constant attention to each tree made rubber collection extremely labor intensive. Earlier European depredation, however, had left most rural areas of the Amazon devoid of human population.

The scarcity of local labor had direct impact on the organization of the rubber trade, on the social relations involved in tapping and collecting, on the costs of extraction and the distribution of profits, and on the capacity of the Amazonian rubber trade to sustain itself or to generate other, more progressive, forms of production.

Initial response to international demand for rubber could be satisfied by peasants and laborers settled near or within the established urban centers. Response to the rapid increase in demand and in prices required exploitation of more distant trees and of a much expanded labor force (Weinstein, 1980). Though Indian groups which had survived in a few areas of *terra firme* tapped and sold latex (Murphy, 1960; Leacock, 1964), in most areas it was necessary for the *seringalistas* (the owners or lessees of the extraction areas) to import labor from outside Amazonia. This was a slow and expensive process and significantly retarded the development of the commerce in rubber. It was only through a climatic accident, a long and especially severe drought in the Northeast of Brazil, which forced many peasants to accept recruitment and transport to the Amazon in the 1870s, that the *seringalistas* and rubber merchants were able to keep up with world demand as well as they did (Melby, 1942).

The influx of rubber tappers from the Northeast increased demand on an agricultural system whose initial precarious condition had already been aggravated by the attraction of Amazonian peasants to the rubber trade (Bastos, 1975). Rubber profits were so high, and the cost of importing labor so great, that many *seringalistas* prohibited the imported tappers from growing their own food so that they could dedicate themselves exclusively to tapping and processing latex. This meant that much of the food they ate was imported from outside the Amazon. In addition to being enormously expensive, the resulting diet was also vastly unhealthy. Almost all food was dried or canned. Various travelers in the Amazon who visited tappers' huts commented on the miserable quality of their food and on the lack of balance in their diet (da Cunha,

1913; Wolf and Wolf, 1936). De Castro (1952) estimates that at least half of the tappers fell victim to beriberi. Dietary problems surely contributed to the high mortality rates of the tappers (Melby, 1942). Even the wealthier merchants and *seringalistas* in some outlying posts suffered from dietary deficiencies.

The problem of food for the rubber boom was so great that the government of the State of Pará attempted to induce European farmers to migrate to and settle in an area close to Belém, the Zona Bragantina. A railroad was built from the city to the proposed area, but the government had little success with its project. One group of settlers refused to get off the train when they saw the difference between what they had been promised and what they were being given. Others stayed only briefly. The railroad was completed far behind schedule, only shortly before the collapse of the rubber boom, and did little to solve the food shortage which the rubber boom created (Muniz, 1916; Cruz, 1958; Anderson, 1976).

The imported tappers were kept totally dependent on the *seringalistas* who had recruited and transported them and who kept them in debt servitude by advancing their transport, provisions, and tools at inflated prices against the very low prices set for their rubber output (da Cunha, 1913; Furtado, 1963; Weinstein, 1980). This dependence was maintained by the threat of violence against tappers who attempted to flee without paying off their accumulated debts.

The *seringalistas* controlled both the tappers' exchange of rubber and their provision of subsistence goods and tools. The *seringalistas* themselves exchanged this rubber and received provisions within the closed vertical exchange system of *aviamento*. In this system export firms provided trade goods and credit to *aviamento* "houses." These houses traded goods down through a series of intermediaries (*aviadores*), who advanced the goods to other intermediaries against eventual repayment in the rubber which would be traded up through the same sequence. *Aviadores* at each level in this chain maintained control through the constant indebtedness of the *aviadores* at the next level down. The export houses were the only part in this system in contact with external markets and credit sources, and they were able to set internal prices for both merchandise and rubber because of their monopoly on goods, credit, and access to foreign markets. The exchange imbalance which this control gave to the firms was aggravated through the *aviamento* system, as the prices of goods the tappers received were inflated at each of the multiple intermediary levels (Santos, 1980; Weinstein, 1980).

All capital went into, and all profits flowed from, these hierarchically organized, vertically integrated, monopsonies. Capital achieved control over the product through debt relations with the producers and traders rather than through ownership of the means of production. Local surplus value was directed to investment in the means of exchange, i.e., boats, docks, and warehouses, or to extravagantly conspicuous consumption (Collier, 1968) rather than to development of the forces of production. Various British firms attempted to organize rubber collection, but the combination of the locally dominant classes' opposition to and interference in their direct access to land and the reduced productivity of rubber tappers under a wage-labor regime (Weinstein, 1982) led to the failure of direct British control over extraction. Foreign capital was subsequently limited to credit to export houses and the construction of export infrastructure.

This extraordinarily costly and inefficient system of control could only function in a situation of low demographic and economic density (Bunker, 1979). Weinstein (1980) shows that working and living conditions were better, and *aviador* control much less, close to established urban centers. As the remoter rural areas had been severely depopulated, most of the *aviadores* could control the supply of all essential goods with little or no threat of competition from established agricultural communities. The low density of rural population in the Amazon was therefore a major factor in both the high cost of rubber extraction and the extreme concentration of the profits which flowed from it.

Weinstein (1980) has shown that large portions of the Amazonian elite were deeply concerned about the effects of the rubber boom on the rest of the regional economy. Different states attempted to restrict the flight of labor into rubber tapping and the flight of profits to foreign markets. None of these interventions and oppositions was sufficient to curb the profligate group of merchants and traders who benefited from the rapidly expanding rubber market. The rising costs of extraction and exchange were more than compensated for by the rise in prices (Santos, 1980). It was also, however, the steady rise in prices, along with a growing appreciation in Europe of long-term industrial demand for rubber, which inspired the long, costly, and uncertain process of adapting the wild rubber trees of Amazonia for plantation cropping in Asia (Brockway, 1979).

The Amazon's rubber boom was doomed when the English succeeded in adapting rubber trees to plantation cropping in Asia. As soon as Asian rubber came on the market in sufficient quantity, the high costs of the Amazonian extractive system priced its rubber off the market. Within less than a decade, Amazonian rubber fell from supplying close to 100 percent of the world market to supplying only 20 percent (Santos, 1980a).

The most common explanation of the Amazon's loss of the rubber market is that a fungus peculiar to South America (*Dothidella ulei*) spreads rapidly through closely planted rubber trees, thus making the more efficient plantation cropping impossible in the Amazon (BASA, 1966). In fact, there are methods of grafting which make the Amazon rubber trees resistant to this disease (Sioli, 1973). Various groups of Indians discovered effective close-planting techniques (Casement, 1912). Peasant communities near Santarém have maintained successful stands of rubber trees for many decades. Individual holdings here are small— at most, 2,000 trees—but contiguous lots of row-planted trees stretch across many miles and provide a much better living than is available to most Amazonian peasants (author's field observations, 1978, 1980). Tree grafting is labor intensive, however, so the Amazon's labor shortage made the development of rubber plantations highly unlikely.[3]

Plant disease is a formidable obstacle to the development of rubber plantations, but it is not insuperable and is certainly not an adequate explanation for the Amazon's failure to compete with Asian rubber plantations. Rather, it was the lack of a rural population which prevented plantation cropping. The near absence of rural communities meant that tappers were recruited from great distances and worked in conditions of isolation and dependence on the *seringalistas*. Their isolation and dependence, in turn, left them susceptible to debt servitude and extreme subordination to closed systems of exchange which could respond to increased demand only by exploiting more distant and therefore more costly sources. Both the extreme concentration of income and the rapid collapse of the rubber boom in the Amazon, therefore, can be attributed to the depopulation which an earlier mode of extraction had brought about. In their depredation of the natural and social environment the Portuguese colonizers had severely restricted the range of possible economic and social responses to the international demand for rubber. The rubber boom repeated the pattern of original colonization—the rapid enrichment of a small group followed by a sudden collapse and enduring poverty.

The rise and fall of the rubber economy in the Amazon cannot be explained without reference to a number of phenomena and processes central to world-system analyses. The rapid development and change of center technologies in industry and science, themselves dependent on the accelerated accumulation to which unequal exchange with peripheral economies contributed, created both the demand for rubber and the capacity to transform it into a plantation crop. British political control over large parts of Asia was an essential condition for the establishment of rubber plantations and the recruitment of labor there. Major parts of a large region's social and economic organization were profoundly altered in order to extract commodities which could be sold for profit in capitalist markets.

Important as capitalist markets were in determining the exchange values for which rubber was extracted, though, the mode of extraction and exchange organized in the Amazon was profoundly noncapitalist in the social relations which it engendered and in the ways that the surplus values realized from it were invested—or squandered. Nor did the ways that finance and industrial capital were organized at the time in the industrial center greatly affect that organization of that mode of extraction. Except for the ability of the industrial states to impose a treaty of international navigation on the Amazon River—an arrangement which affected trade more than it did production—effective intervention from the center was limited to the establishment of export and credit infrastructure at the points of embarkation.

The very processes by which rubber was domesticated and transferred to Asia point to the crucial distinctions between the ways in which land and labor were controlled within different modes of production in different parts of the world. The British efforts to transfer rubber from one mode of extraction to another mode of production indicate world-system, or core nation, response to the diversity of modes of production, rather than systemic determination of modes of production through an international division of labor. In the case of the Amazon, even though market opportunities inspired the local reorganization of modes of extraction, the specific socioeconomic forms that modes of extraction took were influenced more by the socioeconomic and environmental conditions created by prior local modes of production and extraction than by the political and economic characteristics of the capitalist world-system.

The aftermath of the transformation of rubber to a plantation crop does, however, show the special relations between productive industry in the core and the extractive processes in the periphery on which industrial expansion and technological development depend. U.S. imports of rubber doubled from 51 million pounds in 1899 to 101 million pounds in 1910. They more than quintupled, to 567 million pounds, between 1910 and 1920 (U.S. Bureau of the Census, 1949). They continued rising to over 800 million pounds by 1925, but the rate of increase never equalled that of 1910-20, the period immediately following the introduction of plantation rubber. These figures suggest that until plantation rubber became available in large quantities, the limited supply of rubber and the sharply rising costs which resulted from expanding the scale of extraction in the Amazonian periphery seriously restricted the expansion of rubber-dependent industry and technology in the world-capitalist center.

The history of the rubber boom and of its precipitous collapse also suggests an important reservation about recent cross national surveys which measure economic growth over periods ranging from fifteen to thirty years (see, e.g., Bornschier et al., 1978). Table 1 shows that the steady rise in both regional product and in per capita income were closely related to the export of rubber. If the rubber economy had generated any parallel economic development, the collapse of rubber prices would not have led to so precipitous a decline to levels approximating those prior to the boom. Short-term measurement of income growth—i.e., over periods of fifteen to thirty years—up to 1910, however, would lead to erroneous conclusions about Amazonian development at this time. Extractive economies may produce dramatic rises in regional income, but these tend to be ephemeral. The brief time periods used for comparative analysis of economic growth may disguise the transitory nature of such prosperity.

The extractive basis of this prosperity and the highly skewed distribution of profits to the top of the *aviamento* system underscore the

Table 1. Rubber Exports, Rubber Prices, Population, and Regional Income, 1820-1920

Years	Rubber Exports[a]	Total Population	Population Active in Exploitation of Rubber[b]	Average Price, Fine Rubber/ Belém[c]	Gross Regional Income[d]	Per Capita Income (Cr$)	Per Capita Income (US$)
1820		137,017			29,877	171	29
1830	156	128,896	1,733		23,428	182	31
1840	418	129,530	4,180		37,603	290	49
1850	879	200,391	7,325		97,628	487	83
1860		278,250	14,888		191,701	689	117
1870		322,909	28,010	2,574	332,529	1,030	175
1871	6,765			2,574			
1880		389,997	42,337	2,600	633,666	1,625	275
1881	8,506			2,600			
1890		476,370	73,119	2,950	476,370	1,998	339
1891	16,650			2,950			
1900	23,650	695,112	107,500	8,678	1,359,479	1,956	332
1910	34,248	1,217,024	148,907	10,050	2,320,338	1,907	323
1915	29,772	1,151,548		3,570	462,085	401	68
1920	23,586	1,090,545		2,400	473,111	434	74

Source. Based on data and estimates in Santos (1977). See Santos, 1977: 213, 216, 310-43, for methodology and sources of estimates.

[a] In metric tons. This includes exportations in transit from neighboring countries until 1876 and from 1919 exports from all of Brazil. The proportion of rubber from outside of the Brazilian Amazon during these two time periods was insignificant, however.

[b] Based on rubber exports and calculations of productivity/tapper. Santos uses two alternative formulas and so arrives at two somewhat divergent hypotheses. The figures included here seem to be the most plausible. These figures do not include administrative personnel. See Santos (1977:41-85) for full discussion.

[c] In reis/kilo. The price is the simple mean of high and low prices on the Belém market. Until 1900 the figures are based on two-year averages.

[d] In 1972 values of Cr$1,000.

problems noted earlier in the labor- and wage-based theories of unequal exchange espoused by Mandel and Emmanuel. At the height of the rubber boom, the labor incorporated in the extraction of high-priced rubber was presumably less than the labor incorporated in trade goods of equivalent price from the industrial center. The inequality of the exchange in rubber was not that the Amazon was exporting more labor for less labor, but rather was in the different levels of articulation between rubber extraction and other economic activities in the Amazon and between the transformation of rubber and other economic activities in the industrial core. High-priced extractive commodities such as gold and diamonds invert Mandel's and Emmanuel's formulations; realization of their market value requires relatively little labor. In the case of the Amazon, as in many other extractive peripheries, this reduced the possible consumption linkages to local productive economies. The paucity of such linkages was aggravated by the low levels of remuneration to the tappers and by the *aviadores'* nearly total control of the exchange of rubber for provisions.

Given the low levels of local consumption linkages to the tappers and the tight vertical control over exchange, it is not surprising that the major infrastructural consequences of the rubber boom were the development of ports and docks in Manaus and Belém, together with a hypertrophy of expensive urban culture represented by elegant hotels, large theaters, and an elaborate opera house (Collier, 1968). These, too, decayed as regional income fell after 1910.

The Amazon after the Boom: 1910-50

The rubber boom collapsed when plantation rubber pushed prices down, but, as in the case of colonial conquest, the boom had transformed the social and natural environments in ways which would affect subsequent uses to which these environments could be put. As in the first cases considered here, external markets for primary goods continued to influence these uses, but the modes of production and extraction, which were organized in response to exchange opportunities, directly affected the distribution and organization of human populations and further altered the physical environment on which these populations depended. These effects, in turn, set limits on the capacity of subsequent modes of production to respond to new international exchange opportunities in ways which would increase, rather than diminish, the local forces of production.

Though some of the imported tappers returned to the Northeast after the boom, many stayed on and reverted to a mixed subsistence and exchange economy based on various combinations of horticulture, extraction, and hunting and fishing. Their primary connection with markets was through a continuation of the *aviamento* system. *Aviadores* supplied both food and implements such as fishing nets, gun powder, or tools, as well as goods such as kerosene, at the beginning of the productive season and took their payment in kind at the end of the season. As in their predecessors' relations with the tappers, the *aviadores* determined both the price of the goods supplied and the price of the goods received. Once again, rates of exchange were highly unfavorable to the producers and contributed to the perpetuation of their indebtedness (Santos, 1968). The internal exchange relations characteristic of a mode of extraction oriented to external market opportunities persisted in impoverished form after the external market collapsed, but they were primarily geared to rural-urban rather than export trade. Rubber was still tapped and exported, but no longer generated the revenues it previously had. Together with Brazil nuts, it provided an extractive cash supplement to subsistence (BASA, 1966).

Trade was carried on for a wide range of products — some cultivated, such as manioc, rice, and bananas; some gathered, such as rubber, Brazil nuts, and a number of other oil-producing nuts; some hunted, such as turtles, manatees, caymans, and jaguars; and fish, which was commonly dried. In the 1930s Japanese immigrants introduced jute, which was an important part of the rural economy until synthetic substitutes lowered its price, and later black pepper, which has become an important export crop. Pepper is still largely controlled by a few small Japanese communities that have broken away from the *aviamento* system by forming their own marketing cooperatives.

Ross (1978) has pointed out that market pressures and the loss of indigenous technology keep a major portion of Amazonian peasantry on the more fragile, less productive *terra firme*. All the marketable crops, except jute, are grown on *terra firme*, but its soils and the existing technologies cannot support the relatively dense populations which were brought there by the rubber boom. Rather than staying dispersed through the jungle, these populations have concentrated in riverine communities, or closer to Belém. These riverine communities left large parts of the *várzea* unexploited or used them only for cattle pasture during low water. Such settlement patterns facilitated trade, but dense settlement patterns in, for example, the Zona Bragantina or certain areas near the confluence of the Tapajós and the Amazon rivers led to annual cropping of *terra firme* with excessively short fallows. The result was rapid soil deterioration, pest and weed invasion, and drastically reduced agricultural yields.

Rubber, Brazil nuts, jute, and black pepper continued to be exported, but the low prices of rubber and the limited sources of the other exports restricted dominant class involvement and the effects of these export economies on the region as a whole. Except for a flurry of national state activity to increase rubber exports when the Japanese captured Malaya in World War II, the region was largely withdrawn from the world market. Direct U.S. funding of programs to support rubber production in the early 1940s did result in the establishment of a regional health care program, however.

National and international demand for skins of jaguars and caymans also provided export opportunities for some areas of the Amazon during the 1950s. Local response to these opportunities depleted these animals as earlier exploitation had devasted the manatee and turtle. Once again the reduction of fauna had profound effects on other parts of the ecosystem and further impoverished human communities. Fittkau (1970, 1973) has shown that the slow metabolism of the cayman, a small crocodilian, is crucial to maintaining nutrient levels in rivers of the Central Amazon. The caymans eat fish swimming up the Amazon to spawn and then slowly excrete them into the nutrient-poor mouth lakes of the Amazon's affluents. Thus, the decimation of a predator that consumed fish actually reduced fish populations and limited the protein supplies for local communities. As Sioli (1975) notes, Fittkau's explanation serves as an example of the complex ecological interrelations of the vast Amazonian river system—and of possible unintended consequences of unbalancing them. The complex relations between coevolved and interdependent species mean that overexploitation of particular plant or animal resources in response to external demand may reduce or eliminate a series of other species. The resulting disruption of entire biotic chains may impoverish present economies, which use these resources, and limit future uses of resources for which demand or need may emerge. Prior impoverishment, such as occurred with the collapse of the rubber boom, may heighten the propensity of local populations to overexploit the resources for which there is effective demand and thus perpetuate cycles of progressive destruction and underdevelopment.

The poor soils of the *terra firme* and the small proportion of the Amazon Basin made up of *várzea* and other favorable habitats would never have allowed dense population or extensive agronomic exploration of the entire region. Lathrap's (1974) description of hierarchical settlement and trade systems along the various tributaries based on and controlled by densely settled, relatively complex, and politically superordinate communities on the mouthbay *várzeas* does, however, suggest far more effective and flexible ways of using the environment than the extreme urban concentration and the fragmentation of settlement along the river, which resulted from the first two extractive cycles that followed the Amazon's incorporation into the world system. Settlement patterns based on the richer *várzea* settlements could have extended into, and exploited, the *terra firme* in ways which complemented and were supported by the *várzea* settlements. A graded *várzea–terra firme* hierarchy would have been able to supply labor for various enterprises in the area and to develop a series of economic linkages with them. The history of the rubber boom would have been very different if dense, productive mouthbay settlements had provided labor and food for rubber extraction or plantation further up tributary rivers and onto the *terra firme*. The demographic and ecological consequences of extractive export economies made this impossible, however. Instead, riparian areas were settled by dispersed groups relying on subsistence economies that were not integrated into the *terra firme*.

The *terra firme* was finally to be incorporated into the national and international systems by a network of roads and airports controlled from outside, with little or no connection to rivers, after 1950. In addition to the extra costs of occupying the *terra firme* by road, without support from *várzea* communities, the roads opened the *terra firme* to exploitation by far distant centers of population and enterprise. The dominant groups in these areas were unfamiliar with the Amazonian environment; the technologies and organizational systems they used had emerged in a very different ecological and economic system, and they had little long-term interest or stake in the Amazonian region. The *terra firme* was thus opened up to the center-south of Brazil, which by this time had developed a considerable industrial capacity, and effectively cut off from articulation with the *várzea*. The resulting forms of occupation allowed the establishment of new forms of extraction which continued the social and environmental disruptions of earlier cycles.

NOTES

1. Reanalysis of the archaeological record and of the early European chronicles of exploration and battle, together with the recently completed Projecto RADAM (Brasil, 1976) analyses of SLAR images for the entire Brazilian Amazon, has resulted in drastic upward revision of earlier estimates of indigenous population size and density prior to European conquest. Even though the chronicler of the 1539 Texeira expedition calculated that this party had encountered over 1 million Indians, and though Antônio Vieira calculated populations of over 2 million in the lower Amazon alone as late as the seventeenth century (Batista, 1976), many scholars ignored or dismissed these and similar indications of precontact population density. Some of the estimates published in this century ran as low as 500,000 people. See Meggers's (1971) arguments that the tropical environment of the Amazon had an extremely limited carrying capacity as an example of extrapolation of temperate-zone biases.

2. Smith (1974:93) estimates that even after half a century of exploitation

and reduction, at least 48 million turtle eggs from the upper Amazon and the Madeira alone were still being crushed yearly during the 1860s.

3. The Ford Motor Company established rubber plantations at Fordlandia and Belterra on the lower Tapajós River in 1926. Prior to the European conquest, this area had supported one of the densest and most complex of the Amazonian societies (Palmatary, 1960). Ford's main problem and a key reason for its eventually abandoning these projects were the difficulties and expenses of importing a labor force to these now depopulated spaces (Russell, 1942).

CHAPTER 3

The Modern State, Capitalist Expansion, and Amazonian Extraction

The initial mode of extraction, imposed and supported by colonial intervention, was organized by an exogenous dominant class in response to center demand for spices and animal oils. Following its collapse and a long period of stagnation, a new extractive mode was organized by a fraction of the locally dominant class to take advantage of core demand for rubber. It also required direct articulation of these locally based dominant groups with buyers from the core, despite the Amazon's formal inclusion within Brazil. Since 1950, however, exchanges between the Amazon and international markets have increasingly been mediated by the Brazilian state. As the Brazilian economy became more highly capitalized, more autocentric, and more industrial, the Brazilian state availed itself of technologies developed within the world industrial center. It enhanced its own transport, communication, and administrative capacities and became able to extend these capacities toward its own frontiers.

State mediation and intervention have not led to economic and political incorporation of the Amazon into the Brazilian nation, however. The depopulation, environmental disruption, and demographic and economic dislocations brought about by the previous modes of extraction created the conditions for both large-scale capitalist enterprise and government economic planners to treat the Amazon as an empty frontier from which profits could be rapidly and wastefully extracted with little regard for, or sustained economic participation by, existing socioeconomic or environmental systems. Contemporary modes of extraction in the Amazon have increased gross regional income, but they have done so in ways which will lead to their own collapse and which are so disrupting ecological and human systems as to limit the possibility of future modes of production to respond to new opportunities for either economic exchange or social reproduction.

State intervention in the Amazon has followed two main policy imperatives: first, the direct promotion of revenue-generating economic activities, and second, the maintenance of order through the assertion of legitimate state authority. The first imperative predominated in government policy through the 1960s; then, in the early 1970s, the state initiated a sustained attempt to control and direct the capitalist expansion which its own policies had stimulated. The second imperative has consistently been subordinated to the first, however, both through the termination of certain control and social welfare programs and through the redirection of other programs in favor of large-scale enterprise.

The directions and changes in government policy have been very much influenced by the forms and functions of the state bureaucracy. National state programs in the Amazon are carried out and shaped by the activities of various specialized bureaucratic agencies. Many of these agencies function over the nation as a whole; others are organized as regional bodies under direct national state control. The structures of these organizations have essentially been extensions of structures which emerged in the Brazilian national center, although the representatives of these agencies were placed in local positions in which they made locally effective decisions. Similarly, the locally based managers and agents of national and international firms can make locally effective decisions.

As in the colonial period, external political forces established the position and supported the power of locally dominant groups. Changes in communication and transport technology, however, tied these representatives of extraregional corporations and governments more closely to the controlling agency than had been the case in the rubber boom. These groups also became local actors, transforming local modes of extraction and production in response to external demand.

Economic Growth and the National State

While the Amazon's economy and society languished in the aftermath of the rubber boom, the center-south region of Brazil moved rapidly through relatively prosperous agricultural exports toward extensive but vertically unintegrated industrialization, based in large measure on foreign capital (Love, 1980; O'Donnell, 1978; Cardoso, 1975; Evans, 1979; Baer, 1979). Throughout the present century, finance and industrial capital first emerged from and then increasingly lessened the relative importance of the export of primary goods such as coffee. The state acted both to foster and protect export economies and then to promote industrial growth. It pushed to break out of an economy which was seen as excessively dependent on primary exports and too susceptible to declining terms of trade by turning, after World War II, to a policy of import substitution which depended on attracting foreign investments (Baer, 1979).

The shifting balance of political and economic power from agrarian classes and regions to industrial classes and regions precipitated political crises, which were aggravated by major differences in regional rates of development. Regional resistance to national centralization of power, the increasing subordination of agriculture to urban-industrial food and capital requirements from the 1950s, the increased concentration of ownership of land, and, the displacement of peasants created major social tensions and fostered violence in many rural areas (Martins, 1980). In 1964 the populist government of Joao Goulart, which had permitted and sometimes encouraged political action by workers and peasants, was overthrown by a centralizing authoritarian regime. This military regime allied itself with international capital and attempted to provide an attractive and secure environment for it (O'Donnell, 1978).

During the entire postwar process of industrialization, and more rapidly after the establishment of the centralized authoritarian regime, the state created new institutions and government agencies to articulate the increasingly interdependent sectors of the economy. These processes had three central effects which were crucial to the ways that the national state mediated between the Amazon and world markets for a limited number of resources.

The first of these was a close alliance between the state and both international and national capitalist sectors, in which each of the three depended closely on the other two, despite significant opposition and conflicts between them. It is especially important to note that this alliance, together with the autonomous development of both the state and of local industry, strengthened and expanded all its members (O'Donnell, 1973, 1977, 1978; Cardoso, 1975). Baer (1979) and Evans (1979) have shown how the state has assumed essential entrepreneurial and regulatory functions, taking key initiatives in industrial development by establishing state enterprises and fiscal subsidies and incentives.

The second effect was that the state apparatus evolved in directions which responded simultaneously to the needs of the developing industrial base in the Brazilian center and to the needs of the state. The increasingly specialized and interdependent sectors of the economy and the need for exports to finance a growing foreign debt expanded the state's functions in the maintenance of economic order and integration. The state's fiscal and entrepreneurial functions fostered a complex administrative apparatus based on state-controlled banks and specialized development agencies. Banks and banking regulations became more and more important in the handling of foreign trade and distribution of foreign bank loans, the management and control of multiple exchange rates and exchange controls, and the manipulation of the different interest rates through which the state attempted to influence the direction of the economy. Banks also became central to national state initiatives and programs to overcome regional inequalities by providing special credits, subsidies, and fiscal incentives to private enterprise through regional planning agencies in the less developed areas of the country (Baer, 1979).

The third effect was the expanded intervention of the state to subordinate agriculture to the needs of industry. The growing industrial sector needed expanding, predictable sources of cheap food in order to keep wages low, while the state subsidized and encouraged large-scale export agriculture. Returns to small-scale agriculture declined while incentives to large-scale agriculture improved. The resulting aggravation of highly concentrated land-tenure patterns heightened social and political tensions in various rural areas (Cehelsky, 1979; Foweraker, 1981). Piecemeal attempts to respond to the various economic and political problems in the agricultural sector led to the proliferation of specialized agencies to facilitate particular aspects of the commercialization of agricultural production and commerce (Schuh, 1971). A series of federal agencies were created to regularize land titles and to resolve tenure conflicts; special agricultural credit programs were established through national, regional, and state banks; a commission was established to set and administer minimum prices for staple crops; a public company was founded to extend warehousing facilities for crops; and a national level association subordinate to the Ministry of Agriculture with separate agencies in each state was established to provide rural extension services.

Most of these specialized agencies emerged in response to particular needs in the rapidly industrializing center-south. They therefore corresponded to a particular type and stage of capitalism. At the same time, however, their organization and their assigned goals reflected state initiatives to transform, rather than simply to maintain, existing relations of production. These were deliberately modern, and modernizing, agencies. They were functionally specific, were oriented to commercialized agriculture within an increasingly industrial context, and employed bureaucratic procedures "rational" within the context of the disjuncture between dependent capitalist industrial and agricultural development. These agencies and the programs which they were carrying out were all part of an attempt to modernize the less industrialized parts of the Brazilian economy. Such agencies emerged and functioned in modes of production which were increasingly modern and capitalistic. At the same time they served the state as a vehicle to reorganize relations of production and of exchange in ways the state saw as compatible with, and preparing the conditions for, the development of capitalist modes of production. Thus, these specialized agencies of the state were geared to the modes of production predominant in the center-south region where they emerged and to the needs of the state there. They were not adapted to the fragmented, dispersed, and tenuously connected settlement and institutional patterns which the previous noncapitalist modes of extraction had created on what was to be the new Amazonian "national" frontier.

The development of increasingly energy-intensive economic and administrative systems in the Brazilian center generated complex problems whose solutions required complex and energy-intensive solutions. These included the expansion and strengthening of a large and complex national state apparatus. The state's enhanced power and size depended on its varied alliances with powerful national and international business interests. These alliances engendered an administrative apparatus comprised of multiple, functionally specific agencies geared to the requirements of a modern capitalist industrial state and economy and to developing the commercial agriculture necessary to an expanding urban population. They also contributed to a growing foreign debt, which followed dependence on foreign capital for import-substituting industrialization. In contrast, the Amazon's extractive economies, which dispersed social and natural energies, maintained simplified, low-energy institutional forms. These differences have all contributed to the growing discrepancies between the Amazon and the Brazilian center and to the ways that the state, and its capitalist allies, have mediated betwen the Amazon and international markets (Davis, 1977; Martins, 1981).

The Amazon has increasingly been used as a stopgap solution to imbalances in the Brazilian national government's programs for rapid industrialization and the socioeconomic integration of the country. During the past two decades the Amazon has come to represent a great reserve of natural resources to government planners searching for ways to reduce the foreign indebtedness caused by Brazil's heavy reliance on international capital. Mining, lumbering, and ranching concessions granted to various multinational and large national corporations have been seen as an effective way to tap these resources (Mahar, 1979) and to attract foreign equity capital. The state's goals for the Amazon were also shaped by its own political preoccupations with territorial security and internal order. As the idea of an Amazon rich in natural resources was incorporated into national economic policy, the old fear that other nations might wish to control these resources was resuscitated (Reis, 1968; Tamer, 1970; Pereira, 1971). The mechanization of agriculture in the center-south and recurrent droughts in the Northeast had swelled the ranks of the already numerous landless peasants of Brazil, increasing political tensions and demands for land reform which the state hoped to alleviate by opening Amazonian *terra firme* to colonization (Cehelsky, 1979; Moran, 1981; Bunker, 1983).

Central government plans for the Amazon, either as a solution to balance-of-payments and population problems, or as a region to be protected, have involved direct government investments and massive subsidies to private enterprise there. Like the earlier extractive cycles, recent changes in the Amazonian economy have developed as local responses to international demand for raw products, but this response has been accelerated and intensified by the national state's acute need for foreign revenues and political legitimacy. The state's political and fiscal programs to satisfy these needs have established new, locally dominant groups and then greatly enhanced their capacity to dislocate local populations and reorganize access to natural resources and the physical environment in which they occur. The Amazon passed from being an extractive periphery of European and North American economies to being the peripheral frontier for the Brazilian economy. Brazilian capitalists and the Brazilian state expanded their control over land and labor in order to accelerate the extraction of value and profits from natural resources. Local groups again reorganized the physical and social environment, but this time they depended on the initiative and support of a powerful national state and of the large corporations they represented. This particular response reflected a national mode of production in which the state assumes key entrepreneurial and credit functions and in which groups of private entrepreneurs control both the economic and political resources to appropriate vast areas of land and portions of state revenues. Like previous cycles, this one has led to growth in conventional economic measures of the regional product and in per capita income (see Table 2), but this growth can only be transitory, because it depends on the depletion of natural resources, on the disruption of the surrounding natural environment, and on the dislocation of human populations (Cardoso and Müller, 1977; Bunker, 1983). I argue in this chapter that if natural values were included in these calculations, they would show that losses to the region probably surpass the value of additional monetary income.

This income growth has emerged from new variations of earlier extractive economies, wedded to massive inputs of tax credits and other federal disbursements. It has not yet reached the income levels achieved during the rubber boom and has little prospect of avoiding the same forms of collapse. Mining, large cattle ranching, and lumbering are all

Table 2. Regional Population, Gross Regional Income, and Regional Per Capita Income, 1910-70

Year	Total Population	Gross Regional Income[a]	Per Capita Income (Cr$)	Per Capita Income (U.S.$)
1910	1,217,024	2,320,338	1,907	323
1920	1,090,545	473,111	434	74
1939	1,463,330	983,356	672	119
1950	1,844,655	1,315,275	713	121
1960	2,601,519	2,347,366	902	153
1970	3,603,860	3,637,446	1,009	171

Source. Based on data and estimates in Santos, 1977.
[a] In 1972 values of Cr$1,000.

being promoted in ways which maximize short-term profits and minimize the possibilities for long-term, self-sustained development.

Total population has also grown rapidly since 1950, but this population is concentrated in Belém and Manaus, which have grown far faster than their capacity to absorb labor, and in the towns and cities which have sprung up along the newly opened highways through the *terra firme*. Recent peasant migrants, displaced by the advance of large, government subsidized extractive industries into the jungle lands they have cleared, constitute the majority population of many new towns. These new urban populations stay on as part of what Hébette and Acevedo (1979) call the "low tertiary" or provide seasonal migrant labor for the extractive enterprises which have displaced them. While total population has grown, many rural areas, including the more fertile *várzeas*, have been losing populations. Rural settlement and small-scale rural extractive and productive economies have become far less stable in the meantime.

The new towns along the highways offer the displaced peasants neither regular employment nor access to land. Because of their recent rapid growth and general poverty, they also lack sanitary, medical, and educational services (Hébette and Acevedo, 1979). Few of the peasants are able to compete successfully for jobs in the large cities, where unemployment and underemployment are already high. The situation of the migrant laborers (*peões, volantes*) is perhaps the worst of all. Subject to exploitation, fraud, and violence by the middlemen (*empreteiros, gatos*), who contract their work and transport them, neither their wages nor their working and living conditions are subject to any labor law or police supervision. Few ranchers or farmers are disposed to provide even minimally adequate shelter for workers who spend as little as three weeks in any one place. By 1975 an estimated 80,000 landless peasants were working in these conditions in the Amazon (Cardoso and Muller, 1977).

Development Programs and the Persistence of Extractive Economies

The national government has used three forms of stimuli to capitalist enterprise in the Amazon (1) publically financed construction of infrastructure such as roads and docks; (2) concessions of resource rights to foreign companies; and (3) tax credits and fiscal incentives to Brazilian companies. Early national government development programs funneled revenues to local state governments and public enterprise to develop transportation and communications systems and to make investment credits available for agriculture. SPVEA (Superintendency of Planning for the Economic Valorization of the Amazon), founded in 1955, operated under the federal logic of the civilian regimes which controlled the national state at that time. It funded preexisting regional organizations controlled by locally dominant political and commercial groups. SPVEA's funding was considerably below the amounts originally decreed (Mahar, 1979:8-9), and it was accused of extensive corruption and inefficiency. Starting in 1959, separate national state programs initiated road-building programs from the Brazilian center-south to the Amazonian Northeast and Southwest.

SPVEA was discontinued after the military coup of 1964, and the SUDAM (Superintendency for the Development of the Amazon) was established in its stead. SUDAM was established under direct national control within the Ministry of the Interior and patterned after SUDENE, a similar agency in the Brazilian Northeast. Most of its high-level staff was also recruited from SUDENE and other national bureaucracies. Its own resources, its ample jurisdiction, and later its control over credits and capital subsidies far greater than the total capital previously accumulated in the Amazon (Skillings and Tcheyan, 1979) gave the SUDAM more power than the corresponding agencies of the local states. The regional bank, the Banco de Crédito da Amazônia, which had been created out of the regionally controlled Rubber Development Bank, was transformed into BASA, the Banco da Amazônia, S.A., with mixed private and national state ownership. This bank, which administered fiscal aspects of SUDAM programs, contributed to the eclipse of previously established local powers.

Concessions to foreign companies were most significant prior to 1968;

domestic capital became more important as the industrial base of Brazil expanded. In 1966 the government established a program of fiscal incentives to be administered by the SUDAM, which allowed firms to place up to 50 percent of their corporate tax debt in blocked accounts which could be used for investment in approved projects in the Amazon (Katzman, 1976; Kleinpenning, 1977; Mahar, 1979). The SUDAM programs made massive amounts of capital available for investment in enterprises which were able to displace established local economies without reabsorbing the displaced labor (Table 3).

The earliest national government initiatives for generating foreign revenues in the Amazon were based on mining concessions to foreign companies. In the early 1950s ICOMI, a consortium made up of Bethlehem Steel (49 percent) and a group of Brazilian companies (51 percent), began exploiting the manganese deposits in Amapá, the territory north of the Amazon delta. Tin mining started in Rondônia in the southwestern Amazon in 1959, but in this case was first undertaken by individual miners (McCrary, 1972:82).

Katzman (1976:454) has characterized both the impact of these mining operations on the gross regional product and the limited secondary growth which mining stimulated in the rest of the economy as follows:

> The enclave nature of the mining economy is illustrated by comparing the growth of Amazonian output before and after mining began. Throughout the period 1947-1956, the region's output grew about 3.8 percent per annum, about 2 points below the national average, and only slightly higher than the Amazonian population growth rate. After 1956, growth spurted and began to exceed the national rate through 1963. If the value of mineral exports were subtracted from the post-1956 growth curve, the old trend line continues (Villela and Almeida, 1966:177-179). If man-

Table 3. SUDAM Fiscal Incentives, 1965-78

Category	Number of Projects	Total Investment in Approved Projects (Cr$ million)	Approved (Cr$ million)	Disbursed (Cr$ million)	U.S.$ Million	Disbursed as Percent of Approved
Industry	182	14,801	6,543	3,020	348[a]	46
Livestock	337	9,715	6,810	3,690	391[a]	54
Other[b]	51	7,647	2,211	973	97	44
Total	570	32,163	15,564	7,683	836	49

Source. SUDAM, 1979, elaborated by Skillings and Tcheyan (1979:58).
Note. Cr$ values at current prices; U.S.$ values derived by converting annual cruzeiro values at annual average exchange rates.
[a] Minimum estimates of capital investments per job in enterprises receiving fiscal incentives: industry: U.S.$34,000; livestock: U.S.$63,000.
[b] Agro-industry, tourism, transport, energy, education, and telecommunications.

ganese or tin mining had significant multiplier effects, the subtraction of mineral exports would have left additional generated income above the old trend line. Direct evidence of import of food and manufactures into the two territories confirm more directly the enclave nature of mining.

Further, the development of mining has decreased the ability of this sector to absorb labor. While the value of production rose from Cr$104,000 in 1960 to Cr$1,149,000 in 1968 (constant values, 1949 = 100), total employment in mining had fallen from 1,831 to 596 (IBGE, 1977:410). This shift has largely been the result of government policies promoting mineral extraction to help alleviate Brazil's acute balance-of-payments problems. Fiscal incentives for advanced technologies were made available through SUDAM to mining operations, and in 1971 the government prohibited placer mines in Rondônia, creating considerable unemployment there.

Actual extraction and export of minerals, as well as government and private investments in infrastructure and exploration, have contributed heavily to total regional income, although extraction—and income—are concentrated in a few, relatively small areas. In 1967 the federal government removed a clause limiting manganese extraction to 1 million tons/year from its contract with ICOMI. Manganese made up 82.7 percent of industrial income in the territory of Amapá in 1970, rising from 687,358 tons in 1957 to 1,606,696 in 1978 (IBGE, 1980). The state's support for capital intensive techniques accelerated extraction; cassiterite production in Rondônia rose from only 61 metric tons in 1957 to 6,909 metric tons in 1978 (IBGE, 1980) and is projected to reach 15,000 metric tons or more by 1990 (Goodland, 1980:13). In 1970, even before the large-scale development of capital-intensive extraction, cassiterite made up 50.9 percent of total industrial income in Rondônia.

Recent discoveries of extensive iron and bauxite reserves and major government initiatives to promote their exploitation will heighten the impact of mining on the Amazon's economy. Massive investments in exploration have already been made in the huge iron ore deposits in the Serra dos Carajás, the rich bauxite deposits on the Trombetas River, and kaolin deposits in Jari, all in Pará. Projections for the amount of investment in the Serra dos Carajás project range from U.S.$1 billion (Mahar 1979:111) to U.S.$4.3 billion (Dayton, 1975:91), and, in addition to the ecological destruction inevitably associated with actual mining, the 876-km railway "will . . . create an impact that will exceed its 70-m width" (Goodland 1980:13), including the expulsion of indigenous and peasant populations and extensive deforestation (over 2 million hectares) for fuel-producing sugar cane plantations (Pinto, 1982). Government plans for Carajás call for the establishment of associated mineral transformation and other industry in the area, but the absence of other locational advantages makes it unlikely that such development could be sustained after the mines themselves are exhausted. The associated development plans will, however, aggravate the ecological disruptions and the conflict over land, as well as impose a heavy foreign debt burden on the project.

The bauxite development along the Trombetas River is anticipated to begin producing 3.35 million metric tons per year of high-grade ores, rising to 8 million metric tons per year (Goodland, 1980:12), with its projected cost estimated at U.S.$2.7 billion (Dayton, 1975:101). Despite optimistic projections that ecological destruction at the Trombetas site will be minimal and ambitious plans to produce food locally to supply company personnel (Goodland, 1980:13), early evidence indicates this mining project will have a significant impact on a far larger area than that immediately involved in mineral extraction. The massive influx of personnel and the resulting strong market for beef at both Porto Trombetas and in neighboring Santarém have encouraged the deforestation of extensive areas of jungle for large-scale cattle ranching in the surrounding areas. Not only has the local economy become thereby tied to what is probably a relatively short-term boom cycle, but the cattle-raising system, based on native *várzea* grasses, is being displaced, and the Brazil nut groves and small-scale staple-crop agriculture that allowed general peasant participation in the local cash economy are being eliminated (Bunker, 1981a).

The mining of nonrenewable resources accounts for a major part of the increase in regional income. Minerals have directly contributed Cr$375,169,000 (1975 values) in regional income in 1970, or 13.9 percent in the growth in regional income since 1960. Salaries for exploration and for the management of government and private support programs have also increased mining's share of regional income. Mining has remained largely an enclave economy, generating few forward or backward linkages. The mines, and what urban infrastructure they foster, can be sustained only as long as the deposits remain. The manganese reserves in Amapá are already approaching depletion, and the Trombetas bauxite deposits are expected to last only an estimated sixty-five years (Goodland, 1980:12), i.e., less than the seventy years which elapsed from the beginning of the rubber boom in 1840 to its collapse in 1910. The associated infrastructure of docks, railroads, and residences which they have generated, and which have also contributed to regional income, will lose some, or all, of its present utility.

The same factors that limit the long-term utility of this infrastructure increase its short-term costs. Most of these mines are in relatively remote locations, so rail and road lines are long. The mining enterprise is also associated with plans for hydroelectric dams to provide energy for mineral reduction, too. In addition to the high financial costs of these undertakings, the flooding of large areas of forest for dams and the opening up of forest for power, road, and rail lines take land out of potential agricultural production, waste lumber, disrupt the regenerative cycles of various animal species, and disrupt the hunting and fishing resources available to indigenous and peasant groups (see Aspelin and dos Santos, 1981:160, for areas flooded). The Tucurui Dam, the largest ever built in tropical forest, is planned to provide power for the Carajás mines. Now nearing completion, it will flood areas used by both peasant and indigenous groups. The rail, road, and power lines associated with the Carajás project will cut through ranching, Indian, and peasant land in one of the most fought-over areas of the Amazon (Pinto, 1982). In addition to disrupting hunting, it will also destroy large Brazil nut groves, which provide a cash supplement to the subsistence of the Gaviões Indians who live in the area. "The railroad will require a corridor at least 60 to 70 meters wide which will also slice through the Mae Maria Reserve from west to east, in another strip about 20 kilometers long, again parallel to the PA-70 highway, but this time about 10 to 12 kilometers to the south of it. The railroad would alienate another valuable part of their only cash income base, further deplete hunting possibilities by displacing the game and disrupting its habits, and effectively slice the reservation into four separate pieces" (Aspelin and dos Santos, 1981:81).

Another major area of government disbursement—and another important source of increased regional income since 1959—has been an ambitious road-building program to provide an infrastructure for the Brazilian government's development plans for the Amazon. Although it includes 59 percent of national territory, the Amazon Basin had no road connections to the south of Brazil until the late 1950s. The transfer of the capital to Brasília, in the central part of the country, was a first step toward integrating the nation around its geographical center instead of along its coasts. From Brasília, roads were built north to Belém, in the early 1960s, and to Pôrto Velho and Rio Branco at the southwest end. In the 1970s, under the Program of National Integration (PIN), massive investments were made to connect the Atlantic coast with Peru. The Transamazon highway south of the Amazon cost approximately U.S.$500 million to construct and more to maintain. Another highway along the northern frontier was budgeted at Cr$400 million (1972 values) but was not completed because of cost overruns (Mahar 1979:19). These major road systems stimulated further expenditure on secondary and feeder roads. While the huge costs of these undertakings added directly and indirectly to regional income, their long-term economic contribution to the region is limited by the predominantly extractive character of the economic activities which the roads have stimulated.

In addition to accelerating the mining of nonrenewable resources, the roads have stimulated predatory lumbering of valuable woods, with no attempt to replace them with equally valuable species, and large-scale pasture formation. Artificial pasture formation and herd management do, of course, involve human intervention in the production of valuable goods, and so ranching is not a "pure" extractive activity. However, Hecht (1981), has shown that most pastures formed in the Amazon are economically viable only as long as nutrients are released by the remnants of the burned or rotting vegetation. In this sense ranching in the Amazon does depend directly on the extraction of natural values. It also shares the other characteristics of extractive economies, including locational impermanence, the expulsion of earlier forms of noncapitalist social and economic organization, low levels of labor absorption, and pronounced disruption of energy transformation processes in affected ecosystems. All ranching economies are partially extractive, but these characteristics are intensified in the Amazon. For these reasons, I will treat ranching in the Amazon as an extractive economy. That it is not purely extractive does not limit its significance in this analysis, as its effects on Amazonian social formations and ecosystems derive far more from its extractive than from its productive aspects. Lumbering and large-scale cattle ranching have repeated the devastating effects of earlier extractive cycles on the natural environment and on rural populations. Increasingly, they aggravate the "demographic vacuum" which legitimated their wastefully land-extensive "frontier" expansion into the Amazon.

The combination of access to fluvial transport, the greater fertility of the *várzeas*, and the availability of aquatic protein concentrated the Amazon's population along the major river courses. The government's new roads traversed sparsely settled upland areas. Contact with road-building crews and the settlers who followed them brought a new wave of epidemics and violence to the indigenous groups who occupied the remote *terra firme* and threatened the tenure and subsistence of isolated peasant groups who combined horticulture, vegetable extraction, hunting and fishing along the upper reaches of tributaries to the Amazon rivers which the roads traversed (Davis, 1977; Velho, 1972, 1976; Moran, 1981).

The modern capitalist forms of production and exchange, together with the corresponding social relations, legal institutions, and functionally specific bureaucratic agencies (which were firmly established in large parts of the agricultural and industrial sectors of the south-central region of Brazil), were still incipient or nonexistent in much of the Amazon, especially in the rural areas (Santos, 1979; Sawyer, 1977). Land-tenure institutions reflected the noncapitalist modes of extraction and production specific to different rural areas. Rights in land were governed by customary usage or by a variety of deeds or authorizations, some dating back to the colonial era, others granted later by state or municipal governments. Actual boundaries tended to be vague, even in deeds certifying legal ownership, though holding size might be specified. Extensive unclaimed areas devolved to the individual states.

Central government decisions to connect the Amazon to the rest of Brazil with highways changed land use and land rights drastically. The completion of the Belém-Brasília highway in 1959 provided access to extensive *terra firme* lands and opened these lands to the market economy. A massive immigration by dispossessed peasants from other regions, especially the Northeast, where mechanization and capitalization of agriculture had disrupted traditional forms of land tenure and created a growing rural landless class, resulted. These peasant migrants used the new road to exploit markets for *terra firme* crops such as upland rice. They continued, however, to combine extraction and hunting with agriculture. Their forms of land tenure and their exchange systems paralleled those of longer established Amazonian peasant modes of production and extraction (Velho, 1972).

An influx of large ranching and lumbering enterprises quickly followed the peasant migrants. Using their greater political and economic power, and frequently resorting to violence, they were able to take control of the land which the peasants had cleared and then to take advantage of the labor reserve which their actions created (Velho, 1976; Ianni, 1979; Hébette and Acevedo, 1979).

Existing land-tenure institutions were not adapted to treat land as a valuable negotiable commodity on the scale that these sudden changes required (Mendonça, 1977; Santos, 1979). The state government sold vast tracts of land in a disorderly and frequently corrupt fashion.[1] The *cartórios,* licensed land-registry offices, were swamped both by legitimate requests to transfer properties flawed by earlier unregistered sales and inheritances and by demands to register and sell fraudulent titles. Banks were caught in the dilemma of an increasing and profitable demand for agricultural credit in a situation where the conventional guarantees—of titled property—were either unavailable or unreliable. The banks exerted increasing pressure on both the state and the national bureaucracies to legitimate the land claims of the large-scale capitalist enterprises which were borrowing money from them with little regard for the legality of their claims.

The establishment of an authoritarian and centralist regime in 1964 created the conditions for further disruptions and changes in land-tenure institutions. In 1968 the central government, acting through the SUDAM, extended its program of fiscal incentives to large ranching enterprises in the Amazon (Mahar, 1979). As the SUDAM was not obliged to consider the validity of titles for the land on which its enormous subsidies were to be applied, their immediate effect was to aggravate the already severe land-tenure crisis. The absence of modern tenure guarantees left both the newer and older peasant settlements extremely vulnerable to repeated expulsion by large enterprises (Velho, 1976). As Martins (1975) has explained, these settlements formed a highly mobile demographic front. They provided cleared land and cheap labor for the expanding capitalist enterprises, which continuously followed and displaced them.

The large ranching and lumbering concerns used various tactics, such as purchasing old or lapsed titles, forging and fraudulently registering deeds, buying state lands, or simply occupying the land, to assert legal claim to lands which the peasants had settled. In addition to subverting prior land-tenure institutions, they also subverted the state's control of its own armed force. In collusion with local police and military detachments, they forced the peasants to abandon their lands by of-fering small sums for the clearing, building, and planting which the peasants had done and then used violence to remove those who would not leave (Foweraker, 1981; Pinto, 1978, 1980; Martins, 1980, 1982; Ianni, 1979). Some of these dispossessed peasants remained as em-ployees for the burning and clearing of land for pastures. Some pushed farther into the jungle, disrupting settled indigenous groups, and started the process of clearing—and eventual expulsion—over again. And some, including many whose employment ended when the pasture clearing was finished, settled in the towns which sprang up along the highways and became part of a transhumant labor force, migrating with the seasonal cycles of burning and harvesting, or moved to the already swollen larger cities[2] (Cardoso and Müller, 1977). (See Table 4.)

The establishment of cattle ranches along the new roads devastated huge tracts of forest, compacted and eroded the soil, and created new microclimates—drier and hotter than previously—in the areas of most intense deforestation. These grass monocultures are highly susceptible to plant and pest invasion; their economic life may be as short as eight to twelve years (Hecht, 1979). The exogenous grasses do not germinate effectively in the Amazonian climate, so the pasture deteriorates rapidly. Ranchers eager to maximize their returns on investment before the pasture deteriorates completely overstock and overgraze, thus inten-sifying ecological damage (Hecht, 1981). The areas cleared are too large to permit recolonization by plant species capable of recovering the soil,

Table 4. Urban Population and Growth in Amazônia

	1950			1960			1970		
City Sizes	Number of Cities	Urban Population by Size Category Number	Percent	Number of Cities	Urban Population by Size Category Number	Percent	Number of Cities	Urban Population by Size Category Number	Percent
To 5,000	86	120,387	23.54	99	152,845	17.34	109	186,239	12.27
5,001-20,000	10	76,278	14.91	17	162,039	18.38	27	265,025	17.47
20,001-100,000	1	89,612	17.52	2	52,509	5.96	5	207,026	13.65
100,000-1,000,000	1	225,218	44.03	2	514,028	58.32	2	858,737	56.61
Total	98	511,495	100.00	120	881,421	100.00	143	1,517,027	100.00

Source. IBGE, 1977:244-45.

however, so these areas may be permanently lost to any future human use (Goodland and Irwin, 1975; Denevan, 1973).

One condition of the fiscal incentive contracts was that the entire 50 percent—the legal maximum—of each project's land must be cleared (Pinto, 1977). In the case of the cattle ranches—the largest of which range from 300,000 to over 600,000 hectares—this has involved huge areas.[3] Neither the government nor the ranchers have been willing to invest the time or money necessary to cut and transport the vast timber sources in these areas, so the land is usually cleared by burning. Estimates of the usable wood thus destroyed run as high as 3.5 million hectares (Pinto, 1977), out of a total of 6.6 million hectares which have been cut and burned for pasture. Of the 14,000-kilometer strip bulldozed for the Transamazon highway, scarcely a single cubic foot of lumber was sold (Moraes Victor, 1975, cited in Goodland, Irwin, and Tillman, 1978:276).

In addition to disrupting human settlement, wasting lumber, extinguishing species, and ruining upland soils, pasture formation may indirectly reduce *várzea* productivity downriver. The soils eroded from the newly formed pastures flow down various of the Amazon's tributaries, where they are deposited in the slower waters of the confluences. This sediment could create a damming effect in the nearly flat lower rivers. This would increase flood levels and delay the river's fall, thus impeding cultivation in large areas of the *várzea*, reducing growing seasons on the rest of it, and inundating riverine settlements that were previously above the normal high water level.

The wasteful use of land is sanctioned in other ways besides the SUDAM's approval and financing of pasture formation. The various local states can sell their public lands to private individuals at a legally established rate defined as "the value of the naked earth" (*valor da terra nua*). This means that the state assigns value only to the land itself and not to anything, such as trees, which may be growing on it. The resulting low prices of the land, in turn, make possible the rapid profits which can be gained by burning off forest vegetation and planting pastures. Even when lumbering was officially promoted following the second Amazon Development Plan of 1974, timber projects were not integrated with pasture formation, and predatory methods continued in those areas that could be cut most profitably. State support and fiscal incentives have increased revenues from lumbering and made timber the major source of the Amazon's foreign earnings, but they have left unchanged the rudimentary cutting and transport techniques which lose approximately 60 percent of the lumber cut to decomposition (IBGE, 1977:377). Even selective logging destroys far more lumber than is actually used because of tightly integrated canopies and the lianas which bind trees, together with the shallow root systems of most tropical species (Hecht, 1981:78). Especially valuable species such as mahogany are exploited beyond the possibility of subsequent regeneration. Logging machinery and roads contribute to both soil compacting and erosion (Hecht, 1981:77-78).

Unlike mining and lumbering, large-scale cattle ranching has contributed relatively little to the growth of regional income. The rapid deterioration of pastures has kept herd sizes and marketing low. Productivity is only slightly higher than in the traditional cattle-raising systems based on natural grasses in riverine areas. Pompermayer (1979) concludes that the major attraction of Amazonian cattle ranching for the large corporations in south-central Brazil is in the subsidies it provides them for land speculation; there is also some evidence that firms have been able to deflect some of the fiscal incentive moneys available to more profitable investments in other areas. State land sale and fiscal incentive policies thus create a climate favorable to rapid exploitation and sale of land. Profits available from land speculation and the manipulation of credits and fiscal subsidies allow ranchers to treat the land with little or no concern for its long-term utility (Mahar, 1979; Hecht, 1981).

The growing government expenditures on salaries and facilities for the agencies which disburse the fiscal incentives and carry out the state's development programs, however, have contributed significantly to the growth of regional income. In fact, the growth in government expenditure is the largest single factor in the increase of regional income. The government has invested heavily to establish, maintain, and staff a modern administrative infrastructure for its multiple development programs. Government expenditures increased from 9 percent of regional income to 14.2 percent in 1972. The income class which shows the next largest increase in this period includes the privately employed lawyers, accountants, and economists, many of whom were formerly employed by the SUDAM and other government agencies, who worked for consulting firms whose major business was to prepare plans and projects for companies which wished to seek fiscal incentives or who carried out special research projects for the government agencies (Mahar, 1979:57, table 3.3). Directly and indirectly, government expenditures have contributed to the rapid expansion of the tertiary, the most dynamic income sector since 1960. To the extent that increased government expenditure results from the implementation of government programs to support extractive enterprise, the associated increase in income will last no longer than the state's commitment to these projects.

Even the government programs to develop nonextractive enterprise may have relatively transitory effects. Fiscal incentives have been applied to industry, primarily in Belém and Manaus, the two largest cities in the Amazon. A free trade zone (FTZ) was established in Manaus, so industries which locate there may benefit from both fiscal incentives and freedom from import tariffs. These industries have tended to concentrate on capital-intensive processes, frequently displacing prior labor-intensive enterprises. Further, the nature of the incentives distorts investment decisions, stimulating investments that are only profitable as long as the incentives are maintained. This results in an absence of either vertical or horizontal linkages between these industries and other dimensions of the regional economy and heightens the flow of income out of the area (Mahar 1979:134-35). The Manaus FTZ, in particular, appears to diminish the "multiplier effects of public and private expenditures in the region [due to] import leakages" (Mahar, 1979:68) and has resulted in a chronic balance-of-payments deficit (Mahar, 1979:144, 147). The export-oriented, capital-intensive industries encouraged by the policy of fiscal incentives and an absence of import barriers do contribute significantly to regional income and product, but they tend to drain resources from the rest of the region. They act as a "pole of attraction" for rural inhabitants, thus dampening economic activity in the rural areas and further attenuating internal commercial and productive linkages (Mahar, 1979).

There is little apparent linkage between the extractive and urban industrial economies, except for a limited amount of investment in wood products encouraged by a strong international market for Amazonian timber (Mahar, 1979:69). SUFRAMA (Superintendency for the Manaus Free Trade Zone) approved nineteen projects in wood products between 1968 and 1975, with an investment of Cr$429.1 million (1975 values), or 11.3 percent of the total projects it approved. These projects employed 3,747 people (Mahar, 1979:155). SUDAM, up to mid-1976, had approved seventeen new wood products projects and the expansion of six projects, with an investment of Cr$972.7 million and Cr$337.0 million (1975 values), respectively, or a total of Cr$1,309.7 million (Mahar, 1979:107). However, this production of wood and wood products made up only 1 percent of sales in the Manaus FTZ in 1966, or Cr$4.3 million (1975 values), falling to 0.2 percent in 1973, or Cr$1.4 million (Mahar, 1979:149).

This brief review of the effects of government financed infrastructure and of direct and indirect government subsidies to capitalist enterprise shows that, far from breaking the environmentally and demographically disruptive cycle of successive modes of extraction, government activities have intensified the rate and effects of extraction and are no likelier to generate self-sustaining autonomous development than were the previous modes of extraction. These extractive economies contributed to a rise in regional income from Cr$2,488.5 million in 1950 to Cr$4,441.2 million in 1960 and Cr$6,882 million in 1970 (1975 values). Increases in per capita income were less impressive, rising from Cr$1,348 in 1950 to Cr$1,707 in 1960 and Cr$1,909 in 1970 (1975 values). When the increase in regional income is compared to the contribution of ecologically self-depleting extractive economies and of politically tenuous government expenditures, however, it becomes quite clear that whatever development this income change reflects is likely to be precarious and self-limiting.

Mining, which depletes the resources on which it depends, and which accounted for 15.3 percent of SUDAM-approved industrial investment through mid-1976 (Mahar, 1979:107), accounted for 13.9 percent of regional income growth between 1960 and 1970, rising from 0.8 percent to 5.5 percent of regional income between 1960 and 1970. Figures for lumber from Pará, which accounts for approximately 80 percent of the Amazon's total production (IBGE, 1977), show a fourfold increase in value from 1960 to 1976, by which time lumber constituted about 12 percent of total industrial and mining income (CONDEPA, 1975). Present logging methods are highly destructive and severely diminish the regenerative capacities of the most valuable species and the most accessible forests. Government expenditure accounts for major shares of income growth and capital formation during this same period. Fiscal incentives and tax credit disbursements from SUDAM alone equaled 20.7 percent of regional income in 1970 and equaled 58.4 percent of the increase in regional income between 1960 and 1970. Major investments in infrastructure, particularly road and dam construction, have also contributed to the growth in regional income. Investment in the Transamazon highway and PIN were to average Cr$756.8 million (1975 values) a year beginning in 1971 (Mahar, 1979:19). A single foreign-owned enterprise, the Jari project, totally financed by the Brazilian subsidiary of National Bulk Carriers, estimated investment expenditures to 1979 at U.S.$500 million, potentially reaching U.S.$1 billion by completion of the project (Mahar, 1979:111).

Exact disaggregation of the specific contribution of such fiscal incentives and of the total yearly contribution of self-depleting extractive enterprises to regional income is impossible within the Brazilian government's regional economic accounting system, but it is clear that major portions of the growth in regional income are either dependent on government expenditure, which may end with changes in policy, or are generated by extractive economies, which will eventually terminate themselves. It is reasonable to assume that all of these factors also generate and sustain indirect employment, whose contribution to regional income can continue only as long as do the government programs and extractive industries on which they depend. When these figures are adjusted for population growth of 95 percent (from 1,844,655 in 1950 to 3,603,860 in 1970), the per capita income growth not directly dependent on mining, fiscal incentives, government service, and roads is likely to be insignificant or negative. These gross income figures also mask the consequences of increased concentration of land tenure (Santos, 1979); of peasant expulsion from land and loss of subsistence bases; of rapid urbanization (IBGE, 1977); and of net out-migration from certain areas of the Amazon (Wood and Wilson, 1982). These meager results, moreover, have been brought about at considerable cost to the natural environment and its future utility. The income curve adjusted for extraction-related, and therefore necessarily self-depleting, economies is probably flat or negative. When resource values are added to the environmental costs of these extractive economies, it is clear that more value is leaving the region than is returning in trade and other transfers. If we had the data necessary to calculate the effects of these economies in terms of energy flows, both as energy immediately consumed and as energy incorporated into useful social and physical organization, rather than simply in exchange values measured in income, the adjusted relation between values produced and values destroyed would probably be sharply negative.

These results also came at considerable cost to social order. As lumbering and ranching enterprises gained title to land and attempted to control it for extraction and for speculation (Hecht, 1981; Mahar, 1979; Pompermayer, 1979), they used the power of the state—both through modern land-title and judicial institutions and through the state's apparatus for violence—and their own private control of hired gunmen to dislocate peasants who held land in these areas. Peasant resistance to the armed employees and military and police allies of the lumbering and ranching concerns led to increasing, and increasingly publicized, violence. Land conflict had been a major factor in frontier expansion in other parts of Brazil (Foweraker, 1981), and the continuation of such disturbances created an embarrassment for a modernizing authoritarian regime whose public legitimacy relied in part on its regulation of social conflict (Martins, 1980, 1982; O'Donnell, 1973). The Amazon became a new center for such conflict. At the same time the continued expulsion of peasants, who then moved to new uncleared areas, and the location of ranching, mining, and lumbering enterprise in previously inaccessible areas created further pressure for the opening up of Indian lands, both those in formally established reserves and those not formally recognized.

The state had undermined its own legitimacy by promoting rapid capitalist expansion in areas where it could not control violence. The institutions on which the state depended to maintain order in the national center extended only tenuously into the Amazon. The potential for violence was heightened by the extreme imbalance between competing sectors, which government subsidies to large companies created in areas where a history of extractive economies had impeded the development of stable populations and productive systems. Indeed, the state's action had itself tended to weaken the previous nonmodern, noncapitalist institutional bases of land tenure, access to resources, and the control of violence.

Simultaneously, the state was facing crises resulting from the extreme, and increasing, concentration of land tenure in other parts of Brazil. It attempted to resolve both of these problems by directly regulating land tenure in the Amazon, first, to control violence and bureaucratic irregularity there, and second, to promote the resettlement of landless peasants from other parts of Brazil. The following chapters analyze the ways that the state imposed modern land-tenure institutions on the Amazon in order to achieve these goals, the ways that subsidized enterprise interfered in this attempt, and the organizational difficulties which the state confronted in implementing its own programs. In order to analyze these problems, it is necessary to consider various characteristics of the modern capitalist state and of its bureaucracies. The Amazon presents a limiting case for various theories of the state precisely because of its extractive history and because of the discrepancies in social and political organization between the Amazon and the increasingly energy-intensive, industrialized, and modern center of Brazil. In order to understand the actions of the national state in the Amazon, we must take into account the organization and operations of the bureaucracy which was formed as the Brazilian national state responded to and fostered the development of an industrial economy in close association with foreign and domestic capitalists. These bureaucratic forms were distinctly modern, both in the functional specificity of particular bureaucratic agencies and in the attempts to regulate the relations between different sectors of agricultural and industrial economies. These agencies extended their modern procedures and structures into the Amazon, where few of the institutional bases around which these agencies were organized existed.

While the focus of the next chapters is on the process and the distortions of modernization through these bureaucratic agencies and on the specific effects of modern bureaucracies, it is impossible to understand the forms and the effects of this modernization without reference to the demographic, ecological, and infrastructural results of the extractive economies through which the Amazon had participated in the world economy. Government programs made the Amazon an economic periphery to the Brazilian center. They also made the Amazon an institutional periphery by transferring directly the administrative and procedural forms which regulated bureaucracies in the capitalist center directly to the noncapitalist Amazon. These forms did not remain intact, however. The very different physical and social environment in which bureaucrats were obliged to work in the Amazon profoundly distorted the intended organization of their agencies and programs. These programs modernized without necessarily achieving intended results. They did, however, extensively affect social and economic organization in the Amazon.

It was through the emergence of the modern national state that the Amazon was subordinated to the mediation of the Brazilian center in both its internal organization and in its relation with external markets. It was through the actions of this state that new locally dominant groups—the bureaucrats of federal agencies and the managers and representatives of international and national companies as well as individual entrepreneurs—achieved the power to reorganize local modes of extraction and production. Finally, it was through the struggles and alliances between different modern bureaucratic agencies and the newly dominant groups with and against different segments of the earlier established social classes in the Amazon that national government programs were carried out, often with results far different than those envisioned by government planners. All of these struggles and actions were shaped by the structure of the physical and social environments in the Amazon. They were also shaped by the concentration of political, economic, and energetic forces in the modern organizational forms of the central state and their resulting disruption of the more dispersed, far less energy-intensive institutional forms which were peculiar to the Amazon.

The anomaly of uneven development and major regional inequalities within a single nation state poses major problems for theories of the developmental state as well as for the programs of the state itself. Many of the recent Brazilian government development programs for the Amazon have been aimed at establishing modern institutional forms characteristic of capitalist modes of production prior to the establishment of capitalist economic systems. Modernization theories which stress the role of a strong central state in national development (see Higgott, 1980) tend to ignore the profound imbalances caused by modernization programs in countries which have marked differences between the national center and the national periphery. Theories of modernizing authoritarian states in Latin America (O'Donnell, 1973, 1978; Malloy, 1977; Collier, 1979) and of associated dependent industrial development (Cardoso, 1973; Evans, 1979) tend to focus exclusively on the modern capitalist sectors of the societies they describe.

Numerous recent studies of the action of the national state in the Amazon have dealt with this problem by labeling the Amazon a frontier, an area into which the national state, and the nationally dominant classes, are extending their power and influence (Velho, 1972, 1976, 1979; Mahar, 1979; Schmink, 1981, 1982; Foweraker, 1981; Wood, 1980). This label captures important processes of state and capitalist expansion, as well as the particular forms of lawlessness and violence which occur as economic expansion precedes the establishment of modern capitalist institutions. The notion of frontier must be carefully qualified when it is used in the Amazon, however. First, the concept may imply an eventual incorporation of the frontier within the dominant society. I believe that the past and present dynamics of Amazonian extractive systems make this outcome highly unlikely. Second, the notion of frontier may imply the expansion of one system into empty space, when in fact what is described as frontier expansion in the Amazon frequently involves the conflict between two different economic and institutional systems. Finally, the idea of frontier implies linear and progressive expansion. The extractive bases of capitalist expansion into the Amazon is anything but linear; rather, it follows the location of resources for which there is a market. Mining, especially, creates discontinuous and randomly located changes in social and ecological systems. The extractive character of the dominant economies in the Amazon continues to disrupt both natural processes of energy use and coordination. The flow of energy out of the Amazon impoverishes natural and human systems there while it accelerates economic processes in the Brazilian and other industrial centers. Both the imbalance of extraction-production interdependencies and the internal dynamic of extractive processes can only enhance the subordination of the Amazon to the Brazilian center and the disjunctures between the subordinate and the dominant system. I prefer, therefore, to look directly at the implications of the Amazon for various theories of the developmental state and then to consider the relevance of the notion of frontier within this general framework.

NOTES

1. Of the 6,987,567.0 hectares of land sold to private buyers by the State of Pará between 1924 and 1977, 6,481,042.8 hectares (92.7 percent) were sold in the five-year period between the opening of the highway in 1959 and the revolution in 1964 (based on data from Santos, 1979). The revolution greatly reduced the massive state land sales, though the states have contested these restrictions and have continued to sell land.

2. The Suiá-Missu ranch serves as one of many possible examples of the different demographic effects of ranching and peasant colonization. This ranch projected eventual permanent employment for 250 men in its proposal for fiscal incentives. These men were to be employed on 678,000 hectares of land, of which 50 percent, or 339,000 hectares, were burned and cleared for pasture. At this rate of employment, ranching would provide 500 jobs on a greater amount of cleared land than 30,000 colonist families have probably cleared and now use (Bunker, 1980b). Actual employment on this ranch is probably less than projected.

3. Land-holding sizes of some of the major beneficiaries of the SUDAM's fiscal incentive policy for agriculture and ranching are as follows: Corporation, holding size (hectares); Jari (D. K. Ludwig), 600,000-1,200,000 (disputed); Suiá-Missu (Liquigas), 678,000; Codeara, 600,000; Vale Cristalino (Volkswagen), 140,000; Bruynzeel, 500,000; Georgia Pacific, 500,000; Robin MacGlolm, 400,000; Toyomenka, 300,000. Though a number of smaller projects, ranging from 4,000 to 17,000 hectares, were approved prior to 1975, the SUDAM decided that only ranching projects of over 25,000 hectares would be eligible for fiscal incentives. This criterion reflects official opinion of the minimum size for economic viability. The average size for these projects at this time was 18,750 hectares (Cardoso and Müller, 1977). IBDF authorizations for clearing in the south of Pará alone, 1973-76, were as follows (all figures are approximate): 1973, 450,000 hectares; 1974, 500,000 hectares; 1975, 267,000 hectares; and 1976, 450,000 hectares. Hecht (1981:68) presents the following data on deforestation in Brazilian Amazonia: area cleared by 1975, 2,859,525 hectares; area cleared by 1978, 7,717,175 hectares.

CHAPTER 4

The Limits of State Power
on an Extractive Periphery

Until 1970 government policy toward the Amazon involved relatively uncontrolled subsidies to large-scale capitalist enterprise. In addition to disrupting the natural environment, government policies disrupted local economies and populations and caused a series of violent conflicts over access to resources and the breakdown of local institutions of order and of land tenure. In this situation the state was impelled to attempt to control and direct the capitalist development that its own policies had stimulated. Simultaneously, it was confronting a situation of increasing social unrest and criticism due to the growth of a landless peasant class and its repression of this class's attempts at political organization in the Northeast. It attempted to respond to these two problems with a program that combined social welfare with political and institutional control.

The much discussed Transamazon colonization projects constituted a departure from state policies of direct support for large-scale enterprise in the Amazon. For a brief period the state attempted to reduce social and political tensions by opening the Amazon to peasant settlement. These policies, however, were part of a more general attempt on the part of state to bring the rapid extension of capitalist activity under control by using the various agencies of the state and the institutional structure which functioned in the rest of Brazil. The social welfare programs were rapidly subordinated to the demands of the state's capitalist allies, but the institutional programs, aimed at maintaining state control and regulation of enterprise, have continued.

These programs and the changes in them comprise a particularly interesting case of the tensions and contradictions between the modern state's need to promote both economic growth and social order (Block, 1977) and in its efforts to achieve both political control and subjective legitimacy (de Janvry, 1981). The peripheral status which extractive economies had imposed on the Amazon greatly diluted the state's political imperative of social order and subjected it to significant interference from powerful private interests.

Debate about the Brazilian government's reasons and plans for building the Transamazon highway from the Atlantic coast to the Peruvian border and for settling thousands of landless peasants along it had become intense even before the project's precipitous beginning. Critics denounced the road "that went from nowhere to noplace" as economic folly, while champions of "national integration" saw it as a crucial step in the economic and geopolitical unification essential to Brazil's realization of its "great nation" potential and to alleviation of its land-tenure concentration (see Tamer, 1970; Pereira, 1971).

Most discussion of the technical, organizational, economic, and political difficulties that hampered construction of the road and the completion of the agricultural colonization projects has been limited to the context of the highway itself. These issues, however, also have direct relevance for a number of wider questions about the capacities of national states to implement development programs aimed at social welfare and distributive justice. Several studies of development in Latin America suggest that the state's efficacy in implementing development programs, especially those designed to favor politically unorganized and economically weak rural populations, may be impeded by interference and subversion by powerful private interests, by the complexity and rigidity of bureaucratic organization, by the inadequate preparation and discipline of bureaucratic personnel, by the diversity of regional, political, and economic systems within particular countries, or by the "softness" of the state itself.[1]

These themes contrast markedly with assumptions underlying recent theories of the corporatist or authoritarian state in Latin America. These theories ascribe considerable autonomy and administrative efficiency as well as an "overarching similarity in structure and organization" (Malloy, 1977:3) to regimes like those of Brazil, Chile, and Argentina. Malloy (1977:16) describes the authoritarian corporatist state as an unpleasant but potentially viable system capable of regulating the economic and social relations of entire nations. O'Donnell (1973, 1975, 1977, 1978) in his theory of the bureaucratic-authoritarian (BA) state maintains that the BA state depends on a shifting alliance with the national bourgeoisie and international capital. He implies that, even though it depends on these allies, the BA state dictates the terms of this alliance and limits private sector access to its own administrative apparatus by maintaining bureaucratic control of higher government positions. He specifically argues that the national bourgeoisie is subordinate to the state (1977:63), even though it is essential to the state's strategies to regulate international capital.

Drawing primarily on data from Brazil, Chile, and Argentina, but including Mexico and Uruguay as well, O'Donnell (1978:6) lists defining characteristics of the BA state as:

1. Occupation of higher government positions by persons who have had successful careers in complex and highly bureaucratized organizations—the armed forces, public bureaucracy, and private firms;
2. Political exclusion, through the closing of channels of political access to the popular sector and its allies both by repression and the imposition of vertical controls on organizations such as trade unions;
3. Economic exclusion, by the reduction or indefinite postponement of the popular sector's participation;
4. Depoliticization, by pretending to reduce social and political issues to "technical" problems to be resolved by interaction between state-controlled organizations; and
5. A stage of important transformations in the mechanisms of capital accumulation, which are part of a "deepening" process of a peripheral and dependent capitalism characterized by extensive industrialization.

Other features (O'Donnell, 1975, 1977) include military predominance, priority of security goals such as elimination of subversion and popular sector agitation, an attempt to create a politically and economically attractive environment for international capital investment, the progressive concentration of income in the upper classes, and a tendency toward bureaucratic expansion and technocratic decision making.

Most of the theoretical considerations of the authoritarian state have emphasized one of its most salient characteristics, its evidently great power. Malloy (1977:16) maintains that the BA state is capable of regulating the economic and social relations of entire nations by "conscious" decision which favors some power contenders over others. O'Donnell does not place the BA state so emphatically in the position of controlling all social and economic relations, but rather discusses its tense alliance with the national bourgeoisie and with international capital. He does, however, attribute considerable autonomy to the state, though he maintains that international capital and, to a lesser extent, the national bourgeoisie also possess autonomy. He refers to mutual control (1977:49) and to the bifrontal penetration of the BA state into the organization of civil society and of the private sector into some parts of government. While insisting on the mutual indispensability of the three allies, O'Donnell nevertheless implies that the BA state controls and regulates access to the terms of the alliance and argues that the national bourgeoisie is subordinate to the state (1977:63), even while essential to it in its control of international capital.

Despite the different emphases and conclusions with respect to the relative power of the authoritarian state, international capital, and the national bourgeoisie, these theories posit that the authoritarian state has sufficient power, control, and autonomy to regulate the economic and social relations of the society. This notion of the authoritarian state's power and efficacy contains the idea, most explicitly formulated by O'Donnell (1977:54), that this type of regime is accompanied by capitalist forms which, though they do "not follow the patterns of growth of the central economies," are "far removed from the archetypal situations of underdevelopment."

The assumption that authoritarian military regimes with highly centralized bureaucratic administrations have created new forms of government with extraordinary degrees of political autonomy and administrative capacity implies that such states could control or obviate the obstacles to effective development identified in various studies of development program failure. Social welfare programs in the Amazon, where a series of extractive economies had enhanced the ability of dominant groups to disrupt human and social environments for their own short-term profits, posed an important challenge to the BA or corporatist state's developmental capacities, administrative efficiency, and relative autonomy. These largely excluded the national bourgeoisie or international firms from direct participation or indirect benefits. The state's ability to implement programs that did not benefit the classes which its earlier development programs had strengthened and that even provoked their opposition or interference would depend on considerable autonomy from powerful private interests and its independent capacity to implement development programs.

The Brazilian government's programs for colonization and rural development along the Transamazon highway brought no immediate benefits to any dominant group or class. Rather, the programs were aimed at relieving the poverty of landless peasants, one of the poorest and politically weakest segments of Brazilian society. These schemes did, however, divert funds from other development programs and thus generated opposition from powerful groups in the sectors affected (Cardoso and Müller, 1977). They also created infrastructure and opened access to valuable natural resources. Various powerful groups attempted to gain control over these resources and infrastructure. Because the extractive history of the Amazon had left most of the region without stable populations or established production systems, these colonization projects were established in areas where both distance and lack of modern infrastructure greatly complicated the task of organizing and administering these projects.

The coincidence of significant civil opposition and major administrative problems in a development program undertaken by a regime that O'Donnell has called "the purest example" of a BA state (1977:53) provides a suitable case for testing the limits of the Brazilian state's autonomy and administrative capacity. Previous studies (O'Donnell, 1978; Evans, 1979) have shown that the regime which took power in 1964 has greatly strengthened its position relative to both domestic and international capitalist groups and that it has achieved impressive administrative and entrepreneurial capacities. These studies, however, have focused on state initiatives in regions of the country and/or in sectors of the economy with "an extended but vertically unintegrated industrialization . . . and a highly modernized urban social structure" (O'Donnell, 1978:9) and in programs in which there was a consonance of interests between the state and at least some powerful private interests. Even within these sectors, Evans shows that the relative influence and autonomy of the state varies with the production and marketing characteristics of different industries. The colonization and rural development schemes along the Transamazon highway present an opportunity to examine the state's degree of autonomy and administrative capacity in development programs which do not enjoy either the support of some powerful private groups or the previous existence of modern organizational supports and infrastructure.

Social Welfare Programs and Government Intentions

The Brazilian state's strong support of economic development based on rapid industrial "deepening" through the concentration of income in the wealthiest classes (O'Donnell, 1978) raises the problem of the government's intentions in creating social welfare programs for the poorest classes. Such programs are relevant to the question of the state's developmental capacity, administrative efficiency, and autonomy only if it can be shown that the state was, at some point, clearly committed to a particular program's success.

Arguments that the government used the colonization schemes to attract an adequate labor force for large-scale ranching, lumbering, and mining enterprises with which it planned to develop the area (Cardoso and Müller, 1977; Davis, 1977) can be easily dismissed. Though some support for the road-building programs came from military and geopolitical preoccupation with the "demographic vacuum" of the Amazon and its subsequent susceptibility to "international covetousness" (Reis, 1968; Pereira, 1971), the long history of spontaneous colonization on

Brazilian frontiers made accessible by road building (Velho, 1972, 1976; Foweraker, 1981; Martins, 1975; Hébette and Acevedo, 1979) indicates that official encouragement to migrate would have been unnecessary to this purpose. Further, despite the relatively rapid abandonment of the colonization idea itself, restrictions on land-holding size in most of the colonization areas remained relatively effective, so migrants to official colonization areas did not constitute as accessible or significant a labor reserve for large-scale enterprise as did migrants to areas along other roads and highways which had not been reserved for colonization. Intense and continued criticisms of these projects from major business interests is further evidence that the colonization projects were not designed as a disguised contribution to large-scale private enterprise in the area. Finally, in contrast to earlier colonization projects, both in the Amazon (Anderson, 1976; Tavares et al., 1972) and in other parts of Latin America (Nelson, 1973; Moran, 1981:6-8), government plans for Transamazon colonization included extensive and costly investment in a comprehensive administrative and physical infrastructure. The enormous budgets allocated to the colonization projects and the massive publicity which accompanied and justified them (see, e.g., INCRA, 1972) indicate a major government commitment to these projects, at least initially.

The apparent inconsistency between these social welfare goals and the government's predominant dedication to rapid industrialization and economic growth through the concentration of income is best explained as an attempt to gain legitimacy and to offset criticism of its policies of excluding the rural poor both economically and politically (Contini, 1976, cited in Moran, 1981). "[T]he state must present itself as the incarnation, as the political and ideological expression, of the general interests of the nation, to which the sectors excluded by the BA unquestionably belong" (O'Donnell, 1978:20).

Despite its great repressive powers and its political exclusion of the majority of the population, the authoritarian state cannot rely indefinitely on its alliance with domestic and international capital, but must somehow stabilize its control by making itself legitimate to other sectors (Linz, 1973; Schwartzman, 1977; Portes, 1979). If the colonization and rural development programs were successful in turning landless peasants into market-integrated small farmers, the government could claim that its economic model was accessible to all classes and an apt vehicle for social as well as economic development. Successful rural development programs would be especially effective in the government's search for legitimacy; they could be used both as a response to national and international criticism of the socio-economic condition of Brazil's rural poor and as an affirmation of the military regime's superiority over previous governments.

This does not mean that the government designed the Transamazon colonization schemes solely to legitimate itself to a politically and economically excluded class of landless peasants. Even if it had managed to settle as many peasants in the Amazon as originally proposed, these programs would have affected only an insignificant part of this class. The use of the colonization schemes as a legitimating device appears rather to correspond to the state's representation of itself as a national state, "working to everyone's long-term benefit . . . for the attainment of the true goal; the grandeur of a nation in which even those excluded and repressed are invited to participate vicariously" (O'Donnell, 1978:20). Roett (1978) captured some of the initial effects of government publicity campaigns when he wrote that the "[c]onstruction of the Transamazonic Highway . . . quickly captured the imagination of the Brazilian people" (152) and when he cited a *Jornal do Brasil* editorial which described "the pride that Brazilians feel over the opening of the nation's new frontier, constituted by the gigantic work of conquering and colonizing the largest empty space on the globe" (153). These publicity campaigns were directed at the entire national population rather than at a specific, politically and economically excluded, segment of the population.

The colonization schemes also served to abate increasing pressure for significant land reform. Feder (1970) and Thiesenhusen (1971) have pointed out that colonization schemes have been used in other Latin American countries as substitutes for the deeper institutional changes that land reform would involve. Certainly the Brazilian military government had strong political reasons to attempt to alleviate the political tensions caused by the growing concentration of land and wealth in the northeastern and southern regions of the country (Cehelsky, 1979). Its curtailment of the previous civilian regime's modest land reform and its veto of land reform proposals made by its own Ministry of Agriculture in 1967 had strengthened the impression that its policies were directed against the rural poor and had created rifts within the military establishment itself (Cehelsky, 1979; Foweraker, 1981; Martins, 1981, 1982). It could partially reduce some of these pressures by the mere demonstration of intent implicit in the large colonization budgets and accompanying publicity of the early 1970s. It can therefore be argued that the Brazilian military government acted in its own interest and independently of powerful private interests in establishing the colonization program. Its ability to carry out these programs, which do not enjoy the support of powerful private interests, thus provides a better test of the limits of the Brazilian BA state's autonomy and administrative capacity than previous studies (O'Donnell, 1978; Evans, 1979).

Central Government Policy and Peripheral Land-Tenure Institutions

Another dimension of the BA state's power, according to O'Donnell (1978:15), is its ability to "deeply transform" society through control of economic, political, and social relations. Of the wide variety of new institutions introduced, the most important to the transformation of Amazonia was the establishment of modern land-tenure, credit, and exchange systems.

The colonization and rural development programs along the Transamazon highway constituted, among other things, a major government attempt to establish a new set of institutions, exogenous to the region, against major temporal and spatial obstacles. The land-tenure, credit, and marketing institutions that had emerged from the sequence of regional modes of extraction, production, and exchange in the Amazon were radically different from those which the government attempted to establish. The tropical environment imposed different constraints than those of the temperate zones where central Brazilian institutions had been formed. Population densities and spatial relationships were also very different in the Amazonian periphery. The 59 percent of national territory officially defined as Amazonia contained only about 8 percent of the national population and produced only about 4 percent of its income (INCRA, 1972). Only within the previous decade had roads connected the Amazon to the rest of Brazil, and there were still large areas accessible only by water or air.

Commercial agriculture had never contributed significantly to the Amazon's market economy. The combination of low population densities and low levels of production had maintained the *aviamento* system intact. Wealth was accumulated and transferred from the rural to the urban areas almost exclusively through control over exchange. Property in land had little juridical or economic importance (Santos, 1979; Sawyer, 1977).

Transfer of land rights through sale or inheritance, therefore, was seldom registered officially. The enormous distances to administrative centers, the lack of commercial value of the land itself, and the frequent absence of the appropriate authorities made the costs of registration far greater than any benefits it might bring. Informal institutions of land tenure based on occupation, use, or sometimes superior force superceded the juridical forms of possession that functioned in the capitalist Brazilian center.

The ranching and lumbering entrepreneurs, attracted by new roads and fiscal incentives, were able to exploit the discrepancies in land-tenure institutions. In addition to the presumptive preeminence of national legal forms and titles over locally established use rights in land, these entrepreneurs had greater access to and influence over courts, police, and army detachments. They were further protected by distance from administrative centers to which local occupants might appeal against their violent expulsion. These factors impeded effective state action to control the violence and conflict.

In 1970 the government of Emílio Garrastazu Médici moved to control the chaotic effects of rapid capitalist expansion into the Amazon by establishing a system of roads through the region that would enable the military to move into the area more quickly; attract other kinds of commercial interests; and thus make it feasible to settle thousands of landless and unemployed families from the drought-scourged Northeast there. In 1971 this plan was followed by the *decreto-lei 1.164*, through which the government imposed national control of all state lands in a 100-kilometer wide belt on each side of any federal highway already constructed, in construction, or planned in the entire Amazon region. This amounted to over 60 percent of the total area of some states.

The National Institute of Colonization and Agrarian Reform (IN-CRA), formed in 1970 by merging three lesser agencies, was given control over the newly acquired federal lands with the responsibility of classifying land tenure, surveying, selling or colonizing, and titling them. INCRA's assigned goal was to impose an order which would control conflict between various segments of the rural population and regularize the possession and use of land in ways conducive to economic growth within modern capitalist institutions of production and exchange (Brasil, 1971, 1974). While INCRA was legally a self-governing agency (*autarquia*) within the Ministry of Agriculture, *decreto-lei 1.164* made it subordinate to the National Security Council, which assumed power over policy toward the administration and occupation of the federal lands in the Amazon.

The national government's expropriation of immense areas of the various states' public lands and the establishment of a bureaucratic apparatus to manage and dispose of them are compatible with theoretical statements that point to the modernizing authoritarian state's attempts to regulate and arbitrate social and economic relations (Malloy, 1977) and the predominance of military administrative control through bureaucratic organization (O'Donnell, 1975). INCRA's administrative structure and its statutory mandates correspond closely to O'Donnell's and Malloy's characterizations of the BA state as depoliticizing social and political problems by subordinating conflicting sectors to centralized bureaucratic control.

INCRA was organized into separate departments, each of which reported directly to different sections of the agency's national headquarters. These departments were directed to seven basic tasks:

1. Examination and validation of claims to occupied or titled land;
2. Survey and sale by public bid of federal lands in lots of up to 3,000 hectares and the sale of larger lots subject to congressional approval;
3. Maintenance of a cadastral survey and collection of the national rural land tax;
4. Supervision and regulation of private colonization companies;
5. Establishment of federal colonization projects;
6. Agrarian reform as defined by the *Estatuto da Terra;* and
7. Promotion and regulation of all agricultural cooperatives.

These diverse mandates obliged INCRA to deal with constituencies directly opposed to each other and to resolve their conflicting demands on its resources. Economic considerations, however, significantly distorted the execution of these mandates. Contrary to what theories of the BA state predict, INCRA's centralist organization and broad mandates impeded rather than promoted government autonomy and administrative efficiency. As will be demonstrated below, INCRA's organizational structure facilitated private sector penetration of and interference in the colonization programs. Further, administration of the colonization programs themselves was so inefficient that the costs to the colonists of complying with bureaucratic procedures were often greater than the benefits they derived from the development program (Moran, 1981; see Chapter 6).

The Question of Autonomy

Part of INCRA's revenues and much of its political influence came from patrimonial control over public lands and taxes. This created direct pressure to allocate its financial and administrative resources to large-scale land sale and title validation rather than to the costly and politically sensitive issues of colonization and agrarian reform. This bias toward large-scale enterprise was exacerbated by direct competition between ranching and lumbering enterprises and peasant or small farm occupation of land. The history of the colonization program along the Transamazon highway vividly demonstrates these contradictions.

In coordination with a major national publicity campaign and the central government's political commitment to the Program for National

Integration (INCRA, 1972), the bulk of INCRA's activities and budget from 1970 to 1974 was dedicated to the ambitious *Projetos Integrados de Colonização* (PIC) along the Transamazon highway. Publicized as a program to give "lands without men to men without lands,"[2] the declared purpose of these projects was to solve the problems of overpopulation in the Northeast and of *minifundização* in the South by settling up to 100,000 landless peasant families in the Amazon. Government directives charging INCRA with supervision of all aspects of these projects provoked opposition from private groups that had benefited from INCRA's other funtions and from other public agencies that perceived this expansion of INCRA's budget and jurisdiction as an encroachment on their own.

The Brazilian authoritarian regime was unable to limit private access to its own bureaucracy. Nor was it able to prevent the public airing of conflicts between its own administrative units. Cardoso (1975), Martins (1977), and Pereira (1977) have all described a major transition in the relations among the "state bourgeoisie," the national "capitalist" bourgeoisie, and international capital. The high levels of the state bureaucracy had grown rapidly in size, strength, and autonomy during the years following the 1964 revolution. In the early 1970s, however, national and international capitalist groups significantly increased their influence on development policy, both through direct pressure on government and by penetrating key positions within the state bureaucracy.[3]

The colonization schemes and the policies restricting the size of landholdings in the Amazon were an immediate and relatively easy target. Under pressure from private interests, the SUDAM, and the Ministry of Planning, INCRA policy and personnel were fundamentally reoriented. INCRA announced in 1972 that it would sell public lands in the Amazon to private enterprise. Cirne Lima, the minister of agriculture, resigned, protesting interference in and restrictions on the colonization projects. The president of INCRA, Moura Cavalcanti, replaced Lima as minister of agriculture. As president of INCRA, Cavalcanti had clearly and repeatedly expressed opposition to Reis Velloso, the minister of planning, and other high members of government who were urging that the Amazon be opened to large-scale private enterprise. In 1973, however, Cavalcanti changed his position to one more compatible with Velloso's; he announced that Amazon development policy had to be modified to encourage "more dynamic" private initiative. In the context of the debate over who was to control land in the Amazon, "more dynamic" enterprise was clearly meant to imply "large" enterprise and signaled Cavalcanti's intention to oppose the legal restrictions on the amount of land that INCRA could sell to any one bidder (Cardoso and Müller, 1977:157-58).

Interagency conflict at the regional level also created blocks to the government's expressed goals for the occupation of the Amazon by small farmers. The umbrella program for the colonization projects, PIN, was to receive 30 percent of the income tax revenues for fiscal incentives which had previously gone to the SUDAM. This posed an evident threat to the SUDAM's predominant position in Amazon development programs. The resulting competition between INCRA and the SUDAM generated various impasses both between these two organs and between the various agencies which received rural development funds from each of them. As this program also threatened the business groups that had benefited from the SUDAM's fiscal incentives and other supports for industry and large-scale ranching and agriculture and mineral extraction, SUDAM found natural allies among the entrepreneurs' associations and interest groups that were demanding access to Amazonian resources and federal subsidies. The superintendent of the SUDAM throughout this time was advocating that economic integration of the Amazon could best be achieved by large ranching projects (Cardoso and Müller, 1977:157-58).

Finally, in 1974, INCRA's president, Lourenço Tavares da Silva, formally acknowledged the major policy changes that had already occurred. INCRA, he said, was opposed to *latifúndios*, but not to large enterprise in itself; consequently, the colonization projects would be oriented toward a "joint composition" with large and medium enterprises (Cardoso and Müller, 1977:181). By this time, colonization budgets had already been cut and the number of colonists to be settled had been reduced to one fifth of the originally projected 100,000 families.

In 1975 INCRA was instructed by the government's personnel department to reduce drastically the number of its functionaries in the colonization programs. INCRA increasingly left assistance programs to other, less powerful agencies and restricted its own activities in the colonization areas to surveying lots and expediting titles, though even in this there continued to be lengthy delays (Bunker, 1979). Many of the original colonists failed to receive titles and therefore could not obtain investment credit from banks. Increasing numbers left the area, selling rights in their lots to other colonists or to the ranchers who were buying land behind the colonization areas.

With the publication of the second Plan for the Development of the Amazon (PDA II) in 1975, the government explicitly abandoned the idea of developing the Amazon through the settlement of small farmers and emphasized instead the establishment of large, highly capitalized ranching and mining enterprises which supposedly would be more effective in generating foreign revenues. By 1976 two presidential directives, *exposição de motivos 005* and *006*, authorized INCRA to regularize titles of up to 60,000 hectares and 3,000 hectares for large and medium enterprises, respectively, whose "paralyzation might hinder the economic development of the region" (Santos, 1979:130-31). In the same year private colonization, to be carried out by land-selling companies under INCRA guidance, was approved. This constituted a major victory for the private interest groups opposed to official colonization. INCRA was authorized to approve sales of up to 500,000 hectares to private colonization companies. By the end of the decade, it had authorized twenty-five such projects in northern Mato Grosso and southern Pará (Schmink, 1981:10).

The government retreated rapidly from the policies proclaimed in its first (1972) Plan for the Development of the Amazon (PDA I), which had emphasized the settlement of small-holding farmers as the solution to social and economic problems. Simultaneously, it granted a series of concessions to large-scale capitalist enterprise in PDA II. These were formalized, systematized, and legitimated by the initiation of POLAMAZONIA, a plan/program which proposed the development of sixteen "growth poles" where development efforts and expenditures would be centered. PIN, with its emphasis on socioeconomic integration, was not formally abandoned, but most of its funds were transferred to POLAMAZONIA. The sequence of events which preceded these policy changes indicates that the state was not able or willing to resist private sector demands, even where its own credibility and claims to legitimacy were at stake.

The government invoked the difficulties of the colonization process itself and the balance-of-payments crisis brought about by Brazil's rapid economic growth and aggravated by the increase of petroleum costs to explain the reduction of its commitment to the colonization projects. While these difficulties were certainly contributing factors, they cannot have been determinative, as numerous other costly development programs for the Amazon continued or were initiated during the same period (Mahar, 1979). In fact, INCRA's *Projetos Fundiários* increased their activities in large-scale land-tenure classification as colonization budgets declined (see Table 5). The SUDAM's disbursements for fiscal incentives in 1975 and 1976 returned to levels even higher than their previous peak in 1970, despite mounting evidence that many of these subsidies were being diverted to other uses—often outside the Amazon—and that the pastures which had been established had an extremely short economic life (Hecht, 1979). The official justifications for favoring large-scale agricultural enterprise at the cost of the colonization projects is especially implausible in light of consistent evidence that small producers market more produce and support more workers than larger enterprises (da Silva, 1978).

INCRA maintained a minimal presence in the colonization projects and aimed at removing them from its tutelage as early as possible. INCRA's functions for the regularization of land titles in ways compatible with modern capitalist modes of production, i.e., in ways which guaranteed that land could be regularly alienated, negotiated, and used as collateral for production credit with minimal social tension through *Projectos Fundiários* and similar activities, were greatly enhanced. These forms of institutional modernization in the Amazon, moreover, have been directly associated with the expulsion of peasants from the land and their reduction to a dependent rural proletariat (Martins; 1981, see also Domar, 1970). Thus, while social welfare programs declined, the state continued those programs which enhanced its own capacity to promote, regulate, and control economic activity, such as land titling and registry, at the eventual cost of further reducing rural populations.

Numerous factors contributed to the curtailment of the colonization programs. Although not determinant, the sharp rise in oil prices, cost overruns resulting from inadequate topographic information about the land the highway would traverse, and the delays in construction—

Table 5. Indicators of Government Activities in Colonization Compared with Indicators of Activities Related to Large-Scale Enterprise, 1970-77

	Colonization—PIC Altamira and Itaituba		Large Enterprise	
	INCRA Budgets (Cr$)[a]	INCRA Personnel	INCRA Land-Tenure Classification— PF Altamira (Ha)[b]	Fiscal Incentives SUDAM Disbursements (Cr$)[a]
1970				632,758,447
1971				561,533,792
1972	128,265,518	1,228		424,298,206
1973	159,330,205	1,651	324,000	477,618,018
1974	119,719,014	833	510,000	487,391,435
1975	112,065,111	700	600,000	923,671,516
1976	95,190,642	517	1,486,200	652,922,274
1977	39,700,639	248	559,700	504,926,063

Source. INCRA, CR-01, FF/FFP; SUDAM, DAI/DPOI.
[a] Values corrected to 1977 equivalents following Conjuntura Econômica, 324 (April) 1978: Index 2, Column 2.
[b] Ha = hectares. *Two Projetos Fundiários*—PF Santarém and PF Cachimbo—were established within the original jurisdiction of PF Altamira in 1975 and 1977, respectively. Figures here include all three PFs.

which increased costs both directly and through the effects of inflation—all made the projects costlier to the state than had been anticipated. These factors, however, do not explain the effects of competing
private sector demands on INCRA's resources, of criticism and political
pressure from powerful business groups, and of the publicly expressed
opposition of various parts of the national state's bureaucratic apparatus. All of these indicate that, in this program at least, the state was
considerably less autonomous than Malloy or O'Donnell suggest. They
further suggest that the Brazilian state's considerable autonomy in its
alliance with domestic and international capitalist groups (Evans, 1979;
O'Donnell, 1978, Cardoso, 1973) may be limited to projects and programs in which there is substantial overlap between the interests of
the state and those of at least some powerful private groups. This is
congruent with Evans's demonstration that the relative power of each
of the members of the "triple alliance" between the state, domestic
capital, and international capital varies with the differential bargaining
power and with the shifting points of common interest among the three
"allies" in different sectors of the national economy.

The effects of private sector pressures and demands on the colonization projects were compounded by a number of highly visible mistakes and failures in planning and administering the colonization
schemes. Contrary to theoretical expectations of the BA state's administrative efficiency and capacity to transform society deeply, the organization of the colonization projects was marked by inefficiency,
faulty planning, bureaucratic indiscipline, and lack of interagency coordination. These administrative problems, which are analyzed in the
following chapters, reduced the chances of program success and further
undermined state autonomy.

In the Amazon the sequence of modes of extraction had impeded
the development of population and productive bases which might have
formed the basis for an alliance with the state in its social welfare and
order maintenance goals. The rapid reduction of social welfare goals
in the Amazon shows that the BA state, as a modernizing, authoritarian
state, was unable to achieve its social welfare goals outside of the
context of the modern economic and political institutions of its capitalist
center.

Other governmental attempts to mediate and regulate the social and
ecological impact of the development it promotes have been as ineffective as its colonization programs. The absence of a strong local
political voice, due to the lack of established and self-sustaining local
enterprise, has weakened national state efforts to balance the strong
political influence of large-scale capitalist enterprises. The various official agencies responsible for the protection of the natural and social

environments of the Amazon are politically and financially weak in relation to the economic interests of large-scale enterprise and the government agencies designed to support them. The National Indian Foundation (FUNAI) has been the target of numerous accusations of corruption and brutality against the Indians it is responsible to protect. It has been notoriously slow in responding to violations of indigenous reservations. One of its most common responses has been to remove Indians to other areas rather than to insist on the expulsion of invading peasants and large enterprise (see Table 6). In some cases Indian groups have been resettled in totally different environments than those to which they are adapted, put into areas too small for the subsistence strategies on which they depend, or even settled close to other groups with whom they have long been at war.

FUNAI is responsible by statute to guarantee the enforcement of various laws protecting Indian life and land. Roads which promote peasant settlement, the extension of ranching, lumbering, and mining, and the spread of new diseases directly threaten Indian life and land. Roads, however, have been the keystone of government development programs and of business plans for the Amazon. FUNAI's incapacity to protect the Indians from the road builders is one of the clearest examples of the subordination of agencies responsible for the preservation of the human and natural environments to other agencies charged

Table 6. Location of Various Agricultural and Ranching Enterprises in Relation to Indigenous Lands

Company	Relation to Indian Lands	Size, Location, and Activity
Jari Florestal Agropecuária: owned by D. Ludwig's National Bulk Carriers	Borders 9 Aparai villages to north and west	600,000 hectares along Pará and Jari rivers in Amapá; cattle, forestry, mining
Swift-Armour-King Ranch: bought by Deltec International Packers	Apparently invaded Tembe, Urubu, and Kaapor reserves	72,000 hectares in Paragominas, Pará; cattle
Volkswagen do Brasil	Borders Caiapó lands	140,000 hectares in Araguaia, Pará; cattle
Fazenda Suiá-Missu: owned by Liquigas	Parque Nacional do Xingu (North), Xavante (South and West)	678,000 hectares in Northwest (Mato Grosso); cattle

Source. Based on Molano Campuzano (1979) and Cardoso and Müller (1978).

with the promotion of rapid industrialization and capitalist expansion (Table 7).

Despite legal prohibitions against road building through reservations, FUNAI has consistently accepted the extension of such roads, even when alternative routes could have been proposed. The legal impediments to a road which the State of Pará is currently building into an area rich in fertile soils, mohagany, cassiterite, and other minerals were solved when FUNAI simply eliminated the southern half of the reservation through which the road was planned to pass. Instead of cutting the reservation in half, which would have violated the law, the road now conforms to legal prescription by forming its southern border. FUNAI acceded to official and private pressures with a legal solution that will increase the eventual impact of the road on the Indians by legitimizing invasion of what was previously the southern portion of the reservation (Bunker, field notes, 1978). Opposition by mining interests has seriously compromised FUNAI attempts to establish new reserves (ARC, 1980, 1981a, 1981b, 1982). The National Department of Roads and Highways (DNER), highway departments of the individual states, and the construction companies that benefit from their contrasts are closely allied with other private groups interested in access to various parts of the Amazon.

The "Highways of Integration," designed to run north to south to connect the Amazon to Brazil's economic and demographic center and east to west to open the jungle for settlement and military security, pass through the territories of numerous tribes. In principle FUNAI agents were supposed to contact, pacify, and relocate, if necessary, the groups whose areas the highways would penetrate. A combination of factors, including budgetary and personnel shortages, FUNAI's dependence on the construction process itself for access and logistic bases, and the construction companies' and the government's unwillingness to extend construction schedules to allow for relocation, meant that in

Table 7. Tribal Areas Affected by Different Highways in the Amazon

Highway	Tribal Area
Belém-Brasília	Gavião, Kraho, Apinayé, Xavante, Xerente
Transamazon highway	Juruna, Arara, Parakana, Asurini, Karao
Santarém-Cuiabá and BR-80	Tribes in Xingu National Park, Kreen-Akarore
Northern Perimeter	Waimiri-Atroari, Yanomami, Atalaia do Norte, Tumucumaque National Park
Pôrto Velho-Cuiabá	Aripuanã indigenous park

many cases road crews entered in direct and violent contact with settled Indian groups, and army detachments were called in to guarantee that construction would continue.

In one case, the Arara, a tribe which had long maintained steady trade and occasional labor relations with the inhabitants of Altamira, a town situated at the intersection of the Xingu River and the Transamazon highway, were so badly treated that they withdrew to the forest. The area where they settled was later ceded for private colonization to a major wheat cooperative in the South. After several Arara attacks on surveyors and road crews who entered the area, FUNAI closed the area, pending the Arara's "repacification."

Another highway, from Manaus to Boa Vista, was completed several years behind schedule because of determined armed resistance by the Waimiri-Atroari. Alternate routes were available, but FUNAI accepted the projected route through Indian lands and allowed construction to proceed before pacification — and much less, relocation — had occurred. As a result, the road advanced as a military invasion. FUNAI's supposed contact and pacification functions were preempted by the army. When the road finally opened in 1977, passage along it was allowed only in armed convoys.

In another widely publicized case, the Ministry of the Interior finally interdicted 7.7 million hectares as a reserve for the Yanomami Indians of the Territory of Roraima and the State of Amazonas in 1982, after several years of intense pressure from international and national organizations. FUNAI had done little until that time to stem the invasion of peasants, ranchers, and prospectors for the area's gold, diamonds, uranium, cassiterite, and other minerals. Business groups, politicians, and government administrators in Roraima continue to lobby for access to the land.

In addition to the beatings, killings, rapes, and theft that resulted from this uncontrolled contact, there was massive contamination by new diseases. In addition to influenza, measles, and smallpox, which contact with Europeans have brought since colonial times, the Northern Perimeter road may spread a fly-borne disease that results in blindness. Davis (1977:101-3) claims that in some newly opened areas, incidence of this disease among indigenous groups has reached 80 percent.

The Brazilian Institute for the Defense of the Forests (IBDF) has been somewhat more aggressive in countering the private enterprises and government agencies interested in big business in the Amazon, but the results of its attempts to enforce conservation laws suggest one reason FUNAI is so careful to accommodate these interests. IBDF has the power of authorization over all clearing, as well as of enforcing laws which protect commercially productive species such as the Brazil nut and which limit clearing to 50 percent of any property. When, however, the IBDF attempted to fine a ranching enterprise owned by Volkswagen of Brazil for an unauthorized burn—detected by Skylab—which IBDF claimed destroyed as many as 25,000 hectares, Volkswagen representatives claimed that SUDAM approval of its fiscal incentives was sufficient authorization, even though they admitted that they had cleared more than they were scheduled to clear in any one year. Volkswagen threatened to pull out of the project if the fine was enforced. It was reported, but not confirmed, that the IBDF agency headquartered in Belém was immobilized during this dispute because the work authorizations of all of its delegates were suddenly suspended pending investigation.

Volkswagen not only refused to pay the fine, but it also attacked IBDF's authority to restrict and monitor forest clearing and to charge fees for its clearing authorizations. The Amazonian Association of Agriculture and Ranching Entrepreneurs—an interest group of 200 major firms which operate in the Amazon based in São Paulo, whose president has boasted that its members control more wealth than any other organization in Brazil—mobilized legal and political pressure to change conservation legislation so that pasture would be considered arboreal cover. IBDF discovered that attempting to fine a major company for violation of conservation laws was not only impractical but also it threatened to undermine the agency's capacity to function at all.

IBDF has suffered similar difficulties in establishing and protecting national parks and forest reserves. Legally, IBDF is obliged to pay for the work and improvements of anyone who has been on reserved land for a year and a day. The first "cleaning" of a reserve is generally fairly simple: peasants are paid off and relocated. This payment, however, becomes an invitation to the so-called industry of possession (*indústria da posse*), in which someone settles in order to be bought out. As the commonest and quickest form of improvement is to burn and clear the land, the establishment of forest reserves quickens the destruction of the forest, at least in the short run. Frequently, this second wave of occupants is financed by local ranchers and businessmen with sufficient political power to make IBDF reluctant to prosecute on the basis of invasion of reserved land. Instead, it pays repeatedly for burned forest.

FUNAI has tutelary authority and responsibilities in relation to the Indians, and IBDF is established to protect the forest. There is, however, no single agency responsible for the protection of peasants. As citizens, peasants do have recourse to the law (Indians, though protected by law, are not allowed to sue for violations of the law). Any Brazilian may, for example, register land which he has occupied "tranquilly and pacifically" (*mansa e pacíficamente*) for ten years and claim indemnification for work done on any land which he has occupied for a year and a day. These legal forms provide the peasants little protection against violent expulsion. Journeys to administrative centers, food and lodging during the processing of papers, and registration fees are enormously costly in a subsistence economy where most surplus production is exchanged directly to pay off prior debts. Surveying land is even more expensive. Large companies have the resources to influence the police and the courts in any case. The Catholic Church has in many areas attempted to help the peasants, but its clergy has been subject to both official and private penalties for these activities. Several priests and bishops have been attacked or tried for subversion.

The bureaucratic agencies that government has employed to control and direct capitalist expansion have been subject to manipulation by the capitalist enterprises which other state programs and agencies are subsidizing. Government programs designed to promote exports by securing rapid profits for favored business sectors have flourished, but in doing so they have contributed to the devastation of the human communities and the natural biotic systems on which any long-term development must depend. Bounded by the legacy of earlier despoliation and confronted by the enormously greater political and economic power of local representatives of international capital, national business interests, and military advocates of "great nation" ambitions, the uncoordinated, understaffed, and underfunded special agencies for the defense of indigenous societies, peasant communities, and plant and animal resources are constantly subverted and marginalized (Figure 1). At best, they win temporary, and very occasional, holding actions. At worst, they serve as a flimsy facade which the government and dominant business interests can use to legitimate their export-promotion policies, pointing to these agencies as evidence of their good intentions and blaming these agencies' failures on the intransigence of the Indian, the lack of initiative of the peasant, and the intractability and hostility of nature itself (Bunker, 1978; Wood and Schmink, 1979).

The present official developmental programs and large-scale enterprises promise to repeat the history of the colonial conquest and of the rubber boom. By subordinating the requirements for long-term reproduction of the social and natural environments to immediate political and economic demands for the rapid transformation of natural resources into exportable commodities, government and business threaten an even more profound impoverishment of the Amazon as soon as these resources are exhausted. Meanwhile, violent conflicts between ranchers, miners, lumbering companies, peasants, and Indians

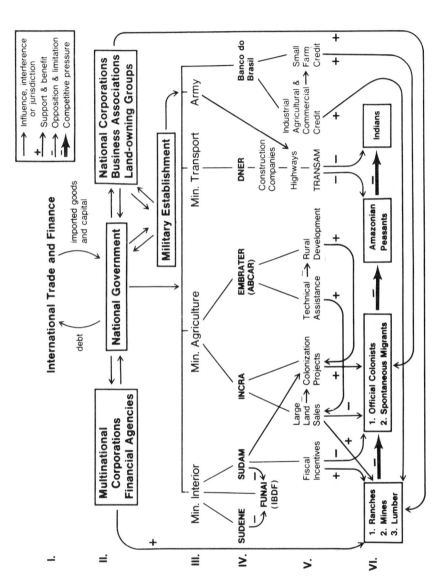

Figure 1. Impact of Government and Business on the Amazon.

continue to undermine the legitimacy of the state. The state has responded with an increased military presence and the establishment of executive groups to control land, implicitly admitting its incapacity to control violence through civil institutions (Schmink, 1982; Martins, 1982).

Cattle ranchers, miners, lumbering companies, and development planners have been able to treat the Amazon as an empty frontier because previous modes of extraction prevented the development of stable human populations able to adapt profitably to their social and natural environments. Colonial trade had destroyed the mixed extractive and horticultural economies that maintained ecological balance by exploiting a wide range of plant and animal resources before European conquest. Local responses to exchange opportunities in the world economy restricted the range and increased the intensity of resource exploitation, in many cases beyond the capacity of species regeneration sufficient to maintain cost-effective extraction. The consequent impoverishment and depopulation of the Amazon set the stage for the boom and collapse of the rubber trade and for the wasteful use of the Amazon as a huge, short-lived, and ultimately destructive pasture.

The role of the national state crucially influenced the forms in which Amazonian modes of production and extraction have been reorganized in response to international systems of unequal exchange. By providing both basic infrastructure and large amounts of capital to large-scale capitalist enterprise, it has accelerated and in some cases created conditions which favor the rapid development of extractive industry. At the same time its own attempts to direct and control the spread of capitalism along its own frontiers and to maintain order in the relations between different claimants to natural resources have been impeded by the use of bureaucratic structures that had evolved within the capitalist modes of production predominant in the central-south regions but that were not adapted to the uses to which the state attempted to put them in the noncapitalist Amazon. The state essentially created the conditions for the subversion of its own bureaucratic apparatus by providing more power to capital than it was able to administer effectively.

NOTES

1. General explanations of these failures, however, are extremely diverse. Different studies attribute cause to a wide range of factors, including the great disparities of wealth and privilege in most Latin American countries, interregional differences in production levels, vested dominant class interests in archaic production systems, the isolation and subordination of indigenous

communities, lack of sufficient personnel with entrepreneurial and organizational skills, distrust between various sectors of the population, the duplicity of international financial institutions, and intervention by multinational corporations (Veliz, 1965, 1967; Anderson, 1966; Furtado, 1965; Herrera, 1965; Lambert, 1969; Feder, 1976; Petras and LaPorte, 1971; McEwen, 1975).

Explanations of the more specific problems of failures in rural development programs are equally diverse. They include obstruction or distortion of program goals, intensification of the exploitation and social dislocation of small-holding farmers (Stavenhagen, 1964; Fals Borda 1970, 1971); manipulation of rural development programs by the government to maintain political control (Cotler, 1972; Feder, 1973); active government opposition to peasant organization (Landsberger and Hewitt, 1968); rural community fears based on a long history of dominant class and government discrimination and exploitation (Huizer, 1969); excessively complex or cumbersome legal mechanisms and bureaucratic procedures (Nisbet, 1967; Findley, 1973); inadequacies of "modern urban" credit institutions in rural settings (Gillette and Uphoff, 1973; Adams, Davis, and Bettis, 1972); unrealistic or inflexible program goals (Tendler, 1973); limited scope and impact of projects (Thiesenhusen, 1971; Findley, 1973; Bunker, 1979); and the insecurity of peasant land tenure (Thome, 1971).

2. This phrase was used in various discourses by President Médici and by the then president of INCRA, Moura Cavalcanti (see INCRA, 1972).

3. The extent and implications of this penetration in the case of INCRA can be shown by the following example: One of INCRA's chief lawyers was also lawyer for a large private firm. An owner of this business publicly stated that the company intended to take over a sugar mill in the PIC Altamira, although the mill was owned by a cooperative and entirely managed by INCRA (personal communication from various INCRA officials).

CHAPTER 5

Power Differentials between Agencies and the Distortion of State Programs

A series of extractive economies left the Amazon devoid of economic and social bases for local resistance to recent predatory capitalist expansion. The Brazilian state's subsidies to modern capitalist forms of extractive enterprise impeded its subsequent attempts to establish long-term self-sustaining economies capable of absorbing and supporting a rural work force. Government programs encouraging large-scale enterprise extended modern corporations' control into the Amazon without reproducing the productive economies from which these corporations and the state itself derived their power. These same corporations then limited the state's ability to implement social welfare programs in the Amazon. The institutional disjunctures between the Amazon and the Brazilian center aggravated these impediments.

The authoritarian regime established in 1964 inherited a bureaucratic system which had evolved during the dependent capitalist formation of the center-south regions. While this regime did alter both the structure and the procedures of parts of this bureaucracy, a great deal of it remained essentially unchanged. The state assigned different parts of its Amazon development programs to agencies whose functions in the center-south most closely corresponded to its perception of necessary tasks in the North. This extension of established agencies into new areas occurred because the state planners knew too little about this unfamiliar environment to devise new bureaucratic forms for the Amazon; because the logic of administration in Brazil was increasingly centralist; and because the various established bureaucratic agencies were not anxious to see rival agencies performing tasks which could be defined as part of their own jurisdiction. Thus, in addition to becoming an economic periphery of the Brazilian center, the Amazon became an institutional, administrative, and political periphery, subject to the imposition of modern bureaucratic organizations and procedures that had evolved in a very different physical, social, and economic environment.

The energy-intensive, expansive, and competitive nature of bureaucratic organization enhanced the disruption and irrational effects of this imposition. The struggles of the various agencies to secure and expand their own budgets and jurisdiction took priority over the achievement of policy goals. The extreme political and economic weakness of Amazonian human communities relative to the resources these agencies controlled left these communities highly vulnerable to the ideological and procedural biases built into these bureaucratic agencies. It also left them little recourse against the policy distortions which interagency struggles for power produced.

The transfer of established agencies to work in the Amazon was particularly significant in the rural development and colonization projects. A series of functionally specific agencies had emerged in the center-south to encourage the integration of agriculture with the expanding urban market there. Separate special agencies were formed to provide particular services such as rural extension, crop price supports, technical assistance, and sufficient warehouses to assure markets. Others fomented and supervised cooperatives, titled and registered land, and carried out official colonization and land reform (Schuh, 1971).[1]

The rural extension agencies, following the U.S. model on which they were organized, were loosely tied to agronomic research institutions based in agricultural colleges. Special emphasis was placed on credit, which was in almost all cases provided to individuals. Banks required guarantees for these loans, so the documentation of land ownership was also a major goal of these agencies.

These agencies essentially facilitated processes which capitalist development in the center-south was already bringing about.[2] Government plans for rural development in the Amazon, however, called for the rapid transformation of entire regions, little affected by the development of capitalist industry and agriculture, which were to be populated by peasant migrants from other regions. The relative independence of the functionally specific rural development agencies, which was appropriate to facilitate the development of capitalist and market-integrated agriculture in the center-south, was not appropriate to the tasks of major state-directed transformations implied by development plans for the Amazon. The prior structure of the agricultural and rural development agencies did not permit the effective central coordination required for such an undertaking. Different agencies responded to different administrative levels, had different fiscal and statutory bases, and operated under diverse patterns of authority. The centralizing tendencies of the authoritarian regime reinforced the subordination of regional and local offices of each agency to its national headquarters, where there was little knowledge of conditions in the Amazon and little contact with other agencies operating there. There was even less contact with the state government agencies with which many of these national agencies also had overlapping functions.

Each agency tended to transfer its own structure and its own procedures to the Amazon and to impose them on its new clients; the result was a haphazard form of modernization. Different agencies and agents of government had been assigned control of resources on which local populations increasingly depended. As access to these resources could only be achieved by compliance with bureaucratic regulations, individual success required rapid adaptation to exogenous modern institutions. Agents in the field typically interpreted compliance with new bureaucratic procedures as a criterion of worthiness to participate in government development programs. Modernity thus became an ideology and a mission of individual bureaucrats, serving to justify both their unequal distribution of public resources and the failure of their less successful clients (see also Wood and Schmink, 1979). Because this bureaucratic perception was fragmented by the specific functions and attributions of each agency, however, the individual bureaucrats were able to ignore the fact that the accumulated costs of compliance for most of their clients were greater than the benefits which enforced or imposed modernization offered them. Competition and bargaining between the different agencies enhanced this bureaucratic insularity.

These agencies also transferred goals, procedures, and technologies appropriate to the economy and ecology of the center-south to their operations in the Amazon. Because of their emphasis on agricultural credit and their orientation to commercialization, there was little interest in the improvement of subsistence crops and strategies, although health instruction—primarily focused on sanitation—was stressed. In many areas, farmers' cooperatives were promoted as a means to encourage commercialization and to return more productive capital to commercial farmers.

Rice, beans, and corn—staples in the center-south—were all aggressively promoted, despite evidence that there was little local market for some varieties of beans and for some of the rice. Manioc, the high-yielding staple of the Amazon which is admirably suited to most of the poorer soils there, was ignored, as were other tropical plants, like bananas, for which there is a steady local market. Except for a limited program to improve the production of jute, an eminently commercial crop, little attention was paid to *várzea* cultivation, as there was little understanding of or sympathy with the technology required. Many agents found the changing, watery *várzea* environment uncomfortable and threatening.

Agents also tended to have little understanding of the vegetable extraction, hunting, and fishing which formed an important complement to agricultural subsistence and income. The special problems of swidden agriculture based on shifting slash-and-burn techniques were also ignored. The emphasis on land titles conflicted with the requirements of extensive periods of fallow. The geometric patterns of land distribution designed for the colonization projects were superimposed on the varied and often broken Amazonian topography with no allowance for the peculiarities of soil types, drainage, or access to water on the individual lots. In one colonization project agents distributed seed that had been tested only in a temperate zone. The seed germinated poorly, and most of the colonists who planted it suffered crop failure, defaulted on their bank loans, and went further into debt trying to feed their families until the next season. Because of their orientation to commercial agriculture, many agents tended to promote a limited number of crops and to discourage the diversified cultivation of numerous species which balanced subsistence diets and which limited susceptibility to pests, plagues, and crop failure.

Some of the individual agents did learn a great deal about local techniques and requirements, but their effective use of this information was limited by agency goals and procedures as well as by the job criteria on which they were judged and which determined their chances of promotion. Frequent transfer of personnel, and the fact that the most effective were rewarded by being posted to urban headquarters, also limited the extent to which individual agents could adapt. Transfers between the colonization projects on *terra firme* and the ecologically, economically, and socially very different *várzea* were a major source of problems.

Thus, agencies organized to operate in an increasingly homogeneous modern capitalist economy were redirected to perform several incongruent tasks in an extremely heterogenous set of rural economies. Furthermore, all of these economies required adaptation to soils, water, and climatic types quite different than those of the ecological zones further from the equator.

Discontinuities in Rural Development Programs

The impediments this haphazard, externally imposed modernization and ecologically inappropriate technology created for effective rural development programs were further aggravated by ambiguities and discontinuities in government policy. The colonization programs were primarily aimed at gaining legitimacy for a national state facing various forms of rural unrest and violence. The remote location of the Transamazon highway assured that these programs would constitute a drain on national budgets out of proportion to any economic return. At the same time, however, rural development programs in other parts of the Amazon had primarily economic goals. The rapid urbanization of the Amazon required cheap, reliable food sources. Thus, part of the rural development programs were aimed at the economic goals of stimulating commercial agriculture in areas accessible to urban markets, while other parts pursued the political goals of easing the social tensions and conflicts over land in other regions of Brazil.

The rural development agencies were faced with a peculiarly diverse set of circumstances. The bulk of their budgets were assigned to the publicly visible colonization projects. These areas, subject to fairly heavy government activity, were relatively immune to the violent conflict over land which occurred in other parts of the Amazon. A smaller portion of their budgets involved their work along the other new roads, where the rapid influx of large enterprise and rapidly rising land values subjected their small farmer clients to explusion. Finally, in some of the traditional areas of settlement along rivers, their main task was to supplant the *aviamento* system, where the extremely low rates of exchange discouraged significant increases in production. In addition, these agencies had to face the series of other problems that had led to the failure of earlier colonization and rural development programs in the Amazon. In some cases their projects were impeded by residue of earlier failures.

Rural development programs in the Amazon prior to 1970 were as sporadic, discontinuous, and marginal as small-scale agriculture itself. The export economy of the Amazon and its position within the national economy do not depend on commodities produced by the peasant farmers there; on the contrary, the economy has expanded by subordinating and expelling these farmers. As the local community has little function in this organization, it cannot serve as a power base from which to make demands on the state.

Both the organization and implementation of rural development plans in the Amazon were subordinate to the political demands and interference of locally dominant land-owning and merchant classes based outside the rural areas affected. At the local level, this subordinate position was reflected in the discontinuation, lack of effective organization and financing, and preemption of small-scale agricultural areas for large-scale enterprise. The administrative, financial, and productive resources involved in rural development programs for peasant farmers in the Amazon were subject to demands and pressures from politically and economically dominant classes (Bunker, 1979).

Many of the Amazon's rural development programs have tried to solve the economic imbalance of excessive concentration of labor in the extractive export economy. Attempts have been made to establish agricultural communities integrated into local markets, in order to lower the costs of reproduction of labor, which were inflated by the near-total dependence on imported subsistence commodities. As the extractive economies themselves have passed through rapid cycles caused by changes in the world market and the depletion of forest products, the conditions of support for such programs have also fluctuated drastically. This fluctuation has impeded any continuous or cumulative process of rural development and, together with the fact that government support for small farmers was largely conditioned by the interests and needs of other classes, has led to insufficient funding, financial and executive discontinuities, and lack of coordination among the various rural development agencies (Bunker, 1981b).

The proliferation of different nationally based agencies after 1970, the fragmentation of responsibilities for rural development, the resulting difficulties of coordination among the agencies, and the diversity of goals did little to improve the effectiveness of rural development programs in the Amazon. The multiple agencies involved in rural development were organized and funded in ways that compromised their orientation toward effective rural development plans or toward a profitable integration of the small farmer into a market economy. Most were in some way patrimonial bureaucracies in the sense of controlling resources and sustaining themselves from the sale of resources or services. Almost all of them served other clients besides small farmers and, because of their funding, tended to be responsive to more powerful economic and political interests than those of the small farmers.

Government Agencies: Hierarchical Power, Dependency, and Exchange

These problems were further complicated by the comprehensive jurisdictional powers assigned to INCRA and SUDAM. INCRA's wide range of derived power gave it great control over various resources crucial to rural development; it was, therefore, able to subordinate other agencies more directly involved in rural development, creating dependency and achieving submission through exchange. However, INCRA was also vulnerable to outside pressures, specifically from the Banco do Brasil and SUDAM, whose mandates encompassed areas of concern broader than INCRA alone; these organizations also had sufficient resources to dominate the agencies directly involved in rural development. The resulting conflict between INCRA and SUDAM aggravated the problems of rural development. This subordinate position of the rural development programs reflects both their divergence from the central thrust of Brazilian development planning, with its emphasis on the concentration of income and of the means of production, and the position, marginal and subordinate, of their clientele, the small farmers.

Structural and organizational constraints on government agencies impeded intervention to create organization and structure conducive to the formation of viable small farming communities. As do all modern bureaucracies, these agencies derived their power—their programs, procedures, and budgets—from higher authority. The greater financial and jurisdictional authority of INCRA, SUDAM, and the Banco do Brasil meant colonization and rural extension programs became relatively minor units within larger agencies that were themselves subordinate to and dependent on other larger bureaucracies for authority and for funding.

Rural development agencies had insufficient power to achieve their stated goals and could only function through contracts and concessions from more powerful agencies. These contracts were worked out in negotiations and bargaining, which raised the costs for these programs. The concessions impeded or deflected the rural development agencies from their assigned purposes. Division of responsibility between multiple specialized agencies aggravated the problems caused by dependency and the need to bargain.

The need to bargain varied between agencies according to their type and scope of power. The position of each agency in the bargaining process reflected its own interests in terms of the mandate imposed by the source or sources of its power. Comparison of these agencies' organization and activities shows some of the ways that relations between the agencies involved in colonization, rural extension, and technical assistance created, in part, the structure of the environment within which the small farmer in the Amazon had to operate. Such an analysis also shows the ways that this environment impeded the formation of politically and commercially effective small farming communities.

In addition to INCRA, the agencies directly involved in colonization and rural extension in the Amazon are:

1. EMATER (Empresa de Assistência Tecnica e Extensão Rural), the local state agencies of a national public company, EMBRATER; its projects included a program of technical assistance to low-income farmers,

orientation and managerial assistance, guidance for agricultural co-operatives, and the preparation of projects for loan proposals.

2. The local state governments' secretariats of agriculture, often involved in extension work and in colonization of state lands.

3. CIBRAZEM (Companhia Brasileira de Armazenagem) a public company subordinate to the Ministry of Agriculture, which maintained a network of warehouses in areas where those provided by private enterprise are insufficient.

4. CFP (Comissão de Financiamento de Produção), an autarchy under the Ministry of Agriculture, which determined the minimum prices to be paid for particular crops and controlled the funding for this program.

5. CEPLAC (Commission for Cacao Cultivation), which derived its revenue from a national tax on cacao exports and was promoting cacao cultivation in the Amazon, in some states independently, in others through contracts with and subsidies to EMATER.

The following agencies were indirectly involved in rural development, but exercised considerable control over other agencies' programs through their control of financial resources:

1. The Banco do Brasil, in addition to administering the minimum price payments for the CFP, provided loans to small farmers in the official colonization areas and near some of the larger urban centers through special agreements with EMATER. Rural development programs absorbed a very small proportion of its resources.

2. The BNCC (Banco Nacional de Credito Cooperativo) made loans to cooperative societies both for their own use and for secondary loans to members.

3. BASA continued its regular credit operations after the failure of its agricultural cooperative program. Its subsequent involvement with rural development programs was minimal, though it did make extensive loans for large-scale agriculture and ranching.

4. SUDAM, the major planning, coordinating, and executing agency for the Amazon, provided limited resources for various of these programs. It was funded in turn by a variety of other federal programs. Its major concerns, however, were with large industrial, mining, and agricultural enterprises.

5. PIN and later POLAMAZONIA were programs rather than agencies, but their directorates controlled funds for which all of these agencies competed. The various state governments, and their own planning agencies, as well as the various national ministries, also provided funds and political leverage.

All of these agencies obtained their power from different sources and at different administrative levels of articulation. In no way were they accountable to any one central planning authority. In fact, the proliferation of *convênios* or interagency contracts in many cases led to an agency's being accountable to several different other agencies. INCRA, an autarchy under the Ministry of Agriculture, enjoyed semi-autonomy, had its own resources, and the power to make decisions, but EMATER, as a "public company in private law" (Pará, 1976), received practically all of its funding already tied to particular projects, either in grants from the Ministry of Agriculture or through *convênios* with the SUDAM and other public organs. It also received revenues from planning work done on commission for banks and private enterprises. The state secretariats of agriculture received funding from the state governments but were also dependent on *convênios* with INCRA and with the SUDAM.

The differences between INCRA and EMATER provide examples of the ways that the different sources and derivations of power between agencies structured the organization of rural development.

INCRA derived power directly from the federal level, both through its budget and in its legally established patrimonial power over federal lands. Though subordinate to the Ministry of Agriculture, its direct control over these lands and its receipt of the monies from both the land tax and its own land sales gave it considerable autonomy from the ministry. It was able to use its derived power in exchange relations with influential economic groups interested in acquiring land. Its benefits from these exchange relations far outweighed whatever it might have gained from well-executed rural development programs, whose clients had few resources with which to bargain.

EMATER, in contrast, derived very little power directly from either the federal or the state level, in terms of funds, authority, or jurisdiction. It had no autonomous control of resources. While a much greater share of its efforts than INCRA's were dedicated to rural extension for small farmers, its derived power was insufficient for accomplishing its own assigned tasks.

In order to function at all, EMATER was forced to operate through a series of exchange relations, defined through constant bargaining with other agencies not primarily concerned with rural development, such as the Banco do Brasil, the BNCC, the local state Secretariat of Agriculture, the SUDAM, and INCRA, as well as with large-scale agricultural enterprises. Its dependence on these agencies and enterprises forced it to shape its programs to their special requirements and to use a portion of its own resources to attract them to further exchange relations. Even in the rural extension programs oriented to the small farmer, EMATER's exchange relations led it to comply with the interests of other sectors. As the small farmers did not have sufficient resources to bargain with EMATER, they had the least influence on its behavior.

The structure in which EMATER had to operate led it to negotiate services which its derived power enabled it to offer in exchange for resources it did not control. Thus, its orientation to the needs of the small farmer, although not compromised as INCRA's was by the tensions of multiple mandates, was still subject to distortions from its dependence on agencies whose primary clientele were based in economically and politically more powerful sectors. Its dependent position left it with insufficient control over resources to program effectively its own activities.

EMATER's mandate was simpler than INCRA's but was restricted by its almost total dependence on other agencies. Its work was frequently interrupted by delays in the funding arrangements established through *convênios.*

The SUDAM, EMATER's major regionally based source of funding, was primarily involved in programs for urbanization, industrialization, and large-scale agriculture. Its support of small-scale farming was so tenuous that EMATER could maintain the financed programs only through collaboration with and submission to other agencies. EMATER was thus relegated to serving as intermediary between the farmer and more autonomous, stronger agencies. Its major efforts in extension were devoted to preparing and accompanying loan requests for the Banco do Brasil, basically acting as the bank's technical assessor. It was constrained to concentrate on rural credit, as an important part of its extension budget came from a 2 percent commission which it received from the bank on each approved loan project. This commission created a tendency to favor large loans and thus concentrate on larger and more prosperous enterprises.

EMATER's program to establish cooperatives depended not only on collaboration with banks but also on the good graces and support of INCRA, which had statutory jurisdiction to supervise all cooperatives. It had to submit requests to INCRA for loans, concession of land to build facilities, and technical assistance. In other areas, it had to renegotiate the old debts of cooperatives which were originally founded by BASA. The need to utilize existing structures, which created EMATER's dependence on INCRA and BASA for its work with cooperatives, was itself a necessary consequence of the limited budget that EMATER received for this program. Once the cooperatives were functioning, EMATER served as intermediary between them and the BNCC in order to obtain credit.

EMATER's extension work was limited by CIBRAZEM's location and operation of its warehouses, because its compliance with the Banco do

Brasil's requirements depended on the farmer's receiving the guaranteed minimum price for his produce, and because the CFP only paid minimum prices where there was an authorized warehouse. Although a public company under the Ministry of Agriculture, CIBRAZEM supported itself by storage charges and was loath to install facilities without assurance of sufficient return. EMATER's dependence on other agencies meant that it had no resource base of its own with which to obtain compliance from CIBRAZEM. As there was no effective pressure on CIBRAZEM, it was usually slow in rectifying the problems it caused for the small farmer.

Coherent organization of EMATER programs was further impeded by its political and economic subordination to the local state Secretariats of Agriculture. Many of EMATER's projects depended on the local state agencies to furnish basic materials, such as fertilizers and vaccines, and were held up by delays in their delivery.

Similar types of negotiation and bargaining had to be carried out by other agencies as well. Because INCRA formally controlled all land in colonization areas, other agencies had to secure authorizations from INCRA to establish their operations. In most cases, this involved relatively simple loan arrangements, but in cases where the agency needed to erect permanent structures the decision had to pass through both the regional and the national offices of INCRA. Rivalries between the representatives at the local and the regional levels frequently complicated and delayed these procedures. EMATER agents assigned to a cooperative established by INCRA in one of the colonization projects spent years bargaining with INCRA for land to build a warehouse, in large part because another cooperative established by another INCRA program opposed the concession to the first cooperative. A cacao nursery which CEPLAC wanted to establish in one of the colonization areas was delayed for over two years while agencies of the state government, EMATER, and INCRA negotiated over location and control. Similar complications beset the plans for experimental stations to be run by a federal agricultural research agency. In the state of Pará, where CEPLAC had been obliged by the state government to operate through special contracts with EMATER, EMATER agents maintained that CEPLAC representatives deliberately delayed fiscal transfers necessary for EMATER's cacao program in order to discredit the agency and regain control of the program (Figure 2).

The convênios and fiscal transfers between agencies frequently meant that the agencies most directly in contact with farmers had the least influence in the establishment of policy and the allocation of resources. This led to particularly severe problems in more remote areas, where communication facilities were limited. Decisions taken by INCRA or

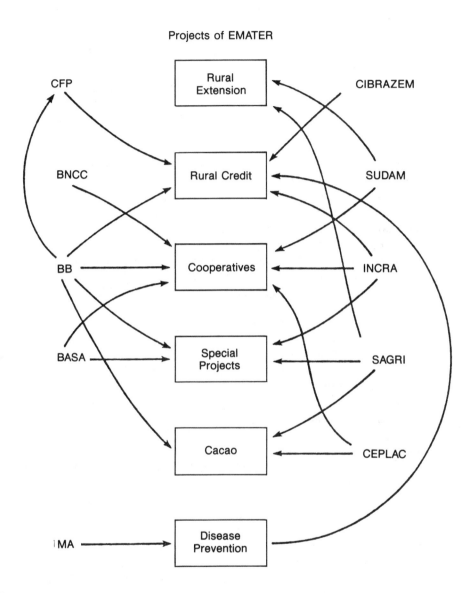

Projects of EMATER

Figure 2. The Major Projects of EMATER. These projects are under conflicting pressures from outside agencies. The arrows indicate which agencies have influence on which projects. A single outside agency may have a positive influence at one level and a negative one at another.

SUDAM to fund particular crops or support particular activities were incorporated into contracts with less powerful agencies, generally in negotiations at the regional level. Project goals were then communicated to the field offices of the less powerful agencies. These local offices had little recourse against inappropriate or impractical goals, as their regional superiors were generally unwilling to renegotiate entire *convênios* with INCRA and the SUDAM. In one instance, this kind of decision making resulted in a local supervisor being instructed to devote over a third of his budget to doubling corn production in an area where no corn was grown. In another case, a branch bank was directed to manage emergency loans for buying cattle in a distant flooded area at precisely the time that local farmers needed to process their crop loans. In order to deal with the emergency loans, this bank had to close its regular credit operations until after the proper planting time had passed.

The interference, discontinuity, conflicting mandates, uncertainty, the drain on personnel time, and travel expenses, which the need for interagency bargaining and agreements created, were exacerbated by the fluctuations, vacillations, and direct reversals of general state policy for the Amazon. One of the executive directions of EMBRATER, in Brasília, who had earlier supervised ACAR-Pará's (EMATER's predecessor) Transamazon programs, told me that he was in a meeting with the planning sector of the Ministry of Agriculture in 1976 when he was informed that the PIN, from which ACAR received most of its funding for the Transamazon, had been ended and replaced by PO-LAMAZONIA. Even though, as he said, one program had simply taken all the money from the other, the entire ACAR Transamazon project was left without any funding. He had not previously been informed of the change in budgetary control. After extensive negotiation, he was able to get renewed, but considerably reduced, funding from POLA-MAZONIA. The negotiations themselves, together with the new accounting procedures and transfer channels which had to be established, took so much time that there was a long lapse in budget and salaries for ACAR's agents and programs. He described the entire process as the same money going through a thousand circles ("O mismo dinheiro dando mil voltas").

He also told me that the decision to transform ABCAR, an "association" directly dependent on the Ministry of Agriculture, into EM-BRATER, a public company, had been an attempt to escape ABCAR's dependence on the good will of the minister of agriculture after a disastrous fight between the minister and the head of ABCAR. He said the result of the transformation, however, had been to subordinate EMBRATER to the local state governments, to CEPLAC, to INCRA, to the Banco do Brasil, and to other specialized agencies to the point that

EMBRATER "was going crazy with *convênios*." The advantages of drawing resources from multiple agencies were clearly offset by the extra work, the delays, and the complexities of multiple bargaining relations. These in turn had been imposed on the new company by demands from these agencies and the private sector that EMBRATER serve other interests than those of small farmers. ACAR was transformed into EMATER at the time the state was abandoning its social welfare programs in the Amazon, so EMATER suffered the consequences of the change in policies that had favored the interests of its primary clients, colonists and small farmers. At the same time it suffered the delays and interruptions in the funding arrangements on which it depended.

The Effects of Interagency Bargaining on Agent Morale

The power differentials and bargaining between agencies at the regional and state levels subjected the field agents of the less powerful agencies to excessive and conflicting or incompatible assignments and to the lack of necessary equipment. The complex funding arrangements that resulted from EMATER's multiple *convênios* frequently left vehicles and boats without necessary gasoline or spare parts because of delays in transferring funds. EMATER agents whose primary tasks and salaries were established by CEPLAC would be requested by their local superiors to perform essential services or to loan their equipment and vehicles to agents paid and financed by INCRA or SUDAM when CEPLAC funds had arrived and the others had not, or vice versa. The considerable solidarity between agents confronting the isolation and hardships of extension work in remote areas was severely strained by the conflict between the performance of the tasks on which the individual agent was assessed and the needs of the local office as a whole.

The frequent delays in salary payments also undermined agent morale. In 1976 delays of budgetary transfers from INCRA, SUDAM, and POLAMAZONIA left some EMATER agents without salaries and without the gasoline necessary to do their work for over six months. Many of the agents were also acutely aware of the discrepancies between the tasks imposed on them by *convênios* and the more general goals of their own agencies. This was especially true of the multiple reports which had to be filed for the various agencies that funded specific projects and for the banks that provided agricultural credit. The forms which agents were required to fill out, and on which most of them believed their career chances were decided, frequently had little to do with their own definition of the tasks they felt they should be performing.

Centrally established policies and goals aggravated these problems.

In order to prevent land-tenure concentration in the colonization areas, INCRA rules specified that no settler could get more land if he already had received a lot. This rule was designed for the newly opened colonization areas, where families received 100-hectare lots. However, it was also applied to older colonization areas assigned to INCRA supervision. In Monte Alegre, a colonization area located in the lower middle Amazon region in the State of Pará, colonists had been assigned much smaller lots several decades before. INCRA and EMATER policies required them to title these lots during the 1970s in order to participate in the rural development programs. The small lots had by this time been overused and the soils seriously depleted. The farmers were not allowed to move to land which new roads were opening up, so they were obliged to assume the costs of surveying and titling these small, deteriorating lots. Agents were aware of the problems this policy was causing but felt obligated to continue the pressure on the peasants to title their land, as the agents' and the agencies' performance was assessed according to number of titles assigned and the amount of credit applied for and used. Similar problems emerged in the soil-depleted areas around Belém and Manaus.

A particularly dramatic instance of the irrationality of centralized policy and procedural controls occurred in the extensive and densely settled *várzea* areas around Santarém. The massive importation of labor to the bauxite mines of Porto Trombetas greatly expanded the local demand for beef. Local merchants sought special PROTERRA loans for pasture formation from the Banco do Brasil. The bank required titled land as a guarantee. The only titled land in the area was in the Brazil nut groves, which provided a substantial part of local peasant income and local export revenues. There were other lands available more cheaply, but as these were untitled, the aspiring ranchers bought and burned Brazil nut groves. This led to the expulsion of relatively dense peasant settlements, direct confrontations, and some violence. The actual revenues produced on the pastures were less than they would have been from the Brazil nuts, but, because the labor absorbed in cattle-management was much less, the income from cattle was much more concentrated (Bunker, 1981a, 1982b). In this case, the unintended results of bank lending policy directly countered rural development goals for the area.

Job-accounting procedures also distorted other agency goals. In 1977 EMATER and several other agencies were directed to initiate a "low income program" whose aim was to increase the income of a third of the farmers in various areas from what was defined as low income to what was defined as medium income. The agents who examined the forms on which their performance was to be recorded soon realized that the only way to assure that they would reach their goals on paper was to select farmers who were already prosperous. Many of the agents I talked to were aware of and disturbed by this distortion of a program whose goals they believed in, but they defended their actions by saying that this was the only way that they could satisfy their regional superiors. Similar distortions occurred even in programs that did not specify income goals. Agents complained that, although they were encouraged to work with the poorest farmers and were repeatedly told that they should not overemphasize agricultural credit, the performance records they were required to submit stressed amount of credit provided. They claimed that agents who did not push a lot of credit were passed over for promotions and for the coveted transfers to urban centers.

This stress on credit created another incentive for extension-agents to work with larger, more prosperous farmers. Bank managers and agents frankly admitted a preference for making larger loans in order to restrict their own operating costs. Large holders were also perceived as more credit worthy and were more likely to be able to afford the considerable costs of titling and registering their land. For all of these reasons, the larger loans tended to be approved more quickly and easily. In some cases agents even urged farmers to apply for credit to buy machinery so costly that there was little chance of repaying the loan.

The establishment of INCRA as supreme authority over land title impeded access to credit for medium-size operations that had previously dealt with banks on the basis of personal trust or on the basis of various land use deeds, authorizations, and titles formerly conceded by either municipal or local state governments. In law INCRA was to accept all valid previous titles, but INCRA procedures were slow and the areas to be administered were vast in relation to the agency's personnel, budget, and other priorities. In many areas there was still considerable doubt and controversy over which areas were under INCRA jurisdiction and which areas were under local state jurisdiction. Banks were usually unwilling to accept earlier titles under these conditions and so favored those who could acquire INCRA titles.

Agents complained frequently of the difficulties that erratic funding, inadequate communication, and delays caused in their relations with the peasants and farmers. Most defined their primary work as convincing their clients to accept new technologies and increase commercial production. They believed that to be successful, they had to establish trust and authority with their clients and that agency problems made it more difficult for the farmers to believe in them. Younger than most of their clients, usually from the ecologically different regions of the center-south, most agents expressed a strong assurance in the superiority of the economic and social values they believed they represented over what they defined as the backward methods and goals of the local farmers. At the same time they felt a strong desire for approval and acceptance by the farmers in whose communities they were temporary and outnumbered newcomers. Administrative breakdowns, errors, and delays made them uncomfortable and resentful of the bureaucracies they worked for, because these undermined the basis of their local authority and acceptance.

Though immensely critical of the organizations they served, few agents expressed any reservations about the value to the farmers of the general goals which they believed these organizations represented. Although they resented the ways that agency errors and inefficiencies undermined their authority, they tended to attribute resistance to their programs to ignorance, laziness, or Amazonian rural culture rather than to the extreme uncertainties that participation in government programs imposed on the farmers.

Program Distortions and Limitations

It must be stressed that large areas of the Amazon were not included in the programs here described. EMATER attempted to distribute its programs geographically, but its very dependence on other agencies limited effective action to the areas where these agencies already operated. The organization of these agencies and their own dependence on economic return for their activities led them to concentrate their resources in certain areas. In Pará, for example, a high proportion of EMATER's personnel and budget were directed to the colonization programs, even though these included only a small proportion of the small farmers in the state (see Bunker, 1978, Tables V-VIII). Because of the low economic and demographic density of the Amazon's rural areas, the small farmers could neither not demand or attract those government services necessary for their integration into the market economy, nor could they influence the efficiency with which these services were provided.

Even where government programs to assist the small farmer were relatively concentrated, the mechanisms used were inadequate and cumbersome. Precisely because these programs depended on power derived from diverse sources, whose major concerns were evidently directed to other sectors of the economy, there were serious contradictions in policy implementation. The limitations on the power derived by the most active agencies reduced their programs to efforts at mediation between other agencies, such as banks or storage companies, which directly controlled crucial resources. By providing services for these agencies, they augmented their own derived power through exchange relationships, at the cost of submission to the more powerful agencies' requirements. The organization which resulted from this type of exchange at the regional and state levels reflected differentials of power between various political and economic sectors at the national level. The agencies which served the interests of nationally and regionally dominant classes by promoting highly capitalized agricultural and industrial activities derived much more power than agencies oriented to small-scale, labor-intensive production. The submission of the latter agencies to the former led to the fragmentation of programs and to the inefficiency with which they were implemented.

Other distortions resulted from the contradictions between the local state agencies' preferred development models and the goals the national state imposed because of its need to legitimate itself through the rural development programs. These contradictions complicated the relations between government agencies and led to failure by imposing high costs for participation directly on the farmer.

In addition to being inefficient and cumbersome, the rural development programs operated through a series of bureaucratic institutions, including land-tenure, commercial, and credit agencies, to which the peasants had to adapt to participate. These institutions' procedures, geared to the regulatory requirements of energy-intensive, socially complex forms of industrial production and exchange, were totally inappropriate for the Amazon. Access to credit for fertilizers, seeds, tools, and labor allowed some peasants to increase production, but the high costs of transport and storage and the forced sale to noncompetitive buyers often so reduced profits that many peasants were unable to pay back their loans or to recuperate the costs of obtaining legal title to land. A large proportion of the costs of rural development was shifted onto the individual farmers, who were least able to afford it.

Because rural development programs generally involve the establishment of modern capitalist institutions, the peasant who does not deal successfully with them is more likely to be injured than helped. The centralizing state-capitalist system imposes new institutions, which reflect its model of the whole economy, and conflicts between the different levels of government result in vacillations and changes in the institutions legitimating and guaranteeing occupation and ownership of land. Adaptation to these rapid institutional changes requires capital, access to information and technical or judicial assistance, and, frequently, political influence. As peasants do not have these resources, they are increasingly vulnerable to exploitation by those who do. Thus, despite their expressed aims, rural development programs in the Amazon become instruments for Brazil's strategy of capitalist expansion through the concentration of means of production. The excessively complex modern institutions which underlie the bureaucracy's standard operating procedures systematically alienate the peasants. Both the fixed costs and special knowledge required for compliance favor large and highly capitalized enterprises, contribute to the expulsion of peasants from their land, and increase discrepancies between rural classes.

Rural development programs in the Amazon respond to the needs of dominant classes rather than to those of the peasants themselves. They have either been aimed at lowering the costs of agricultural products to reduce the labor costs of the extractive industries or to reduce the tensions generated by the extremely uneven distribution of land in other parts of Brazil.

In summary, then:

1. Rural development programs in the Amazon are discontinuous and inadequately funded. Their supposed beneficiary, the peasant class, is too weak, both economically and politically, to force a coherent policy from either the national state or individual agencies.

2. Rural development programs are administered by agencies that also serve development functions for the dominant classes—and the influence of these dominant classes guarantees that the rural development programs figure as a minor part of each agency's total mandate.

3. Rural development programs are primarily oriented to the non-peasant economies and so procedures are established that place heavy costs on the peasants (acquiring a land title, for example) and expose them to further exploitation (requiring the sale of crops to specified warehouses, for example).

4. In taking over agency goals and procedures that worked well in other parts of Brazil (the center-south, for instance), administrators of rural development programs did not consider the disruptive effects that their mandates would have on the peasants and on the ecology of the Amazon.

Complex Bureaucracy and the Failure of the Modern Development State

From their conception the Brazilian government's colonization and rural development programs for the Amazon were subject to attack from powerful civil groups and from that part of its own bureaucracy allied to these groups. Concessions to these sectors and the reduction of colonization budgets in favor of other government programs added to the growing problems of the colonization process itself. The organizational deficiencies of the rural development programs designed to promote the colonization process both lent support to and were aggravated by the capacity of the private sector to interfere in official programs.

Rather than demonstrating effective government control of social, economic, and political relations, the history of these projects reflects private sector penetration of the state apparatus and competition for its resources; bureaucratic inefficiency and excessive complexity; lack of effective governmental control and coordination; the accumulated residues of past political and administrative arrangements; and discontinuities of government commitment caused by shifts in the relative power of different segments of the government itself. These interferences and distortions of colonization and rural development programs indicate that the Brazilian regime was unable to overcome the legacy of extreme power differentials which the Amazon's extractive history had formed and the problems of major regional differences within its own borders.

The environmental and logistical obstacles to the establishment of modern institutions such as registered land titles, formal bank credit, and controlled markets and to the coordination and control of the bureaucratic agencies assigned to implement and regulate these institutions posed a formidable administrative challenge. Rather than responding to this challenge with the administrative capacity required to "deeply transform society," the government was forced to operate through agencies inherited from what Roett (1978) has described as a patrimonial state, a governmental apparatus in which various agencies controlled certain economic and political sectors and derived part of their own political and economic base from that control. The bureaucratic-authoritarian (BA) state was able to mount highly ambitious new programs aimed at transforming the Amazon, but it had to operate through an administrative structure established by earlier regimes and geared to the socioeconomic organization of other areas (Pereira, 1978). Power differentials and bargaining between agencies, rather than centrally established policy, were the primary determinants of actual program decisions.

O'Donnell's model of the BA state predicates its emergence at points of crisis in nations which have attained extended but not vertically integrated industrialization. Extreme regional disparities within Brazil are not adequately accounted for in this model, however. The south-central regions of Brazil are extensively industrialized but the BA state affects and is affected by vast areas within its national boundaries where the economic and organizational systems on which O'Donnell's model is predicated are only tenuously established (Velho, 1976, 1979). Analysis of colonization and rural development programs in the Amazon show that the national state's autonomy and administrative capacity were less than predicted. It also suggests that a comprehensive model of the Brazilian state must take the political and administrative effects of unequal regional development within a single nation into account. The extensive literature on internal colonialism and regional inequality indicates that this problem is shared by many developing countries.

The government's inability to establish the institutions on which its administrative structure and procedures were based, its incapacity to coordinate and redirect the various agencies of its own bureaucracy, and its vulnerability to interference from various private groups and interests show significant restrictions on its autonomy and administrative efficacy in a program initiated outside the organizational and institutional supports of the nation's industrial center and without support from powerful private interests.

Case studies of program outcomes suggest serious restrictions on the state's autonomy and administrative capacity on an extractive periphery, but they also indicate that the national state, its bureaucracy, its ideology, and its developmental goals have had a profound impact on the Amazon. Since 1950, the Brazilian state has crucially influenced the forms in which Amazonian modes of production and extraction have been reorganized in response to international systems of unequal exchange. By providing both basic infrastructure and great amounts of capital to large-scale capitalist enterprise, it has accelerated, and in some cases created, conditions which favor the rapid development of extractive industry. Its own attempts to direct and control the spread of capitalism along its frontiers and to maintain order in the relations between different claimants to natural resources have been impeded by the use of bureaucratic structures which had evolved in the center-south regions but which were not adapted to the non-capitalist Amazon. The state essentially created the conditions for the subversion of its own bureaucratic apparatus by conceding rights and subsidies to capitalist enterprise in a region where locally based economic and political organization was incapable of resisting the predatory strategies of the subsidized entrepreneurs.

The characteristics of this state and of its bureaucratic apparatus may be described in terms of class interests in mediating between and articulating capitalist and noncapitalist modes of production (Foweraker, 1981). They also conform to Smelser's (1963) and Eisenstadt's (1964, 1966a, 1966b) characterization of modernity, especially in the increasing functional specificity of the administrative apparatus and of the social and economic institutions they attempt to impose, as well as in their deliberate orientation toward commercializing agriculture and integrating it with the industrial sector.

Smelser's and Eisenstadt's theories of structural modernization were quite directly imported from their analysis of the social effects of European industrialization. Their assumptions of unilinear evolutionary similarities greatly limited their theories' predictive and prescriptive relevance for Third World development. Their characterizations of structural modernity, however, are peculiarly appropriate to the analysis of bureaucratic forms and processes which are as exogenous to the Third World as the theories are. Bureaucracies can be analyzed in terms of energy flows and energy costs (Adams, 1982). Energy measures (and common sense) can show us that the socially complex forms admirably described by Smelser and Eisenstadt are so costly that their imposition in energy-diffuse social formations accelerate underdevelopment.

Modernity, however, is as polymorphous as modern society is complex. We can describe the complex organization of multiple functionally specific agencies and institutions as modern. We can also characterize as modern the systems of personal and collective knowlege necessary to adapt to, comply with, and take advantage of the rules, regulations, and procedures of this complex organization. The ideologies of the state and of the class fragments allied to it are also modern. I will argue in the rest of this book that all of these aspects of modernity combined in different ways to accelerate and intensify the economic subordination of Amazonian extractive systems to central Brazilian production systems.

While the establishment of modern bureaucracies and institutions in the Amazon has not achieved the developmental effects predicted by Smelser or aimed at by the Brazilian state, they have had the effect of further undermining local institutions and of providing administrative and economic infrastructure to facilitate access to land, natural resources, and credit by large-scale capitalist enterprises. They have thus contributed to the intensification of resource extraction and to the environment and social disruption which it has caused.

The next four chapters examine the ways that the organization, operating procedures, and ideologies of the various modern bureaucratic agencies affected the implementation and the outcomes of different national state programs for rural and agricultural development and colonization in the Amazon. As I have shown, these programs were to a large extent attempts by the state to legitimate itself. The only way that the state could legitimate itself as capable of incorporating the rural and working poor was to establish programs that actually ran counter to its general tendencies toward income and land-tenure concentration. The intended beneficiaries of these programs had little political voice and little economic power. The communities they formed and the agencies which served them were therefore subject to extensive interference from dominant classes and from the bureaucratic agencies whose programs favored the dominant classes. The procedural and ideological modernity of the agencies and of the agents themselves were highly compatible with the ideology and special knowledge of these classes' members and representatives. This compatibility enhanced these classes' ability to dominate and exploit Amazonian communities, because the latter had neither the institutions nor the special knowledge required to deal with complex modern bureaucratic forms. The contradictions between the political and the economic imperatives of the state created a series of major impediments to all of these programs.

The rural development and the colonization programs had much smaller budgets and altered the social and natural environment of the Amazon much less than the programs supporting large-scale extractive enterprise, but they are worthy of extended consideration because they were intended to affect a much larger portion of the local population and because their publicly stated goals of establishing small-scale rural economies with viable links to national and international markets do at least address the major developmental problems of the Amazon, no matter how flawed their actual implementation has been. So far, these programs constitute the only alternative which the state has recognized to the continued, and intensifying, rate of resource extraction and the associated destruction of the environment.

My purpose in presenting the case materials which follow is to show how the modern bureaucratic forms which the state imposed led to program failure: by imposing excessive costs on both state agencies and on rural communities, by facilitating various forms of official corruption, by fostering increased inequality between rural classes, and by imposing technologies that were unsuited to the Amazonian environment. I argue that the exogenous modern forms and institutions were especially detrimental because the previous disruption of human communities by extractive economies left these communities without the political and economic resources to force the powerful state bureaucracies to take their structures, organizations, and needs into account. Modernity as organizational and ideological form becomes the focus of the following chapters because it best describes the disjunctures between the relatively weak Amazonian rural communities and the much more powerful state bureaucracies which increasingly controlled their destinies.

Inappropriate modernity, as the symptom and as the result of the extension of bureaucratic agencies from the Brazilian national center to the Amazonian periphery, is one of the problems which must be resolved before effective development programs can start to reverse the effects of past and present extractive economies. Neither modernization nor its effects in the Amazon can be understood, however, without reference to the ways that world system demand for Amazonian natural resources and the local modes of extraction have affected, and continue to affect, the Amazonian ecosystem. Modern bureaucratic forms effectively concentrate and coordinate vast amounts of human and nonhuman energy. They thereby generate and direct great social power. Their effective functioning, however, ultimately depends on similarly energy-intensive social and economic forms in the society they regulate. These energy-intensive forms cannot emerge in predominantly extractive, energy-losing, social formations. The transfer of modern bureaucracies from the Brazilian industrial center to the Amazonian periphery, therefore, involved the imposition of institutions and agencies whose power was disproportionate to the power generated in endogenous Amazonian social formations. In the absence of correspondingly energy-intensive local institutions with compatible organizational forms, this central bureaucratic power could not effectively direct and regulate; it could only disrupt. This it did, powerfully.

NOTES

1. Barraclough (1970) attributes the proliferation of agricultural development agencies typical of many Latin American countries to the entrenchment of dominant class interests in the Ministry of Agriculture. The government is obliged to create special agencies to carry out rural development programs which do not directly serve these interests. These agencies are subordinate to the Ministry of Agriculture, however, and are thus subject to limits on their own power and resources, their operating budgets, and in the formulation of policy.

2. Peasants, as producers, are clearly marginal to Brazil's export economy, so these agencies were subordinate to other interests in the center-south as well. Between 1950 and 1970 agriculture had declined from 22.8 percent of the gross national product to 17.1 percent, and the percentage of the agriculture labor force from 56.6 to 40.0 percent of the total (Reis, 1975). Export crops account for less than half of Brazil's foreign revenues (IBGE, 1977) and are controlled primarily by large capitalist enterprise.

Expanding capitalist development in Brazil has had the direct effect of constantly dislocating peasant farmers. Both Velho (1976) and Martins (1975) have analyzed frontier expansion in Brazil as a process in which peasants continuously are expelled into marginal areas by expanding capitalist enterprise. According to Martins, a demographic front of expelled peasants precedes an advancing economic front, supplying it with necessary agricultural produce and a supply of cheap manpower. As capitalist enterprise expands into the newly cleared and settled areas, the peasant settlers are once again expelled, and the demographic front advances further. In the terms of Martins's argument, there is little economic or political interest in turning the peasant into a small farmer integrated into a market economy. Rather, the constant explusion of peasants from lands which they have cleared, together with their exploitation, first as producers and later as workers, is an essential part of capitalist development.

The marginality of peasant farmers in Brazil ensures that overall success of national development plans depends very little on their effects on the peasants. While resources per plan or per farmer affected are usually relatively high in Brazil, efforts at rural community development are frequently sporadic and short-lived. The failure of a program is more likely to lead to reduction or total abandonment than to reorganization or reformulation. This tendency is enhanced in Amazonia.

CHAPTER 6

The Cost of Modernity:
Complex Bureaucracy and the Failure
of the Colonization Program

The haphazard imposition of exogenous modern institutions as a precondition for participation in rural development programs run by agencies that controlled crucial material, economic, and judicial resources systematically favored those groups and individuals most able to adapt to the new bureaucratic requirements. At the same time these modern institutional forms provided legal means by which capitalist enterprises could acquire land as a commodity and could appeal to the legitimate force of the state to defend their possession. By establishing juridical procedures for land alienation and ownership, modernizing agencies increased the potential for capitalist enterpreneurs to control both land and labor (Domar, 1970; Martins, 1980). The bureaucratic structures and procedures which the various agencies employed fit well with the notions embodied in most modernization theories. The outcomes of these modernizing programs, however, diverged from their predictions. Because modernity, as bureaucratic organization, as ideology, and as legal forms of relations between humans and of humans to land, has been so important in recent state programs in the Amazon, we must consider the way modern forms are imposed, and the effects of their disjunctures with the socioeconomic forms which previous modes of extraction and production had created in the Amazon.

Theories of modernization, because they are directly derived from liberal explanations and myths of European and North American development, serve as convenient ideological bases for capitalist developmental states. If these states' expressed goals are to achieve economic, social, and political forms similar to those of Europe and North America, they can legitimate their programs by the consonance of the institutional and economic forms which their programs employ with those of the nations which provide them with goal models. The ideological assumption that modernization is associated with political egalitarianism is especially useful to developmental states whose predominant economic strategies are based on the concentration of income, and access to resources, and the political exclusion of workers and peasants.

In the Amazon the legitimating aspects of modernization were most strongly embodied in the official colonization plans. The impact of the modernizing agencies were enhanced in these programs because of their higher per capita budgets and because of highly publicized state commitments to these programs. The colonization programs affected only a small portion of the area which *decreto-lei 1.164* brought under national control and an even smaller portion of the Amazon as a whole. However, the density of agency participation and the intensity of government activity provide an opportunity to examine the processes by which modern institutions were imposed on the Amazon and the effects these institutions had. They also provide an opportunity to assess the utility of modernization theories for understanding the processes of state-promoted capitalist expansion into peripheral and noncapitalist areas.

One of the most consequential of the numerous criticisms leveled against theories of modernization is that certain types of modernity may promote social inequality and/or retard national development. Various studies from both modernization and dependency perspectives have pointed out that the introduction of certain technologies associated with modernization enhances the powers and privileges of the already wealthy at the expense of the already poor, because the relatively high levels of investment necessary to acquire these technologies eliminate weaker competitors and because these technologies eliminate jobs more rapidly than economic expansion creates them.

The negative consequences of modernization have been particularly salient in the agricultural sector. Numerous plans for rural development in the Third World have attempted to resolve this conflict between productive growth and distributive equity by establishing modern institutions such as the titling and registry of land, the provision of formal bank credit, and formally structured crop markets in conjunction with programs to introduce new technologies (Long, 1977:144-84). Such institutions are assumed to equalize opportunities for access to new technologies—at least among the classes with access to land—to break up relations of dominance based on traditional or informal credit systems, and to protect the land tenure of the less prosperous or politically marginal. In this chapter, I address a hitherto neglected aspect of modernization—the economic costs of individual adaptation to these modern institutions. Many of the same cost factors that favor the access of the already prosperous to new technologies may also favor their

access to and benefit from the modern institutions which are incorporated into official development programs to enhance production or
facilitate commercial exchange. In order to examine the proposition
that the differential costs and benefits of individual adaptation to these
kinds of modern institution may heighten social inequality and retard
the developmental goals for which they are designed, I analyze the
costs and benefits of modern institutions for participants in the government-sponsored colonization and rural development projects along
the Transamazon highway.

Inequality as a Problem in Modernization Theories

Few sociological theories of modernization have successfully confronted the tensions between economic growth and social equity
(Wertheim, 1971; Brookfield, 1975). Smelser (1963) and Eisenstadt (1964,
1966a, 1966b, 1970) provide sound functionalist explanations of why
the introduction of modern technology engenders a free and disciplined
labor force and an exchange-oriented agriculture organized around
functionally specific and clearly differentiated social institutions, but
they relegate the resulting dislocations of prior socioeconomic organizations to the status of transitory lags between social differentiation
and social integration. They thus ignore the new forms of social inequality which the adoption of new technologies may bring about
(Wertheim, 1971). Even the rather muted acknowledgment that the lag
between the differentiation and the eventual integration of new, complex, interdependent institutions might be detrimental—at least temporarily—to large segments of national populations disappears from
many of the later attitudinal analyses of modernization. Kahl (1968),
Inkeles (1969, 1971), and Inkeles and Smith (1974) all search for the
values which they suppose will lead individuals to seek and promote
a modern society and which "enable them to understand and accept
the new rules of the game deeply enough to improve their own production behavior and diffuse it throughout their society" (Lerner,
1968:386). These authors do not consider the social dislocations associated with the emergence of and adaptation to modern institutions.
They simply state that modern institutions are essential to economic
growth and that the key problem for national development is the
formation of modern individuals to staff these institutions. (See especially Inkeles and Smith, 1974:316; also critical reviews in Schnaiberg,
1970; Portes, 1976, 1980; Long, 1977; Delacroix and Ragin, 1978).

The assumptions that modern technologies, modern attitudes, and
modern institutions are necessary conditions for economic growth
and social development have been challenged on both empirical and

theoretical grounds. Critics from within the modernization framework have argued that traditional beliefs or socioeconomic arrangements do not necessarily hinder economic growth (Portes, 1973b). Long (1977:30) cites "a growing body of evidence . . . that so-called traditional values and relationships are congruent with development." Portes (1973a, 1973b) and Delacroix and Ragin (1978) conclude that certain "Westernizing" institutions may actually impede economic growth and development by fostering consumption behaviors and individualistic values that limit both the investment and mobilization capacities of national states.

Other studies have shown that the processes supposed to precede or accompany modernization frequently increase social inequality. Technology diffused under government-sponsored development programs tends to be adopted by and to favor disproportionately the more prosperous or powerful (Dube, 1958; Epstein, 1973; Long, 1977). Modernization programs are frequently biased toward industrial growth and have thus fostered the transfer of agricultural surpluses from the rural to the urban sector. This transfer aggravates social inequality by discriminating against rural populations, which are often the national majority (see Varma, 1980:57). Modernization within the agricultural sector, moreover, contributes to rural-urban migratory flows far beyond urban-industrial capacity to absorb the growing reserve of free labor (Shaw, 1976).

Critics arguing from dependency and world-system perspectives have assailed modernization theories for having "served to hide [the] naked imperialism" (Frank, 1969) of the dominant classes in advanced and industrial nations (see also Hechter, 1975; Wallerstein, 1975). From this point of view, modernization is either an ideological blind for or an incidental aspect of the unequal exchange which aggravates social inequalities and retards development in dependent countries.

Though Cardoso (1973) and Evans (1979) have effectively challenged blanket statements that dependency necessarily impedes development, both acknowledge that "dependent development," which tends to incorporate capital-intensive technology and "modern" organization into the most dynamic sectors of the less-developed countries, increases social inequality. Recent cross-national surveys have confirmed the association between transnational corporation investment and inequality in the less developed countries (e.g., Bornschier et al., 1978). Leys (1975) and Feder (1980) have extended these notions to their analyses of rural development planning; they interpret land titling and other attempts to "modernize" rural institutions as the result of the insistence by the World Bank and other international lending agencies on creating capitalist structures more amenable to central state control and world-system exploitation.

The various criticisms of modernization theories have been extensive enough to raise the question of whether there is anything to be learned from further studies of modernization. The answer is that, however much the assumptions underlying various modernization theories have been challenged, modernization remains a prevalent strategy in the development plans of numerous national and international development agencies. Modernization failed as a universally valid prescription for development, but it remains central to the administration, organization, and political ideologies and legitimizing strategies of developmental nation states. Furthermore, most prior studies of the socioeconomic effects of officially instigated modernization have focused on government programs for the direct transfer of technology. Increasingly, however, development strategies based on direct technological transfer have been replaced by strategies of prior or concomitant institutional modernization. These programs of instigated institutional change must also be included in our analyses.

Inequality as a Problem in Modernization Planning

The turn to institutional modernization as a development strategy corresponded to theoretical and empirical criticism of modernization theories. Mounting evidence that direct technological transfers to rural economies might aggravate social inequality and promote rural-urban migrations at levels which required greatly increased social welfare expenditures led many international and national development agencies to shift away from the "improvement approach," which the World Bank in 1960 described as seeking "the progressive improvement in peasant methods of crop and animal husbandry by working on the peasant farmer . . . to induce an increase in his productivity without any radical change in traditional social and legal systems" (cited in Long, 1977:145). This "improvement" approach, based on assumptions that the diffusion of new technologies would foster the sociopolitical changes that Smelser, Eisenstadt, and others had defined as modernization, in many cases gave way to a "transformation" approach based on assumptions similar to those underlying attitudinal variants of modernization theory, i.e., that certain modern institutions would equalize opportunities to benefit from new technologies as well as facilitating their general adoption (see Long, 1977; Varma, 1980; Hyden, 1980).

This shift with its basis in equity considerations was evident in the numerous national and international agency strategies to incorporate Western systems of land titling and registration and of agricultural credit into their rural development programs. Thome (1971), for example, emphasizes equity goals in his review of Latin America programs to provide peasants and small holders with land titles. He stresses tenure security, generalized access to institutional credit, and rights to water—all of which would finally contribute to increasing the production and well-being of the small farmer. He also mentions benefits for the functioning of a modern economy—greater ease of selling or transferring property—and for a modern state—facilitation of enforceable land taxation.

The transformation approach has proved to be far costlier than its technology-improving predecessors (Long, 1977; Killick, 1980). Few of the newly created institutions are directly productive; they require more elaborate administrative structures with greater numbers of trained personnel and absorb a substantial portion of total development budgets. Leys (1975:69), for example, estimates that 16 percent of Kenya's agricultural development budget for 1970-74 was allocated to land surveying and registration. He points out that the titles did not directly contribute to paying off the debt to government which the small farmers and peasants had to assume to participate in the credit programs based on this land titling.

Measuring the Costs of Adaptation

Previous studies of the costs of transforming rural institutions have been limited to analysis of the costs of specific institutions, such as land registry or formal credit. They have therefore overlooked a key characteristic of modern institutions—that their functional specificity necessitates complex linkages within sets of interdependent institutions. In the case of modern institutions established within rural development programs, for instance, institutions of individualized formal bank credit may in turn depend on linkages to institutions of land measurement, registration, alienation, and adjudication, which in turn depend on a series of other institutions for the formal documentation of social identity, and on linkages to institutions of competitive markets for the crops which are financed and for systems of control over the use and eventual repayment of loans. Analysis of the costs and benefits of individual adaptations to modern institutions requires examination of the cumulative effects of all of the institutions with which a particular type of actor must deal. The relevant sets vary between actors; the farmer who needs a land title to secure formal credit must deal with one set of institutions, while the rural extension agent, the land registrar, and the bank director must each deal with different, though overlapping, sets. Analysis therefore requires us to specify the costs of whole sets of institutions for specific sets of actors.

The rural development and colonization schemes along the Trans-amazon highway and in other rural areas of the state of Pará provide a useful case for examining the developmental impact of specific modern institutions. Over 9,000 families participated in these programs; both national and state governments committed relatively large budgets to the projects; the functions of the various agencies within each program were clearly specified, and ample documentation of planning and implementation is available, both in the public domain and in various agency archives.

The strategy designed for the research reported here was to examine the costs and benefits of a particular modern institution, formal credit, for a particular type of actor, small farmers settled in these government sponsored colonization projects. Interviews, direct observation, and analysis of various government agencies' plans and statutes were used to trace the backward and forward institutional linkages to agricultural credit. Once all of the linked institutions had been identified, historical documents and further interviews were used to determine the presence or absence of these institutions, as well as the ways that they, or their functional equivalents, operated in the region prior to the colonization and development programs. Similar procedures were followed to discover the means that the various government agencies had employed to establish and manage the institutions not already in place. Finally, the costs of the farmers' compliance with each of the specialized bureaucratic agencies responsible for the practical implementation of different modern institutions with linkages to agricultural credit were measured; total costs were then compared with returns on the crops financed by bank loans; and the ratio of costs to returns were then compared to gross measures of individual success or failure as indicated by continued access to credit and land.[1]

Central Bureaucratic Organization and Peripheral Land-Tenure Institutions

My analysis of underdevelopment in the Amazon has shown the cumulative ecological, demographic, infrastructural, and organizational constraints that prior modes of extraction and production place on subsequent socioeconomic transformations. It has also shown how the energy flows from extractive to productive economies enhance energy-intensive complex social and economic organization in the productive centers and lead to social and ecological simplification and energy-diffusion in the extractive periphery. This imbalance leaves the extractive periphery susceptible to continued domination and disruption by environmentally destructive enterprise geared to rapid profits rather than to sustained yield. It also leaves it vulnerable to the extension of central bureaucratic and administrative organization, which demands more human energy than the peripheral economy can liberate from direct production or extraction. Energy-losing peripheries cannot elaborate the complex institutional bases which underlie and facilitate individual compliance with complex modern bureaucratic procedures and requirements. The difficulty and extra costs of individual compliance in such a situation are aggravated by policy distortions and irrationalities that accumulate across the imperfectly coordinated specific functions of multiple, exogenous imposed agencies. In other words, the absence of compatible, correspondingly complex endogenous or local institutions (1) makes individual compliance with any particular exogenously imposed agency more difficult and costly, and (2) restricts coordination between agencies, thereby making each agency less efficient and further increasing the cost of individual compliance. These costs and difficulties compound, as individuals are forced to comply with the procedural requirements of multiple agencies in order to satisfy the requirements of each.

These extra costs and inefficiencies are likely to be greatest in the regions least integrated into central economic and institutional forms. Even if the populations of these regions maintain adequate subsistence economies, their accumulation of surplus and their access to cash are likely to be minimal. Therefore, the costs of adaptation to modernity may weigh heaviest on regions and classes least able to afford them.

The Transamazon rural development and colonization program was shaped by four major constraints: (1) the prior institutional system, (2) conflicting demands placed on development programs by different powerful groups in the national center, (3) the complex and costly organizational forms transferred from the center, and (4) the physical environment. All of these affected the costs and effectiveness of establishing modern institutions in the Brazilian Amazon.

Rural development and colonization programs in Pará aimed to integrate small farmers into the national market economy through the institutions of titled, private land ownership, bank credit, and competitive exchange systems. These efforts required a major transformation of local institutions molded by the Amazon's historically peripheral position in relation to both world-core productive systems and the south-central region of Brazil.

Though Pará is somewhat favored in relation to the rest of the region, including as it does the major Amazon port as well as a major financial and administrative center, these effects are largely limited to the capital city, Belém, and its immediate hinterland. The rest of Pará's 1,248,042 square kilometers is sparsely settled and has little or no facility for modern transport and communication. This was especially true of the remote *terra firme* that the new highway opened up.

As I explained in Chapter 5, the new federal agencies the government created and the older ones it redirected to carry out its new programs did not solve the inconsistencies between old and new institutions or the conflicts between different competitors for natural resources. Rather, these agencies simply imposed additional institutional requirements and were themselves riven by the opposing demands of the different groups that claimed access to Amazonian land. The program disruptions and budget reductions which followed the shift back to policies favoring large enterprise further restricted these agencies' capacities for effective action.

The difficulties faced by all of these agencies and the social and economic costs of adaptations to the disjunctive sets of institutions which they imposed were aggravated as it became apparent that many of the technologies these agencies promoted were so destructive of the fragile tropical ecosystem that they could not be profitably sustained (Goodland and Irwin, 1975; Hecht, 1979). Finally, the government's vacillation between using the Amazon as a resource base to solve national balance-of-payments problems via large-scale capital-intensive production of beef, minerals, and lumber for export and using it for settlement and small-scale production by thousands of landless peasants from other parts of Brazil further impeded the establishment of new sets of viable economic institutions.

Peasant cultivation, forest extraction, and exchange through *avia-mento* did not require, and did not stimulate, energy-intensive institutions like titled land, general land registration, systems of formal bank credit, and competitive markets for agricultural produce. Nor did they engender the complex institutions for documenting social identity and personal history that large, complex modern societies require. The national development agencies responsible for colonization and rural development programs in the Amazon, however, employed bureaucratic procedures appropriate to the capitalist economy of the south-central region, where these institutions were fully developed. Their tendency to transfer these procedures and most of their operating assumptions was even greater in the colonization area than in the rest of the Amazon; the high density of rural development activity, which state priorities for colonization prompted, and the legitimating ideologies associated with these projects enhanced bureaucratic assumptions of the crucial value of and need for modern institutional forms and procedures.

Inconsistent Programs and Ambiguous Mandates

The imposition of modern land-tenure institutions constituted a major part of the central government's attempt to control conflict over land and to promote economic exploitation of the Amazon. Assignment of this task to INCRA exacerbated the contradictions between that agency's multiple goals. As I explained in Chapter 4, INCRA was charged, on the one hand, with alleviating the conflict over land tenure according to the 1964 Land Statute (Estatuto da Terra), which stressed use rights in land by virtue of occupation and production. It was also charged with the resettlement of landless peasants and with the establishment of cooperatives for their economic defense. On the other hand, it was expected to regularize and modernize existing and future legal forms of large-scale land ownership in ways which would increase production and revenues. In other words, it was assigned to promote simultaneously the interests of the two groups that competed most directly for land in the Amazon, peasant small holders and capitalist entrepreneurs. Its patrimonial revenues, however, were almost completely dependent on the latter. INCRA's multiple mandates subjected it to political and economic pressures from capitalist groups interested in acquiring lands and made it especially vulnerable to the ambiguities and vacillations inherent in government strategies to use the Amazon both to alleviate the political pressures caused by rapid increase in rural populations and extreme land-tenure concentration in other parts of Brazil and to promote large-scale mining, lumbering, and cattle enterprises whose exports might relieve some of Brazil's balance-of-payments problems.

Conflicting Demands Resulting from INCRA's Multiple Mandates

The contradictions inherent in this combination of social, political, and economic functions limited INCRA's capacity to carry out the government's grandiose plans for settling thousands of landless peasants in the Amazon. In addition to resettling peasants and *minifundistas*, the colonization schemes aimed to transform them into middle-level capitalist farmers by providing access to a wide range of modern institutions. INCRA was charged with settling colonists on lots of 100 hectares, providing perpendicular access roads from the newly opened highway, housing, access to credit, transport, warehouses, health services, education, and technical assistance, both directly and in coordination with other federal agencies.

From the beginning, the colonization programs suffered both from the other demands on INCRA's resources and from direct criticisms and pressures from business groups and other public agencies. These demands and pressures, combined with serious planning errors and construction delays (Moran, 1975, 1981; Smith, 1976), severely impeded the capacity of INCRA the other agencies to coordinate their efforts. This failure of coordination raised the costs of the new institutions and reduced the benefits that most of the colonists received.

Institutional Interdependence and the Costs of Development to the Farmer

Each institution imposed by the official development plan had a bureaucratic counterpart in the agency or agencies responsible for various parts of the colonization and rural development processes. In principle each agency fulfilled complementary parts of the functions on which the government's model of rural development was based. The interdependence of the institutions created an interdependence between the various agencies, which the government reinforced by its delegation of powers and its assignments of programs. Institutions cannot be created by fiat, however, and the insufficient development of the modern capitalist institutions reduced each agency's capacity to carry out its assigned functions. Thus, the official model of rural development imposed a set of modern institutions on the rural population and simultaneously presupposed that these institutions were sufficiently established to permit modern bureaucracies to function in their terms.

Because these modern institutions were highly interconnected and complementary, inefficiencies resulting from the need for each agency to function without its institutional bases were compounded by the interdependence of all the agencies and by the fragmentation of rural development programs and responsibilities among them. None of the institutions could function without the rest: credit required documented social identity, land title, and a competitive market; land title was only possible with documented identity; surveying was only possible if there were adequate roads; the competitive market could only function if there were adequate roads and warehouses, and so on. The organization necessary to establish these institutions was so costly and so complex that the maintenance of schedules and coordination between the various agencies were almost impossible. The institutions themselves, therefore, tended to be established at different rates and in different degrees across time and space.

Further, coordination of the complementary programs was often hindered by conflicting demands on the agencies' resources, as well as by the delays and program distortions that resulted from the power differentials, bargaining, and funding delays described in the last chapter.

Finally, the enormous distances and spaces involved, together with the natural physical barriers of a tropical rain forest, delayed the establishment of the structures necessary to effectuate the institutions and impeded communications within and between the rural development agencies. The Transamazon highway is even now a narrow dirt road during the six-month dry season, when thick dust makes travel on it quite hazardous. During the six-month rainy season, highway traffic is frequently interrupted by washouts, with bridges swept away, and by long stretches of mud which mire vehicles and increase the risk of their slipping off the roadway altogether. Telephone service is precarious or nonexistent. As all of the agencies had their administrative centers in Belém, the difficulties of communication created procedural bottlenecks and delays, as well as policy distortions due to insufficient exchange of information. Because the access roads heading off the highway were not built on schedule and were mostly impassable during the rainy season, many of the agencies' functionaries could not reach more than a small part of the work areas assigned to them. Dispersed location of the field offices of different agencies, disparities in their levels of funding, and the lack of coordinated planning meant that the various agencies frequently worked in different areas. Thus, each agency attempted to establish its part of an interdependent set of institutions without reference to the other agencies upon which its effective functioning depended.

The logic of the attempt to transform peasants into middle-level capitalists required that they adapt to an economic model devised by central government planners and to the procedures of the interdependent but uncoordinated agencies assigned to implement this model. The costs of fulfilling the procedural requirements of this model without having all the necessary institutions in place weighed heavily on the small farmers who participated in the rural development programs. The following examination of the financing-cultivation-harvesting-remuneration cycle illustrates how institutional interdependence created agency interdependence and how the costs of agency procedures and of the breakdown in their coordination were passed on to the small farmer. It shows how the accumulation of these costs led to net loss for most farmers and prohibited the agencies from carrying out their programs effectively.

The Dependence of Rural Extension on Bank Credit

The official model of rural development in Brazil, based on the U.S. county-agent rural extension pattern and adapted to the economic relations predominant in the market-oriented agricultural zones of the more developed areas (Schuh, 1971), is highly oriented to individual agricultural loans. Throughout the 1970s EMATER-Pará (Technical Assistance and Rural Extension Company-Pará) was both the official rural extension agency for Pará and the only organ licensed to prepare agricultural credit projects. Because it was defined as a "public company in private law" (Pará, 1976), it had to sustain itself through contracts, or *convênios*, with other public agencies and with private companies.

It was partially financed by the Ministry of Agriculture, but a considerable part of its budget came from a 2 percent commission it received from the Banco do Brasil for all approved projects. In order to sustain itself, EMATER was constrained to orient its rural extension programs heavily toward agricultural credit.

EMATER's dependence on the Banco do Brasil forced it to function more as an agent of the bank than as a rural extension agency. An EMATER official had to prepare each loan project. This project included an evaluation of a farmer's debt capacity and a phased plan for the application of various portions of the loan. The official was responsible for ascertaining that each phase of the cultivation had been completed before authorizing the farmer to withdraw the next portion of his loan from the bank.

The Dependence of Bank Credit on Land Title

The institution of bank credit requires means of assuring repayment other than the interpersonal guarantees implicit in less formal credit arrangements. The Banco do Brasil demanded guarantees of titled land or capital invested in titled land for its agricultural loans. A partial exception was made for a special INCRA document called a Licença de Ocupação, which was given to an occupant while his title process was pending, but this served as a guarantee only for short-term loans. In the case of small farming in Pará, short-term credit was limited to rice, beans, and corn, the so-called subsistence crops, whose cultivation on a small scale can only be considered even marginally profitable if the farmer's labor is not calculated as a cost. Effective market integration of the small farmer in the Transamazon colonization areas depended on perennial crops such as sugar cane, pepper, and cocoa, partly because of their greater value per volume—an important consideration given the great distances to markets and the precarious and costly system of transport—and partly because of the rapid soil depletion caused by annual crops in the fragile tropical soils. Long-term credit for these crops was contingent on possession of title to the land.

As was explained, the dominant modes of production and extraction in most of Pará did not require the kind of titles which the banks demanded. Pending INCRA's classification of the land's occupation, use, and titling and its subsequent surveying and regularization, the national government's expropriation of the 200 kilometer-wide high-way belt effectively suspended the validity of whatever pre-INCRA documentation might have existed there, and in areas near the highway belt de facto suspension of validity occurred because no one knew whether the land was part of INCRA's jurisdiction or of Pará's.

INCRA's capacity to classify, survey, and register the numerous vast tracts of land under its jurisdiction was limited by the size of its own budget, by shortages of qualified personnel, and by inadequate trans-portation and communication networks. Within this limited capacity, its dedication to the surveying and titling of small farmers' lots was compromised by its involvement with land sales to large enterprises and with its tax collecting activities. In many of the traditional small-holding areas, INCRA had not even begun the demarcation of the land within its jurisdiction, let alone the actual classification and surveying of occupied lands. *Decreto-lei 1.164* effectively annulled a set of land-tenure institutions adequate to the present modes of production and then imposed different institutions adapted to modes of production predominant in other areas, but it could not guarantee that the new institutions would be viable.

Up to 1976, INCRA had expedited no more than 12,800 Licenças de Ocupação (LO) and 4,400 definitive titles (TD). The TDs replaced an equal number of LOs. Many of the TDs and LOs had already been cancelled for reasons of abandonment or transfer. Thus the total number of effective INCRA and documents in all of Pará was considerably less than 12,800. Indeed, the number of effective land documents issued by INCRA was less than the number of new land occupations which it had provoked. Even in the high-priority colonization areas, where rural development programs were concentrated, INCRA's land docu-mentation was slow. Many of the new settlers in the colonization areas still did not have land documents in 1977 (see Table 8); almost none of the occupants of the traditional settlement areas incorporated into INCRA jurisdiction had them (Santos, 1979).[2]

The surveying, tenure classification, documentation, and registration required to implement modern land-tenure institutions throughout both the traditional settlement and the newer colonization areas would have involved enormous expense and would probably have taken years to complete even with major government support. INCRA's commitment to other activities, together with restrictions on personnel dictated by the central government's cost-cutting policies and diminished com-mitment to small-scale colonization, retarded the titling process and restricted it to a small proportion of the land under federal jurisdiction. The various rural development programs, especially those involving bank credit, were in turn limited and distorted, because they were so designed that they could function only within the context of the new land-tenure institutions.

Table 8. INCRA and Expedition of Land Titles in the Colonization Projects (PIC), 1972-77

	PIC Altamira		PIC Itaituba		PIC Monte Alegre	
Year	TD	LO	TD	LO	TD	LO
1972	803	--	--	--	--	--
1973	76	--	--	--	--	--
1974	555	2,281	--	--	--	--
1975	1,071	57	144	383	--	97
1976	254	133	356	622	719	--
1977	70	9	955	55	300	13
Total	2,829[a]	2,480[b]	1,455[a]	1,060[b]	1,019[a]	110[b]

Source. INCRA CR-01/TF.
Note. TD = Definitive titles; LO = occupation licenses. The approximate number of colonists in 1977 (author's estimate) were: PIC Altamira, 4,130; PIC Itaituba, 2,600; and PIC Monte Alegre, 3,000.
[a] Includes cancelled titles.
[b] Includes cancelled LOs and LOs substituted by TDs.

The Dependence of Land Title on the Documentation of Social Identity

The institution of nationally uniform ways of certifying property ownership by title presupposes other institutions for certifying social identity in similarly uniform fashion. INCRA's delays in tenure classification and land surveys resulted in part from its own insistence that an applicant for an LO or a TD present numerous personal documents. These included birth, military service, and voting records, marriage license, tax number, and an identity card, as well as a certificate of good conduct from the police. In order to acquire an LO or a TD within the colonization area, the prospective farmer was required to present both a health certificate and a title search record at each of the several steps in the process to guarantee that he did not own other land. If the legal tenure of his lot was complicated by transfer, he might have to present all of these documents four or five times.

Those institutions which characterize, control, and certify social identity in complex societies were no more developed in the rural areas of Pará than were those institutions which regulate the ownership and use of land as a negotiable good. Few small farmers had all the requisite documents, and a great many had none at all. Nor did the necessary infrastructure exist to enable the rural population to obtain them easily.

The documents themselves were relatively expensive, as were the trips to and delays in the necessary government offices. The time and money spent traveling to different administrative centers were increased because the proper forms or the proper functionary was not present or, even worse, because the necessary records of the stages of life were never kept. INCRA, health agencies, police headquarters, and income tax offices were often located in different and widely distant administrative centers. INCRA's own procedures, which involved the submission of the same documents in three different processes—first for a Guia de Assentamento (Settlement Guide), then for an LO, and finally for the TD—entailed additional delays and the expenses. The complexity of each process and the inadequate explanations of all of the bureaucratic requirements meant that many farmers had to make extra trips to INCRA offices to complete their applications.

Bureaucratic insistence on treating the colonist or the small farmer as if he had lived all of his life within the institutional structure already established in the south-central region of Brazil complicated already costly procedures for obtaining land documents to such a degree that many were unable to do so (see Table 9). Even for those who managed to get the necessary land documents, however, the relations between EMATER, the Banco do Brasil, and various other agencies were either so complex as to make credit unprofitable, or the approval and release of loans so delayed that the funds obtained could not be applied in the proper seasons.

The Cost of Credit

The institution of bank credit assumes a series of procedural requirements and controls. Compliance with these requirements necessarily involves some cost, but if the bureaucracies responsible for the controls do not function effectively, these costs become exorbitant.

The farmer seeking credit had to make at least two trips, and frequently more, to the EMATER office and at least two more to the bank in order to get his credit project elaborated and approved. Even after the loan was approved, however, his access to the money depended on the bank's disbursement of portions of the loan which corresponded to the various phases of planting and harvesting. The bank disbursed each portion upon certification from EMATER that the previous phase was satisfactorily completed. In some cases the EMATER agent's authorization of payment was itself dependent on the authorization of another agency of the Ministry of Agriculture verifying the absence of plant disease.

EMATER did not have sufficient agents for the number of farmers with whom it worked and was frequently subject to long delays in the receipt of money for gasoline and vehicle maintenance from the other agencies with which it had *convênios*. For both of these reasons, the

Table 9. Minimum/Maximum Time and Money Costs of the Steps Necessary to Receive Short-Term Rural Credit: Examples from the Colonization Areas of Santarém, Itaituba, Altamira, and Monte Alegre, 1977

Destination and Purpose	Number of Trips[a]	Distances and Round Trip Time[b]	Transport Costs Per Trip: Cr$	Food and Lodging Costs Per Trip: Cr$	Commission, Charges, Xerox, Photographs: Cr$	Total Costs: Cr$
I. Personal Documents[c]						
Various *Município* Offices	4-8	20-245 km 1-3 days	10-200	30-400	600-800	720-5,600
II. "Guia de Assentamento" and "Licença de Ocupação"[d]						
INCRA	3-6	0-154 km 0-2 days	0-100	0-150	50	50-1,550
III. Elaboration and Registration of Credit Plans and Loan Withdrawals[e]						
EMATER request for projects	1-3	0-172 km 0-2 days	0-200	0-150	---	0-700
EMATER offices receive signed proposal[f]	1-2	0-172 km 0-2 days	0-200	0-150	---	0-700
Banco do Brasil and *cartorio:* register loans, first withdrawal[f]	1-2	20-245 km 1-5 days	10-200	30-650	250	290-1,950
EMATER authorization for second and third withdrawals[f]	2-6	0-172 km 0-2 days	0-200	0-150	---	0-2,100
Banco do Brasil second and third withdrawals	2-4	20-245 km 1-5 days	10-200	30-650	---	80-3,400
Banco do Brasil payment for produce, loan discounted	1	20-245 km 1-3 days	10-200	30-400	---	40-600
Total (I, II, and III)[g]	15-32	160-6,491 km 8-91 days				1,180-16,600

Note. The official exchange rate in July 1977 was Cr$14.26 to U.S.$1.00.

[a] Number of trips and round trip times varied widely in function of delays in the various agencies, certain functionaries not being present, certain forms not being available, long lines or temporary closing of credit offices in banks, mistakes or omissions in filling out of forms by employees of other agencies.

[b] Maximum distances between farmers' residences and various agencies varied in the four areas: in Santarém, to all agencies, 172 km; in Itaituba, 245 km to Banco do Brasil and *município* offices, 120 to INCRA, 70 to EMATER; in Monte Alegre, 80 km to Banco do Brasil, *município* offices, and EMATER, 100 to INCRA; in Altamira, 220 km to Banco do Brasil, 174 to INCRA, 60 to EMATER.

[c] The income tax certificates were valid for only one year; other personal documents had to be obtained only once.

[d] To obtain a definitive title required the repetition of II and registration in the *cartório*, which could cost up to CR$2,000.

[e] The direct costs of elaborations of credit plans and withdrawal of money (III) were annual.

[f] In Monte Alegre and Santarém the trips to EMATER and to Banco do Brasil for each of the three authorizations and withdrawals could usually be combined.

[g] The minimum and maximum totals were clearly highly improbable in individual cases, though they do represent bureaucratic possibilities. Individual farmers tending toward the maximum in any given year were probably those most likely to desist at some point in the process or to be unable to repay bank loans.

farmer frequently had to go to the EMATER office to persuade the agent to sign his authorization without visiting his lot, or he had to wait until the agent finally arrived, thus losing days of work and risking crop loss through late planting or harvesting.

Even after he had the necessary authorization, he might still be subject to delays at the bank, which on occasion closed its credit section for several days at a time while it resolved its own administrative problems and, at least once, for several weeks while it investigated one of its functionaries' embezzlement by falsification of farmers' loan records. Such trips and delays raised the cost of credit greatly. In the case of short-term loans these costs were frequently as high as 50 percent of the loan value and in some cases exceeded it (Table 9). The delays often obliged the farmer to plant dangerously late in the season or to apply his own resources in the first stages of cultivation without any guarantee that he would receive the credit necessary to complete his investment.

Only perennial crops such as pepper, cocoa, and sugar cane provide high enough returns to absorb the fixed costs of rural credit. These crops require long-term investment loans, however, and so were only available to farmers who had received TDs from INCRA. The only exception to this rule was a special program which waived the title requirement for cocoa but which had benefited only a small number of farmers by 1978. For the rest of the farmers who had received only INCRA's LO and could therefore only obtain short-term credit for the "subsistence" crops of rice, beans, and corn, bank credit was more likely to contribute to loss than to profit, since many farmers became so deeply indebted to the bank from failures with short-term loans obtained on the basis of the LO that they were ineligible for the loans necessary for the more lucrative permanent crops if and when they finally got the definitive INCRA title.

The Costs of Overlapping Federal, State, and Município Jurisdictions

New institutions can be legislated, but even in the context of a strong central government the functioning of these new institutions may be impeded by the persistence of other institutions which favor prior established interests. Despite the evident centralizing tendencies of successive Brazilian military regimes, and in contrast to INCRA's great formal power over federal lands in the Amazon, the state and *município* governments still maintained jurisdiction over all transactions involving land, including all credit for which land served as guarantee or mortgage. INCRA's great powers over land included the authority to issue land title and guarantee loans, but the control over land and loan registration remained with the *cartórios* licensed by the various states.

The *cartórios*, located in *município* headquarters, were in fact prebends granted for life and in practice hereditary to private individuals. Once a *cartório* owner received his *ofício*, the state government had little control over his behavior, especially in the more remote *municípios*, and the national government had none at all.

This contradiction of the regime's centralist model resulted in multiple jurisdictions which increased the bureaucratic complications and the costs involved in all transactions involving land. To the already expensive procedures for getting the LO directly from INCRA and registering a short-term loan, which used the crop itself as a guarantee and could therefore be registered in the *cartório* closest to the bank, were added the additional requirements that, when INCRA finally conceded its TD, and every time that the bank accepted this title as guarantee for a long-term loan, a separate trip had to be made to the *cartório* at the headquarters of the *município* in which the land was located.

As *município* headquarters were located along the rivers, the traditional transport routes, and as the colonization projects followed the highway, which cut across *municípios* at a great distance from the rivers, the colonist frequently had to make long and difficult trips along the highway in order to get to the river and then go by boat to the *município* headquarters (see Map 2). In the case of the PIC Altamira, for example, the bulk of the settlement was the *município* of Prainha, whose *cartório* was located in Monte Alegre. In order to register a title or an investment loan, the colonist had to travel 543 kilometers west and north by road to Santarém, a journey of up to twenty hours, and then travel east again for six hours by boat. In 1977 the round trip by bus and boat cost over Cr$600 for transport alone and lasted at least five days. Similarly, most of the colonists in the PIC Itaituba were obliged to travel to Santarém, a distance of up to 400 kilometers, to register their land loans. In addition to being costly and time-consuming, the precarious condition of the highways, with mud in the rainy season and thick dust in the dry season, made the journey dangerous.

Since the *cartórios* were not subject to federal control, and the state government's supervision of them was tenuous, they could easily exploit the small farmer. They had in some cases taken advantage of the colonist's lack of protection and of his haste to return home rather than continue to pay extra days of food and lodging to extort illegally high charges for their services. Until 1978, when various public agencies and a local cooperative joined forces to pressure the state authorities into sending an investigatory commission, the *cartório* in Monte Alegre

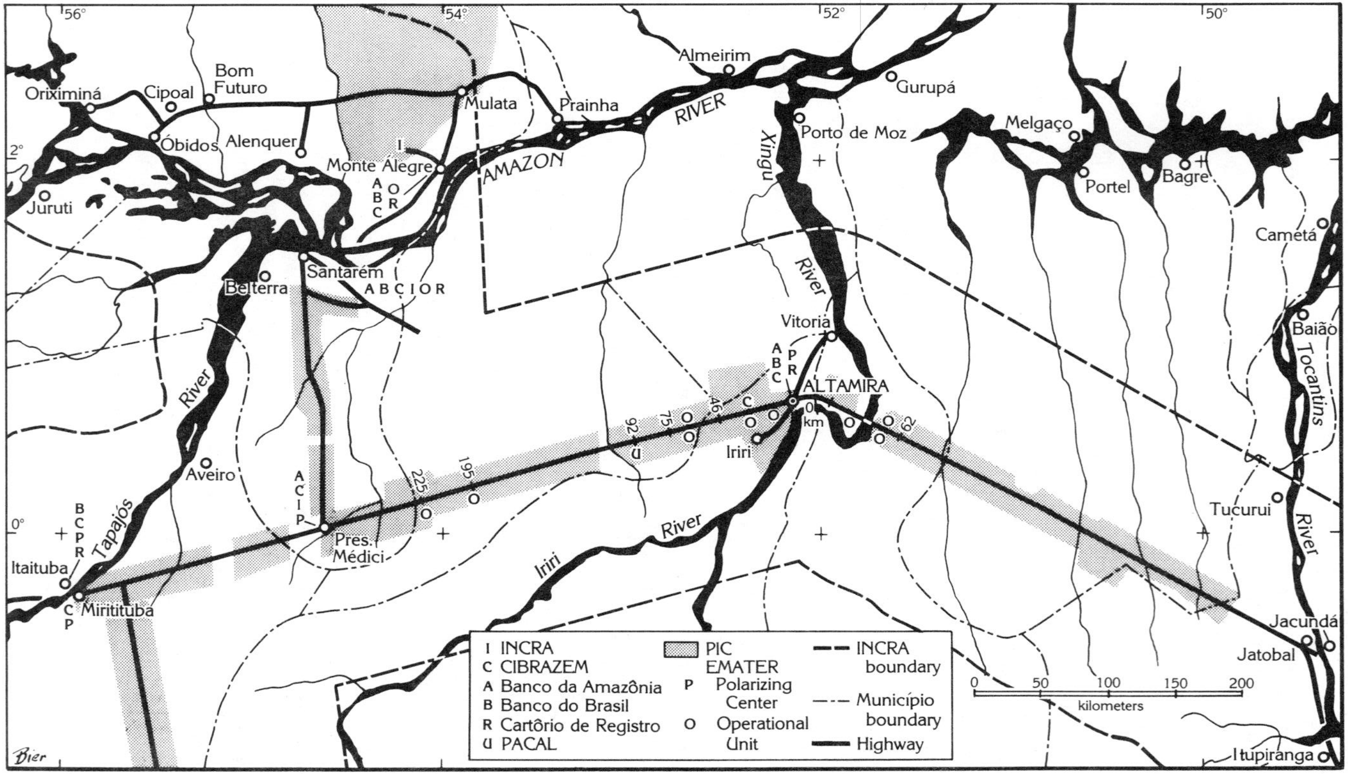

Map 2. COLONIZATION PROJECTS IN PARÁ.

Legend:

I INCRA
C CIBRAZEM
A Banco da Amazônia
B Banco do Brasil
R Cartório de Registro
ɑ PACAL

PIC
EMATER P Polarizing Center
O Operational Unit

— · — INCRA boundary
— · · — Município boundary
——— Highway

Bier

regularly charged colonists up to four times the legal maximum of one minimum salary (Cr$815 in 1977).

Even on the highway itself, or in those *municípios* whose headquarters were located at intersections of rivers with the highway, the offices of the various federal, state, and *município* agents were often widely separated. Being subjected to all three jurisdictions raised the accumulated costs of rural development for the farmers even further.

The Costs of Commercialization

The success of the institutions of titled private property and bank credit depended on the existence of a competitive market, but the temporal and spatial obstacles to the establishment of the physical infrastructure necessary for a competitive market system were particularly severe in the Amazon. In order to pay back their loans, colonists had to be able to sell their produce at a compensatory price. The markets required roads, which were INCRA's responsibility in the colonization areas. Many of the access roads still did not exist four or five years after their projected completion date, and many of those completed became impassable during the harvest season. In the case of subsistence crops the colonists had to be able to sell their produce at the CIBRAZEM (Brazilian Warehousing Company) warehouses in order to be assured of adequate prices. This government company was the only place they could receive the CFP's (Produce Financing Commission) minimum prices. Like EMATER, CIBRAZEM was self-sustaining. It was therefore reluctant to invest in areas where its storage charges could not cover its costs. The CFP's implementation of its minimum price policy was thus restricted to areas which CIBRAZEM determined would be cost effective within its own budgetary constraints.

Even though CIBRAZEM had to act as a business in some respects, it was subject to the controls on expenditure required of all government bureaucracies. All purchases had to be submitted first for approval and then for bidding. The combination of these restrictions maintained CIBRAZEM's capacity well below that necessary for the volume of crops produced in the small-farming areas, especially those outside the colonization projects, and impeded or delayed its installation of equipment which would allow faster rotation and handling of the stored produce. In the PIC Altamira, for example, it was only in 1978 that highway scales were installed, replacing the slow and much more expensive manual unloading and weighing system. An entire warehouse there was idle from 1973 to 1978 for lack of necessary equipment and staff.

The cost of CIBRAZEM's inefficiency was passed on to the farmer. Where CIBRAZEM had no warehouses, the farmer frequently had to sell far below established minimum prices; where there were warehouses, CIBRAZEM delays caused heavy losses to the farmer. At the height of the rice harvest, he might have to spend as many as eight days waiting in line to unload while he paid for the truck's idle time and for his own food and lodging. The cost of transport, of a four- to eight-day wait, of food and lodging, and of the various CIBRAZEM handling charges exceeded half the value of the normal 200-sack truckload of rice during the 1977 harvest, even without counting the value of the farmer's lost work time (see Table 10).

Both the Banco do Brasil and EMATER counted on the minimum prices when they calculated the farmers' debt capacity each year. In fact, the delays at the CIBRAZEM warehouses either cost the farmer so much or forced him to sell to private buyers at so much lower prices that they were a major factor in many farmers' inability to pay back loans.

Table 10 shows the range of possible relations of cost to return on the 1977 rice crop from a maximum possible loss of Cr$20,692 to a

Table 10. Approximate Costs to Farmer of Credit, Production, Transport, Unloading and Processing One Truckload (200 Sacks) of Rice at CIBRAZEM Warehouse in PIC Altamira or PIC Itaituba in Relation to Value Received and Loan Value Owed in 1977

Costs, Sale Value, Profit or Loss	Cr$
Costs	
1. Credit cost	1,180-16,600
2. Production costs: value of loan prepared by EMATER for 7 hectares, for approximate yield of 200 sacks, before interest charges, based on 100 percent of production costs, clearing to harvest, exclusive of transport and commercialization charges.	7,840
3. Interest on loan	350-500
4. Transport: Cr$25-30/sack	5,000-6,000
5. Waiting time paid to transporter; 4 to 8 days at Cr$400/day	1,600-3,200
6. Food and lodging for farmer waiting to unload: 4 to 8 days at Cr$150/day	600-1,200
7. Handling charges: Cr$4.08/sack for 4 handlings	816
8. Cleaning: Cr$1/sack	200
9. Purging: Cr$1/sack	200
10. Drying (from 14 percent to 18 percent humidity)	128-136
Total Costs	17,914-36,692
Sale Value	
Paid to farmer by CFP, Cr$80-105/sack according to quality	16,000-21,000
Profit or Loss	
Range of difference: sale value minus total	(−)20,692-(+)3,086

Note. The official exchange rate in July 1977 was Cr$14.26 to U.S.$1.00.

maximum possible profit of Cr$3,086. Rice was the most profitable crop available to a colonist without a TD and with a clean credit record. If it could be assumed that individual cases were distributed evenly across this range and that all colonists received loans for seven hectares of rice, then seven of every eight colonists would have lost money that year. In fact, the combined physical distances to various administrative centers were roughly even in their distribution. Number of trips and time spent tended slightly to the high end of the intervals calculated here and would have been much higher if all colonists had in fact sought and received loans. The point, of course, is that the colonists at the greatest geographical distances were less likely to get or to be able to repay loans, that colonists who incurred heavy costs in time and money were obliged to desist from seeking a loan and thereby lost absolutely their initial compliance costs, and that the high rates of loan default which these combined costs imposed on farmers excluded increasing numbers from credit programs. The costs and benefits calculated here varied from year to year with weather and crop prices. I was told of both more favorable and of worse years. I doubted the validity of cost estimates people remembered from earlier years, so I did not gather data for systematic comparison across years. People did not seem to feel, however, that 1977 was a particularly bad year, so I think it can serve as an approximate representation of the costs that compliance with bureaucratic procedures imposed on the colonists.

It should be noted that this calculation excluded the costs of procuring land documents. It should also be noted that the chances of loss would be much greater over additional years and that the crucial transition to permanent crops was only possible after liquidation of all outstanding bank debts. Thus, the longer the colonist had to wait for the TD, the less chance there was that it would be of any use to him in gaining access to profitable loans.

Inconsistencies in the Model: INCRA Norms and Capitalist Land-Tenure Institutions

Attempts to resolve some of the disjunctures between new institutional forms, program aims, and incompatible economic relations actually aggravated distortions in the programs. The title situation in the colonization areas was further complicated by INCRA's special regulations there. One of its concerns was to "fix" the colonists on their land. The official model of colonization required that the colonists adapt to modern capitalist institutions and become small farmers. However, INCRA could only assure their permanence on the land and impede the acquisition of large holdings by limiting the farmers' rights or opportunities to sell the lots they received, whose value had been much increased by the publicly financed infrastructure and by the clearing which the colonists had done. In order to impede land sales in the PICs, INCRA ruled that even a colonist with a definite title could not sell his lot until it had been officially "emancipated." Rather, the colonist who wanted to transfer use rights could apply to INCRA to evaluate the improvements made on the lot so that he could sell these, the fruits of his own labor, rather than the land, to another applicant, also selected by INCRA, who could not have another lot in the colonization area. Contradicting its own capitalist model of colonization and rural development, INCRA adopted an anticapitalist policy on land rights in order to discourage the sale or transfer of use rights and to prevent eventual concentrations of land ownership.

In practice, this scheme was enormously cumbersome. Delays of up to four years in the official transfer process were common. However, many colonists wanted to sell, primarily because the value of their production had not kept pace with the value of their lots, which was increased by the arrival of settlers with more capital. Many of these more recent migrants were small farmers from the South who were expelled by the competition from large, mechanized agricultural enterprises. Though their individual lots were too small to be profitably mechanized, or though they themselves could not accumulate sufficient capital to compete effectively there, the sale value of their land was enough for them to be able to bring relatively large amounts of capital to invest in the much cheaper land in the Amazon. Increasingly, the colonization schemes were transformed from a solution to the problems of landless peasants in the Northeast to a means of reducing the resistance of small farmers to land concentration and mechanization in the South.

Because they were not accompanied by effective support programs, INCRA's administrative barriers did not prevent land sales. Rather, a series of informal transfer mechanisms emerged to substitute for the official ones. In some cases the original colonist simply left the lot in return for a sum of money. In others he signed a formal statement of abandonment or transfer and left it with the new owner. In many cases, the original owner signed a power of attorney over to the buyer, leaving the title in his own name. The only real effect of INCRA's measures to prevent sales was to complicate and delay the second owner's ability to title his land and thus get access to investment or long-term credit. Even the documents necessary for short-term credit were difficult for the buyers to obtain. In many cases second and third lot owners exhausted their initial capital before receiving title and were forced to sell, too.

The speculators and large landowners whose access to land the INCRA regulations were designed to restrict were not particularly handicapped by not having documents to the land, as they either had other sources of capital or were not interested in the production of the land itself. It was the small farmers who brought some capital from other areas and who were unable to get credit to follow up their initial investment before their own resources were exhausted who were most severely affected by INCRA's restrictions on transfers.

As the number of abandonments and use-right transfers officially registered by INCRA had by 1977 reached over a third of the lots in the colonization areas,[3] and as the total was certainly much higher than the official figures indicated because of the informal transfers which INCRA did not record, a large proportion of the colonists were excluded from credit programs, directly because of INCRA's delays in titling land and indirectly because of its measure against transfers or because of their inability to repay previous loans because of the high costs of rural credit.

The Concentration of Rural Development Benefits

The net effect of all of these costs and impediments to participation in the rural development programs was the exclusion of growing numbers of farmers, either through abandonment, use-right transfers, or the accumulation of unpayable debts, and the systematic favoring of those few who managed to satisfy all institutional requirements, get land title, and keep a good credit record. In the PIC Altamira, generally considered the most successful in Pará, the total amount of rural credit increased by more than twice the rate of inflation from 1973 to 1977, while the total number of loans was reduced to less than half (Table 11).

The actual concentration of benefits was even greater than Table 11 shows. In the first two years of the colonization program almost all

Table 11. Application of Rural Credit in PIC-Altamira (1973-77)

Year	Number of Plans	Amount of CR$	Equivalent in 1973 CR$
1973	3,048	10,401,772	10,401,772
1974	3,450	18,853,427	14,392,224
1975	1,198	15,157,128	9,341,020
1976	1,512	62,992,219	27,591,632
1977	1,346	96,478,584	28,935,775

Source. For PIC-Altamira, EMATER—Pará, Assessoria de Crédito. For the inflation index that gives the equivalent in 1973 Cr$, Getúlio Vargas, *Conjuntura Econômica*, 31 (Apr. 1977):2, col. 2, and ibid., 32 (Apr. 1978):2, col. 2.

loans were for rice, and there was usually one loan per farmer. By 1977 most colonists who still had access to credit took out multiple loans, one for each crop planted. Approximately one-third of the colonists had more than one loan, and almost all of those had a loan for rice as well. Those few who were able to use the rural credit and extension programs to make the transition from rice to pepper, cocoa, and sugar cane and then remain solvent during the three to four years prior to commercial production[4] had by 1977 accumulated sufficient capital to buy the land and pay the bank debts of their failed neighbors or to invest in trucks and tractors which they used to haul crops they bought from other farmers. The great majority of the landless poor for whom the project was designed had by then returned to their original homes, were working for others, usually on a seasonal basis, in conditions similar to those they had left, or had gone farther into the jungle to try again.

The interdependence, ineffective coordination, and spiraling costs involved other agencies besides those described here, but their full description is beyond the scope of this chapter. Both the interdependence and the breakdown in function and coordination of these agencies stemmed from the imposition of modern institutions geared to production systems typical of more developed areas and from the combination of capitalist and anticapitalist mechanisms peculiar to the colonization projects. The imposition of modern institutions cost most of the population, which had to adapt to them, far more than it gained. Rather than contributing to economic development, these modern institutions led to program failure and aggravated social inequality.

Conclusion

By analyzing complementarity and interdependence within linked sets of modern institutions, the obstacles to their coordinated establishment, their impact on production systems, their degree of congruence with previously existing institutions, and their different accessibility and benefits to various segments of the population, I have evaluated the contribution of modern institutions to socioeconomic development in a particular set of government-sponsored programs.

In this particular case the institutions through which the government aimed to promote rural development led instead to increased social inequality and contributed to program failure. These institutions comprised a new social and economic order into which the government attempted to integrate some members of an excluded, impoverished class. Their interdependence, however, so complicated the programs designed to implement them that the responsible government agencies were not able to coordinate their work and the majority of the rural poor could not adapt to them or assume their extra costs. The inadequacy of transport and communication over a large, sparsely settled, and difficult terrain, discontinuities in funding, and the opposition of economically powerful groups all prevented the full establishment of the set of institutions presupposed by the colonization plans. The new institutions were only partially established—at different rates across time and space—even though they tended to invalidate prior social and economic arrangements. The rural development programs thus brought about rapid but incomplete changes in the institutions legitimating and guaranteeing the occupation and use of land and regulating access to credit. Adaptation to these rapid and partial institutional changes required capital, access to information and to technical or juridical assistance, and, frequently, political influence. As small farmers did not have these resources, they lost out to those who did. The effects of the imposition of modern institutions were directly opposite of the results for which they were intended.

The failure of many of the original colonists and their replacement by more prosperous farmers from other regions were direct results of the high costs of adaptation to a complex set of modern institutions. Such adaptation would have involved some costs in any event, but the government's failure to coordinate the establishment of such institutions increased the farmers' cost of adaptation to each institution and reduced whatever benefits the colonists might have derived from the entire set of new institutions if they had functioned as planned. The costs of adaptation were high, but they were also fixed: They did not vary with the amount of capital invested or the area cultivated. Success, therefore, depended on a scale of operation large enough to offset the high fixed costs of bureaucratic procedures. The colonization projects attracted farmers who had sold land in other regions. These migrants bought rights to the land and to the improvements on it from original colonists who could no longer obtain credit because of past debts. Such purchases became especially attractive after 1976, when more credit was available for the most profitable perennial crops and when many of the worst infrastructural problems had been solved. Complications in the titling process, however, often delayed even a relatively well-capitalized newcomer's credit plans long enough to exhaust his resources and lead to second and even third departures from the same lot.

The rural development programs worked directly against those small farmers for whom the accumulated costs of complying with the bureaucratic requirements outweighed the commercial value of the financed crop. These same programs then exacerbated the inequalities between the farmers who sustained losses on their financed crops and those who, by good fortune, relative proximity to administrative centers, or sufficient capital, had managed to comply with bureaucratic requirements for the documentation of personal identity, land title, and credit for perennial crops on a scale large enough to offset the fixed costs of this compliance. This second group's access to increasing amounts of credit, in turn, enabled its members to buy the land rights of failed farmers in the first group. The rising demand for land increased land prices and made sale a more attractive option for the farmers who did not have access to sufficient credit. For most of those who sold their land rights, however, much of what they received went to pay off bad debts and to finance a move to a new location. Those who stayed in the area usually found little investment opportunity for the small stake they had left, and they frequently ended up working for hire in conditions similar to those from which they had originally been recruited into the colonization programs.

There were several mutually reinforcing causes of the eventual failure of the Transamazon colonization program. Soils and climate were essentially unsuitable for the annual crops which the original planners had supposed would support the colonists. The high costs to government of road construction and maintenance and of developing extension and administrative systems generated significant opposition from politically powerful groups, which demanded other allocations of both public funds and public lands. The severe balance-of-payments problems, which originated in Brazil's dependence on foreign capital for much of its rapid industrial growth, were aggravated by great increases in oil prices after 1973. These events reinforced pressures to exploit the Amazon for rapid economic returns rather than for social welfare goals (Brasil, 1975). Any of these three problems alone would have made sustained, effective implementation of the colonization plans more difficult; together they posed formidable obstacles to their continuity and eventual success. The analysis in this chapter, however, is limited to the effects of the incomplete and partially integrated establishment of modern capitalist institutions on the individuals who had to assume the costs of adapting to these institutions. I have shown that the costs to the farmers of satisfying the bureaucratic procedures required for participation in the colonization and production-support programs were likely to outweigh the benefits of such participation. They accounted for a significant portion of their individual failures and thus for the failure of the original program goals. I have also shown that the relation of costs to benefits of participation in these programs favored more highly capitalized farmers and led to their increasing ability to displace their less prosperous fellows.

This analysis does not demonstrate that modern institutions are necessarily anti-economic for peasants who are trying to become commercial farmers, but it does indicate some of the ways that precipitous or premature modernization may impede development and some of the complexities and pitfalls facing governments that attempt to impose entire new sets of exogenous modern institutions on an unprepared population. Equally important, it also shows that differential access to modern institutions may function to create inequalities that parallel those caused by differential access to modern technology. The inherent limitations of a single-case analysis are offset in this study by the identification of processes and mechanisms whose presence, absence, or degree can be specified in examinations of similar cases.

This study suggests that the relation of costs and benefits of modern institutions is affected by: (1) the relations between specific new institutions and productive systems, (2) the degree of congruence between new and previously existing institutions, (3) the interdependence and complementarity of the new institutions, and (4) the temporal and spatial obstacles which may impede their coordinated establishment. To the extent that institutions are interconnected and complementary, they typically must be established in sets, rather than separately, or they will not function to promote the ends for which they were designed. If there are missing pieces, each separate institution's effect on productivity will be diminished or nullified, even though its costs for the affected population may remain the same.

Modernization programs aimed at the least dynamic sectors or the poorest populations are most likely to result in the incomplete establishment of institutional sets. Government resources are scarce, especially in underdeveloped countries, and subject to multiple demands. Those sectors that are already highly productive and already adapted to and use more complex sets of modern institutions are likely to compete most effectively for these resources. This competition may limit or interrupt the resources which governments can or will commit to institution-building programs in the less developed sectors. The costs of adaptation to the incomplete or disarticulated sets of institutions which result from political and budgetary restrictions on such programs are likely to be transferred to the target population, whose production levels are probably too low to sustain such costs.

The specific focus in this chapter has been on the costs of individual participation in and adaptation to modern institutions. It should be clear, however, that establishing and maintaining these modern institutions involved considerable direct costs to government, and to specific agencies as well, and that the high rate of individual failure and land sales increased these costs. The intensely modern procedures employed on the Transamazon highway absorbed over three-fourths of the rural development budgets for the entire state of Pará and, even so, benefited a minority of the 9,000 families in the various colonization projects.

The practical implications of this study depart little from common sense; careful and coordinated scrutiny of all aspects of the plans for the colonization projects and of the ecological constraints under which they would operate should have been adequate to foresee most, if not all, of the outcomes reported here. Practically, therefore, this study may serve best as a caveat that modern institutions which work well for regions, or groups, whose economies are modern may fail for regions and groups whose economies are not modern. It also stands as a reminder that institutions must be planned as sets, rather than as the separate domains of disparate public agencies. The theoretical implications, however, invite more discussion. Where previous studies have suggested that some aspects of modernization may retard development, they have either focused on indirect effects of modern institutions, such as increased consumption, resistance to mobilization, or a tendency to migrate (Portes, 1973b, 1976), or they have interpreted the imposition of exogenous modern institutions as a reflex of more fundamental economic dependencies which tend to maintain underdevelopment (Delacroix and Ragin, 1978:135-36).

The analysis in this chapter outlines specific economic processes through which modern institutions directly retard planned development and increase social inequality within a specific population. Its findings are compatible with models of unequal exchange within a world economic system. The interaction between the world capitalist market and local modes of extraction and production and the recent mediations of the dependent capitalist Brazilian state led to the demographic and political conditions under which the colonization programs were attempted. The capacity of modern bureaucracies to impose new sets of institutions and the inability of Amazonian communities either to moderate their impact or to afford the cost of adapting to them are compatible with my model of ways that unbalanced energy flows enhance organizational complexity and social power in productive economies and decrease them in extractive economies.

The analysis in this chapter, however, does not rely on this model to explain the internal processes which led to the failure of these particular development programs. Thus it avoids the problems involved in analogous extension to the local level of models developed to explain unequal exchange between nations (see Portes, 1976, 1980). Rather, this chapter demonstrates that the economic effects of politically and administratively imposed modern institutions can be assessed within the framework of modernization theories if we examine directly observable economic and political behaviors of the national state and different classes. Indeed, the analysis suggests that the peculiar contradictions between the imperatives of economic growth and subjective legitimacy which the national state seeks in its rural development programs must take modernity, as ideology and as bureaucratic organization and procedure, into account. It also suggests that the concepts of functional specificity, differentiation, and social complexity, which inform Smelser's and Eisenstadt's structural theories of modernization, are essential for analyzing the effects of certain kinds of state intervention in noncapitalist economies, but that the phenomena to which these concepts refer may have highly irrational results which these authors did not anticipate. Such direct observation of internal process necessarily limits us to the close analysis of specific cases, whose particular characteristics may not lend themselves to direct generalization. Nevertheless, this kind of analysis does allow us to incorporate statements about process into our examinations of highly abstract concepts such as modernity, change, and development.

NOTES

1. The costs are not only narrowly economic, although these costs are the ones treated here, but they also include the social disruption and suffering resulting in part from the violent competition over control of the resources made accessible by publicly financed infrastructure, credit subsidies, and fiscal incentives opened up for profitable exploitation, and for which the central state's institutions were not sufficiently developed to control (Foweraker, 1981).

2. In some areas of traditional settlement, the imposition of INCRA as the normative agency for land title has actually disrupted previous sytems of bank credits for agriculture. In these areas some ranchers and farmers received credit on the basis of various land documents and/or personal prestige with the banks. Even though these documents may have presumptive validity until contrary decision by INCRA, their effective value is annulled if a bank manager decides that he needs the security of the INCRA title. Thus the INCRA delays put even those rural enterprises which were formerly working with bank credit at a competitive disadvantage with those more recently established that had INCRA documents.

3. Author's estimate based on various INCRA documents.

4. Of the perennial crops, only sugar cane produces in its first year; however, it is the most restrictive, as it depends on proximity to a sugar mill. In 1977 less than 400 farmers grew sugar cane on commercial scale in the colonization areas of Pará.

CHAPTER 7

Collaboration, Competition, and Corruption in Two Colonization Projects

The disjunctures, discrepancies, and distortions of rural development organization and policy that resulted from the power differentials and bargaining between agencies and from the haphazard imposition of modern institutions created multiple problems within the field offices of the various development agencies and forced major departures from normal bureaucratic procedures and expectations. The isolation of the rural communities, the distance from and the difficulty of communication with agency headquarters, and the close contact in which field agents lived with their own superiors in the small towns in which they worked gave their superiors control over agents' personal lives, well beyond the bureaucratically defined limits of their authority. At the same time the requirements of community acceptance impelled supervisors to concern themselves about the off-job conduct of their subordinates. All of these factors combined to extend the agent's relations to the agency into most aspects of his personal life and magnified the difficulties that organizational disjunctures imposed on them.

These same circumstances also provided opportunities for corruption and official deviance. Obviously, some violations of agency procedures, regulations, and norms occurred in order to facilitate the agents' work or to relieve the farmer-clients from impossible requirements. Agents required to verify farmers' compliance with their credit projects frequently filled out forms without visiting farmers' lots to avoid delays in financing. This shortcut solved problems of lack of transport, bad or impossible roads, excess work, or personal indisposition, but it greatly increased the risks that credit would not be used for its stated purpose. Agents might also fill out forms for crop production estimates without verifying their information. On the negative side, agents used agency vehicles for their own purposes and used their bureaucratic positions for personal monetary gain by providing professional services for a fee to large enterprises not qualified to participate in programs established for low-income farmers or by exorting money directly from their small farming clients.

Public control of crucial resources, the close living and working relations of rural development agents, and the distance of their work sites from central administrative control affected the forms and the effects of corruption. The analysis of corruption on the Transamazon, like the analysis of modern institutions, shows that the phenomena which modernization theories discuss have important effects on the outcome of development plans, but that the explanations of these phenomena suggested by modernization theories do not work for these cases.

Corruption aggravated the inefficiencies and distortions resulting from the delays and omissions of the various interdependent rural development agencies. The Banco do Brasil suffered embezzlement, and some of its agents received kickbacks. Some INCRA personnel demanded bribes for access to good lots or expedition of the titling process. Many functionaries of the various agencies purchased lots in the colonization areas, either through power of attorney or in the name of relatives or spouses. They thus contributed to the inflation of land prices which encouraged many colonists to sell their use rights. These functionaries occupied particularly favored positions to get bank loans, to avoid the long lines at the CIBRAZEM warehouses, to receive special technical orientation, and to benefit from other government assistance programs through the informal exchange networks that emerged among the lot owners in the various agencies. These networks became sufficiently dense to impede the agencies' willingness to bring pressure to bear on other agencies whose inefficient performance created difficulties in the work of the rest. The private prosperity of numerous agents depended on interagency good will, which created considerable pressure against criticism or complaints to administrative headquarters.

Some government agents also bought crops directly from the farmers. Usually working through employees or partners, in some cases their own relatives, they could take advantage of their special relations with CIBRAZEM personnel to avoid the long waits in line and the CFP's regulation restricting minimum price payments to the producers themselves or to buyers who could prove that they themselves paid the minimum price. They could thus achieve a high rate of return and a rapid turnover on their investment. With some crops, such as pepper and cocoa, market prices were so much higher in Belém than on the highway that the agents made returns of up to 50 percent even after paying for shipping. CIBRAZEM employees also colluded with the private sector intermediaries to accept the rice they bought at low prices from the farmers. In addition to distorting official policy, this corruption aggravated the delays that motivated the farmers' sales to private buyers.

The government employees were in an excellent position to buy good land, to develop it, and to buy crops from other farmers, both because they knew how to work the agency system and because they had a secure, and, for the region, relatively large income to invest. They received free housing and use of official transport for at least part of their travel. Their access to credit as lot owners and their rapid return as crop buyers magnified the power and effect of their basic capital. Collectively, these agents' corruption had considerable impact on the areas they worked in. What is particularly interesting about corruption in the colonization projects, however, is that its incidence varied enormously between projects. This variation requires further explanation than that provided by modernization alone.

Violation of administrative rules and procedures by government officials may constitute a major obstacle to the effective implementation of national development programs. Whatever positive functions bureaucratic corruption may have in bending inappropriate or excessively rigid regulations or directives (Merton, 1957; Leff, 1964; Scott, 1969; Nye, 1967), realization of central planning goals is impeded to the extent that individual functionaries can change or negotiate their assigned tasks (Weinstein and Weinstein, 1982). Official corruption and the imperfect hierarchical control which it indicates occur in all state apparatuses, but many authors suggest that it is a particularly acute problem for the less developed nations (Bretton, 1962; Myrdal, 1968; McMullan, 1961; Bayley, 1966; Huntington, 1968; Horowitz, 1972). Their explanations for why this might be so are not particularly satisfying, however, and many are seriously flawed by the evaluative comparisons between industrial and nonindustrial societies implicit in modernization theories. They tend to attribute corruption in less developed countries to the lack or weakness of modern traits in either the bureaucratic apparatus itself or in the individual attitudes of bureaucratic agents. Neither the explanations that characterize the state in less developed countries as "weak," "soft," "patrimonial," or "prismatic" nor those that emphasize the failure of universalistic norms to overcome the particularities of kinship obligations, ethnic group loyalty, or regional identity can account for the different degrees of official corruption which have been detected in settings with similar social, cultural, and political characteristics, or even within the same country at different points in time or in different locations. Adequate explanation of such differences depends on organizational and behavioral—rather than on generic or cultural—variables.

Rather than considering corruption as reflecting different degrees of modernization, it is more plausible to assume that official corruption will occur in any bureaucracy unless the advantages or gains that illicit behavior provides are outweighed by negative consequences. I believe the degree of informal, interpersonal opposition or cooperation within and between official agencies is a key factor in determining the incidence of official corruption. Opposition between the functionaries of government agencies serves to reduce corruption by assuring the mutual vigilance of the actors involved and by preventing the opportunities for collusion or acquiescence that are necessary for corruption to occur. This thesis can be examined by comparing the organization and the extent of official corruption in the agencies involved in two different rural development projects along the Transamazon highway.

In order to examine this thesis, I follow a strategy used by Blau (1954) to analyze the different effects of competitiveness and cooperation on performance in a bureaucracy. Blau held other variables constant by studying two different sections of a public employment agency in which the duties of the functionaries were essentially alike. In this study I compare the degrees of corruption in two different colonization and rural development projects run by the same agencies involved in the same basic tasks and bound by the same official procedural prescriptions. Agency organization was identical in the two projects, and the agents in each project were recruited from the same populations and had similar work experiences, social and economic status, formal education, and regional origins. None of the agencies involved distinguished between personnel assigned to work in either of the two projects; rather, positions in each project were filled from the available personnel already in each agency as the need arose. There is a crucial difference between Blau's research case and this one, however. Blau analyzed the effects of interpersonal competition and collaboration within two offices of the same agency on illicit procedural behaviors engaged in to enhance the recorded work rates and other criteria that determined promotion and tenure. I analyze the effects of competition and collaboration among the functionaries of different agencies on the level of activities expressly forbidden by their employee status or which involved illicit use of agency resources or authority for their direct monetary gain. Illicit procedural conduct similar to that described by Blau occurred, but it was related to structural incompatibilities between the tasks assigned to agents and the agencies' goals and procedures and the resources available to carry them out. In the projects analyzed here such procedural violations were viewed as a solution to inappropriate regulations rather than as a means to personal gain and were common to all of the projects investigated.

Both of these projects were equivalent units—"integrated colonization projects" in the Brazilian government's National Integration Program. Various federal and state development agencies were assigned specific tasks in each of these projects. The project offices of each agency responded directly to their respective state or national headquarters. The projects were thus administratively equivalent and independent of each other. Recruitment and assignment of functionaries were controlled by headquarters, so each agency's project offices were staffed from a common population. The small-farming settlers in each project were drawn from similar populations. Program policies were centrally determined and simultaneously imposed on each project. The preexisting physical and social environments were quite similar—both projects were set up in primary forest, recently opened up by the new highway—and, except for a two-year difference in starting dates, the time periods analyzed here are the same. In one of these projects, however, a large number of functionaries illicitly exploited their agencies' material and jurisdictional resources for their own personal gain, while in the other this type of corruption was effectively controlled. This strong contrast between the behaviors of public officials within highly similar geographical, political, administrative, and temporal frames, together with the extreme geographical isolation of each project, provides a useful case for analyzing the effects of interpersonal behaviors and relations on corruption, as it effectively "holds constant" contextual variables such as the nature of the state and cultural variables such as kinship obligations, ethnic identity, or regional bias.

I avoid the question of the relative prevalence of corruption in underdeveloped countries as essentially unanswerable, both because of the extreme imprecision of actual measures of corruption and because different societies diverge in their definitions of corrupt behavior (Bayley, 1966). By defining official corruption as the illicit use of public agencies' material and jurisdictional resources, the violation of agency rules and procedures, or the failure to follow official directives for personal gain, I avoid problems of cultural relativity. Rather, I focus on corruption as an organizational problem, taking as a point of departure ideas derived primarily from Crozier's (1964) and Dalton's (1959) analyses of bureaucratic conflict and from Homans's (1950, 1974), Blau's (1964), and Olson's (1965) notions of exchange. These studies suggest two modalities of organization behavior: first, a perpetual struggle by actors to expand the authority, scope, or influence conferred by the positions which they occupy; second, a series of accommodations or exchanges worked out between actors in which the continuation of rewards to any one of them depends largely on the continued satisfaction or, alternatively, on the effective fear of either loss or punishment, of all the rest. If this is so, corruption is most likely to occur in situations characterized by high degrees of collaborative exchange between individual bureaucratic agents and is much less likely to occur where these relations are marked by antagonistic opposition. Organizational variables can then account for the predominance of either of these two modalities. In order to examine this proposition, I analyze the relative degrees of collaborative exchange and opposition among the functionaries of different government agencies and the effects these had on the incidence of corruption in the two colonization projects.

Toward a Theoretical Explanation of Corruption

Numerous theoretical approaches could easily incorporate positions based on antagonistic-collaborative relations in order to explain the emergence and maintenance of official corruption (e.g., Simmel, 1950, 1955; Coser, 1956; Dahrendorf, 1958, 1959; Bottomore, 1965), but a combination of conflict and exchange perspectives seems especially powerful. Public agencies depend on functionaries' compliance with the responsibilities and norms which define their positions and functions, prohibit private use or ownership of agency resources, and prescribe obedience to legitimate authority (Weber, 1947; Barnard, 1938; Selznick, 1949). Public agency control over significant resources which individual functionaries may be able to use in their own interests, however, provides one of the necessary conditions for collaboration and exchange among these functionaries (Blau, 1964; Homans, 1950, 1974; Olson, 1965). Because the correction of an agent's malfeasance or omission usually depends on clients or colleagues appealing to other functionaries, in the same or in other public agencies, excessive solidarity within or between public agencies increases the possibility that functionaries may use the agency's control over resources to benefit themselves at the client's (and the agency's) cost.

Executive control over significant resources provides opportunities for collaborative exchange between functionaries, but bureaucratic hierarchies and the delegation of authority within them may also stimulate struggles for power and dominance within and between public agencies. In contrast to those studied by Blau (1964), Homans (1950, 1974), and Olson (1965), the bureaucrats described by Crozier (1964) and Dalton (1959) are perceived to operate under the strategies of a zero-sum game, in which their own prestige, the possibility of promotion, and access to organizational resources depend on increasing their own strength and the strength of their departments and on weakening that of their competitors. Both of these analysts found that bureaucrats (individually and in groups) use areas of uncertainty not covered by the rules and omissions, errors, or shortcomings of other individuals and groups to increase their own areas of action and authority and to control additional organizational resources. Crozier (1964:156) described those strategies as follows: "Each group fights to preserve and enlarge the area upon which it has some discretion, attempts to limit its dependence on other groups and to accept such dependence only insofar as it is a safeguard against another and more feared one, and finally prefers retreatism if there is no other choice but submission. The group's freedom of action and the power structure appear clearly to be at the core of all such strategies."

The strategies described by Blau, Homans, and Olson, on the one hand, and by Crozier and Dalton, on the other, do not reflect totally discrepant theoretical positions but rather describe two different types of possible bureaucratic behavior. These different types of behavior can account for both the emergence of corruption and for the spread and persistence of corrupt activities.

Discovery and Discretion in the Study of Corruption

Evidence of corruption first emerged while I was collecting data on the effects of agency interdependence on project performance. It had become apparent to me that in one of the projects—Project A—the director of one of the agencies refused to report the omissions and inefficiences of another agency to his agency headquarters, even though these were impeding his performance. Attempts to elicit an explanation from him created obvious tension; an agent standing behind the director signaled me to change the subject. This agent—whom I had already interviewed several times—later explained that the director could not complain about other agencies' performance because his involvement in various corrupt activities made him highly vulnerable to reprisal. The agent was then willing to list the various forms of official corruption and to explain how they worked, but would not say which other agents were involved. With this information I could elicit information about corrupt activities from the colonists and other agents over the next eighteen months, though I made no attempt to gather systematic data until the end of the field work, and I never broached the issue of corruption directly. I traveled extensively with various agents, and I frequently stayed overnight in agency houses; I knew many of the agents well and could observe them closely. A great deal of information gathered from conversations between agents was later used to formulate questions about the activities of particular agents who appeared to be engaged in illicit activities.

A number of agents—both corrupt and those opposed to corruption—were willing to discuss corrupt behavior more openly as it became clear that I already knew a lot about it. Nine agents were willing to discuss their own corrupt activities, and multiple reports were used to corroborate the activities of others who were not so forthcoming. Five agents who had attempted to complain about corruption in their own and other agencies were willing to provide further details and to explain how their own complaints had been blocked at the project level. Finally, a large number of colonists mentioned official corruption but in most cases were unwilling to name corrupt agents. A lot-by-lot analysis of land ownership in selected areas at the end of the research revealed that at least half of the public agents and over 80 percent in one agency in Project A had bought lots legally reserved for colonists. Attempts to determine the precise number of agents involved in illicit crop buying so aggravated the anxieties provoked by my land-ownership survey that the effort was not concluded, although it was possible to identify at least 25 percent of one agency's field staff as having engaged in this activity. Information about the other types of corrupt activity analyzed here—which included extortion from colonists for assignment to lots with good soil, drainage, and road access or for rapid access to the warehouses which provided official minimum prices as well as the use of government vehicles to transport crops—is based on mutually corroborating reports by various public agents and colonists. In all of these interviews I attempted to elicit specific dates of alleged corruption to permit later analysis of the emergence and evolution of these behaviors.

I followed similar procedures in Project B, the other project that replicated all of the administrative, geographical, and ecological characteristics of Project A. Interviews were conducted with ninety-seven agents in the two projects; twenty-seven of these were interviewed at approximate three-month intervals over a period of two years.

Interagent Networks and Differential Risk in the Emergence of Corruption

The first question raised is how and why corrupt behavior emerged in Project A and was controlled in Project B. Agents in Project B reported that they routinely informed their project directors of omissions and malfeasance in their own and in other agencies and that these complaints were routinely referred to higher authorities if they could not be resolved at the project level. Following the clue provided by this marked contrast with Project A, I sought indications of differential interagent solidarity in the two projects.

I found that housing arrangements and the distribution of residence created marked differences in the personal relations between agents across agency boundaries in the two projects. In Project A residence patterns promoted extensive interagency networks of friendship, co-operation, and collaborative exchange. Residence patterns in Project B, however, created considerable social distance between the agents of different agencies.

In Project A colonists were first settled in widely dispersed "agrovilas," integrated communities for colonists which also served as support bases for the various agencies. As a result, individual agents of the several agencies lived as neighbors in a series of small, self-contained planned communities. There were ample opportunities for collaboration and cooperation in improving their own living conditions, developing social relations, and sharing work activities. Agents from different agencies visited farms together, shared rides into the town that served as ad-ministrative headquarters, visited each other after work, and lent each other tools and equipment.

The interaction between agents in Project A was heightened by the formation of a very active social club in the administrative center—and by the fact that the administrative center was the only place where agents could go for weekend relaxation. Marriages also occurred across agency lines. Thus, the members of the different agencies collaborated with each other to satisfy many of their work, residential, and recre-ational needs. All of this led to complex exchange networks between them.

The colonists themselves, however, preferred to live on their own lots rather than in the agrovilas. Thus, when Project B was initiated a year later, the agrovilas were not built there. The major agencies es-tablished their main residence bases in three different administrative centers, so that most members of each agency resided in close proximity to each other and far from members of other agencies. Furthermore, none of the administrative centers offered the joint recreational centers or other shared attractions of the Project A administrative center. Project B, unlike Project A, was located a relatively short distance—about 100 miles over precarious but usually passable roads—from a major town which offered a wide range of diversion. Agents tended to go there with other agents of their own agency, but they were not dependent on each other for amusement once they arrived.

The consequences of these very different social relations were evident in the reactions to the first type of corruption which occurred in either of the projects. INCRA officials were in charge of distributing lots to the colonists. Differences in soil fertility, topography, and distance to the main road and to administrative centers created great variation in the potential value of different lots. In both projects INCRA officials attempted to extort payment from colonists for preferred lots and, in a smaller number of cases, attempted to dispossess colonists living on particularly desirable lots in order to settle a relative, friend, or prosperous ally there.

Redress for individual colonists depended on access to other officials of the same or of other agencies. As access to administrative centers was difficult and relatively expensive, redress could best be sought through the agents with whom the colonists had routine contact. In Project A these tended to be agents who were living in close proximity to and working with the corrupt INCRA officials. Colonists interviewed in Project A reported that their complaints were met with only counsel to be silent, threats of expulsion, or the withholding of other benefits and support.

In Project B, on the other hand, colonists who complained of extortion or of lot expropriation by INCRA officials found ready allies in EMATER agents, whose usual response was to take the complaint to their own supervisors, who in turn brought these matters to the attention of the INCRA supervisor. Four different agents and two colonists spontaneously and independently recounted an early incident in which the EMATER project director reported the INCRA project director's refusal to sanction an INCRA agent—his relative—for illegally expropriating a colonist's lot. All reports said this accounted for the continued "bad blood" between the two agencies in Project B.

Similar sequences of events distinguished Projects A and B in the other forms of corruption that emerged during the colonization process. Agent crop-buying and lot purchase started within the first two years of each project's development, but they were rapidly checked in Project B. Complaints from agents in various agencies resulted in immediate cessation of the corrupt practice or, in three cases, transfer. No formal complaints were recorded in Project A, however, and the corrupt practices became fairly common. Again, colonists in Project A reported that their complaints or reports to other field agents were ignored or resulted in threats.

That field agents lived in close proximity to their supervisors in Project B and that most lived at some distance from their supervisors in Project A do not account satisfactorily for the difference between the two projects. Most attempts at corruption in Project B occurred in the agent's work areas, where they were as far removed from supervision as were the agents of Project A. Furthermore, all of these complaints were made by other field agents following reports by colonists themselves. Finally, in Project A, there was as much corruption close to the administrative centers as there was farther away from them. In fact, as noted earlier, some of the Project A directors were themselves corrupt.

I examined several alternative explanations of the different levels of illicit behavior in the two projects, such as possible effects of recruitment patterns, nepotism, differential opportunities for illicit behavior between agencies, and the possibility that different procedures for reporting agents' work schedules or procedures governing tenure and promotion might affect opportunities for corruption. None of these possible explanations, however, fits the case. Agency directors at the project level had no control over recruitment; their influence on staffing was limited to the right to recommend transfer or dismissal of an agent and this required them to show cause. While there was evidence that political and family pressures affected a relatively small number of employment decisions in several of the agencies, these pressures only functioned at the hierarchical levels where employment decisions were made, that is, at the state, regional, and national levels which provided the population from which project-level functionaries were drawn. There was no evidence that political and family considerations entered into assignment of an agency employee to an office in one of these projects or elsewhere, except in the sense that political leverage might have helped to avoid assignment to these projects, which were generally considered undesirable because of their remote locations and the general lack of social amenities. Such considerations, however, were applicable to both projects.

Nepotism can also be dismissed as an explanation. In each project there were a few cases of relatives working in the same agency, but in neither project was there any evidence of kinship between project-level functionaries and their supervisors beyond the project. This lack of evidence cannot be absolutely conclusive because these and similar questions could not be asked directly, especially with reference to specific agents, but sufficiently good rapport was established in so many wide-ranging discussions that it is highly unlikely that such cases would not have been mentioned if they did occur.

The different organizational histories, culture, and procedures in the various agencies themselves did provide different opportunities for illicit behavior, but, because the same agencies functioned in each project, these differences cannot account for the different levels of corruption between projects. Procedures and forms for reporting task completion and the criteria for tenure and promotion were also identical within agencies. Blau (1954) concluded that different criteria for promotion and for reporting work were significantly related to the different levels of illicit behavior he discovered between two offices of the same agency. The directors of the offices he studied, however, had far greater procedural discretion and far more control over the promotion and tenure of their subordinates than did the project-level agency directors in this case. We can also dismiss the effects of prior political and economic arrangements in the areas where these projects were established. The projects themselves were established in sparsely settled jungle and indigenous and peasant occupants of the area were soon expelled (Davis, 1977, Moran, 1981). Administrative offices were established in small towns that were already near each of the colonization offices, but prior social organization in these areas was radically changed by the influx of government officials and colonists, who far exceeded the original inhabitants in both number and in political and economic power. Finally, because the analysis covered each project from the date of its inception, there is no previous project history to account for.

Comparison of the emergence of corruption in these two projects supports my argument that corruption results from organizational and interpersonal variables rather than from varying degrees of bureaucratic or attitudinal modernity. Individual collaborative exchange relations across agency boundaries enhanced the possibilities of official corruption by reducing the incentives for individuals, and therefore for agencies, to report the illegal activities of others and by creating a cohesive front against which it was much less likely that the victim of corrupt practices could seek redress. In the contrasting case antagonistic relationships between government agents of different agencies reduced the possibilities of official corruption by sustaining incentives for individuals and departments to watch for and report the illegal activities and omissions of others and by creating a situation in which a victim of corrupt practices had multiple opportunities to find bureaucratic actors interested in using his complaint against the functionaries of other agencies.

Reinforcement of Collaboration and Surveillance

My second task was to explain why the corrupt practices initiated within collaborative exchange relations increased. The opportunity to extort payment for favorable lots ended when the settlement phase was completed, but the difficulties confronted by the colonists predisposed many of them to sell their lots. The precarious conditions of the access roads and long lines at the warehouses encouraged them to sell their crops to private buyers below the established minimum prices. Both of these conditions provided agents with ample opportunities for illicit personal gain. Increasing numbers of agents in Project A bought lots: At the time of field work over 80 percent of the agents in one agency were owners, in some cases of several lots. Crop buying not only spread, but it became centrally organized as soon as the slower growing perennial crops of high value (particularly cocoa and pepper) began to yield. By that time, former field officers who had engaged in these illegal transactions had risen to supervisory positions and were able to use a wide network of friendships with other agents, including their own subordinates, to coordinate, systematize, and extend the various illicit sources of profit.

The director of one of the agencies in Project A was the major partner in, and his brother was manager of, a local company which bought over 60 percent of all the cocoa produced there until 1977, when other buyers took a share of the market. Most loan proposals prepared by EMATER also indicated this same company as the source of the agricultural implements to be purchased with the loan monies. Much of the cocoa this company bought was delivered by agents in agency vehicles. At least a fourth of this agency's functionaries regularly received illicit commissions for crop buying, for channeling agricultural purchases paid for with loan monies through the company, and for including unnecessary items in the credit proposals they prepared. The store would pay the colonist a portion of the cash value of such items and then collect the entire amount from the bank. This procedure, which the colonists accepted because it gave them access to cash, was clearly illegal and inflated the colonists' indebtedness beyond repayment capability. In addition, the direct participation of some agency supervisors in these types of corruption permitted the extension and coordination of the corrupt practices, making them more profitable, more regular, and less subject to risk for the individual agents. It also made it more dangerous for colonists or for other agents to complain or protest.

One of the main reasons for the rapid spread of corrupt activities in Project A was the growing evidence that agents could engage in them with impunity. Various agents interviewed mentioned that colleagues who had bought lots or crops from colonists had kept the lots or crop-sale proceeds without suffering any sanctions. They had seen other agents repeatedly using official vehicles to transport the pepper and cocoa which they had bought. The experience of having their own complaints about malfeasance in other agencies stop with their own immediate supervisors, together with the more affluent lifestyles of some of the corrupt agents, had also worked to convince them that there were considerable opportunities for profit and little danger of punishment in corrupt activities.

The existence of corrupt practices created new opportunities for illicit gain. The agents of the various agencies controlled access to resources which they could exchange among themselves. Thus, for example, any agent who bought a lot might need the collaboration of an INCRA agent, who had control over registering the lot, to avoid reporting his illegal tenure. This was often accomplished by permitting the legal forms, such as power of attorney or registration, to be listed in the name of a relative of the agent buyer. He could also benefit from (1) the assistance of the EMATER agent for technical agricultural orientation or the preparation of credit proposals; (2) the willingness of bank agents to approve bank loans; and (3) the collusion of the CIBRAZEM agent to accept his crops — or those he had bought from colonists — at the official prices and without the need to wait in line. The interdependence of the agencies thus created opportunities for corrupt agents to provide illicit access to their own agency's resources in exchange for illicit access to other agencies' resources. This increased the interdependence between the corrupt agents, their willingness to acquiesce to and even promote the corrupt behavior of agents in other agencies (even at the cost of their own agency's performance), and their cohesion in the face of complaints from settlers.

There were also various types of fraud which required the collaboration, or at least acquiescence, of the agents of various agencies, and, in some cases, the acquiescence or protection of supervisors. These frauds included: (1) charging more against a colonist's credit account than was actually paid and keeping the difference; (2) kickbacks on unnecesssarily expensive implements such as tractors bought on credit; and (3) bank collusion with private rice buyers who took out low-interest loans for nonexistent rice plantations. Participation in this system of exchange by members of all of these agencies was essential to prevent official complaints or disclosure of corruption; it also increased the profitability of lot ownership for the individual functionary. Credit theft and use of credit for unnecessary tools or in exchange for cash also increased the indebtedness of individual colonists and made them more likely to sell their lots.

The extent and scope of corrupt behavior in the major agencies and the direct involvement of high-ranking personnel in at least some of them functioned to prevent complaints or disclosures both within and between agencies. Agency control over the fate of individual colonists was sufficiently great and access to the appropriate official channels for complaint so difficult that their sporadic protests were consistently suppressed or contained within the project. Particular agents opposed to corrupt practices were restrained by pressure from their colleagues and fear of their superiors and also by the selectivity of their opposition. There were cases, for example, of lot owners who were opposed to bribery or to crop buying or of agents who opposed lot ownership but who had used their positions and contacts to settle and later help their relatives. While they could express personal disapproval of behavior they considered corrupt, they themselves were too vulnerable to other

charges to afford an open accusation. They also depended on cooperation with other corrupt agents for much of their own profit. The
interdependence of corrupt agents impeded solutions to the breakdown
in the coordinated performance of tasks. While the functionaries of
each agency perceived that their own performance was hampered by
inefficiencies in other agencies, they were reluctant to complain to their
regional headquarters for fear of disrupting the networks of individual
collusion and silence.

The existence of corruption and the evident impunity of corrupt
agents from sanctions stimulated a number of agents to encourage
relatives to move to the project as lot owners and businessmen. The
special relations between agents in Project A meant that illicit pref-
erential treatment could be arranged in procuring lots, in getting credit,
and in gaining access to other agencies' services. Relatives could be
attracted to the project by the offer of special help, and, once they
were there, they provided a trustworthy basis for the silent partnerships.
The agency director mentioned above, for example, could solve some
of the potential problems of not being able to appear as owner of
record of his company by counting on family loyalties to protect his
interests there. Thus, while the culture of kin relations—understood
as general within similar classes in Brazil and thus within the population
from which agents in both projects were drawn—was constant between
the projects, expanded opportunities for illicit gain encouraged the
migration of agents' relatives to Project A. Once these relatives were
there, they further enhanced the agents' opportunities for illicit gain.
So while the culture of kinship remained constant, the existence of
corruption in Project A increased residential proximity to and economic
collaboration with kin there. Marriage ties across agencies enhanced
the effective strength and scope of kin ties.

The reporting of corrupt practices in Project B, on the other hand,
served to increase the social distance between the agents of the various
agencies and transform the relationship into one of antagonistic surveillance. That colleagues within their agency had been sanctioned
because of reports by agents from other agencies, the knowledge that
their performance was subject to similar surveillance, and the realization
that settlers could find a willing ear for reports of malfeasance introduced tension into the relations between agents working in the same
area. Furthermore, as the fact of surveillance effectively eliminated
opportunities for illicit gain, performance within the agencies was the
only means of gain open to the agents. To the extent that their own
performance depended on the successful operation of their counterparts
in other agencies, they were inclined to complain not only about specifically illegal activities but also about poor performance or omission.

In this sense agents working in the same areas were mutually threatening.

Finally, that corrupt behavior was perceived as highly likely to be
reported and to lead to embarrassment for the agency itself, to discredit
the agency with the settlers, and possibly to bring sanctions on all of
the agents led the agents themselves to discourage corruption within
their own agencies. New agents were clearly informed about the risks
of corrupt behavior, and the project's reputation for not allowing corruption spread among the agents based in other areas. I could only
document two cases of functionaries buying crops; both were stopped
within their own agency before this was reported outside. Similarly, I
was able to document only three cases of functionaries buying land in
Project B. In one of these cases, the functionary was obliged by the
director of his agency to resell the lot. The other two functionaries
who bought lots were transferred out of the area.

Further, agents in Project B tended to take the colonists' side in
complaints against other agents and in some cases helped the colonists
organize formal protests. For example, two different CIBRAZEM functionaries in Project B attempted to exploit the storage and handling
limitations of their warehouses by demanding payment from settlers
for a place in line, and the crop classifiers demanded payment for
giving a reasonable classification and thus assuring a compensatory
price for their produce. CIBRAZEM functionaries also colluded with a
number of private crop buyers. The INCRA director twice protested
directly to CIBRAZEM regional offices and each time effected the removal of the CIBRAZEM manager. When the problem continued, functionaries of both INCRA and EMATER helped a settlers' cooperative
to organize and publicize a formal protest. This provoked an on-site
investigation by CIBRAZEM officials and assurances that they would
exercise greater vigilance over their own personnel.

Because interagent surveillance impeded corrupt practices in Project
B, the mutual dependency and resultant tolerance which protected
corrupt agents in Project A could not develop. As none of the functionaries who remained in the project were able to sell crops—either
their own or those bought from colonists—to the CIBRAZEM, there
was no incentive for them to protect CIBRAZEM functionaries against
the settlers' accusations of corruption. On the contrary, the EMATER
agents had strong reasons for supporting such accusations. The longer
a settler had to wait to deliver his rice and the larger the bribes he
had to pay in order to do so, the less likely he was to be able to pay
back his bank loan. As EMATER agents were responsible for these
loans, and as their possibilities for promotion were to some degree
dependent on their success, it was in their interest to eliminate all

possible obstacles to the settlers' selling their crops at a profit. In contrast to Project A, there was no alternate system of gain available to them by acquiescing to CIBRAZEM corruption. Similarly, there was no incentive for them to acquiesce to their colleagues' buying the farmers' crops, as this practice would also have reduced the settlers' eventual profit.

Thus, a key factor in explaining the different incidence of corruption in the two projects appears to be the disposition of individual agents and agencies to react against the corrupt practices of others and to support settler protests of deviant official behavior. As there were no other sources of profit that collusion would have made available in Project B, each agent's own best interest was served by restricting the opportunities for corruption of others. The few incidents of accusation and subsequent sanctions were widely known among all of the functionaries in Project B and served to restrict corruption further.

This comparison between the extension and maintenance of corruption in Project A and the control of corruption in Project B supports my argument against different degrees of modernity as an explanation of corruption. Corrupt activities in Project A strengthened the cohesion between individuals and agencies, as the rewards available from corrupt practices and the growing number of individuals involved heightened their mutual dependence on collaboration, acquiescence, and silence. Furthermore, an increase in the number of agents involved in corrupt practices also meant greater social pressure on others to engage in or tolerate the existence of these practices. This pressure increased as already corrupt agents were promoted to supervisory positions. This cohesion and resulting social pressures reduced the incentive to complain about inefficiencies and omissions in other agents' performance, even though an agent's job efficiency depended on other agents' activities.

On the other hand, when corrupt practices were initiated within the context of the antagonistic surveillance described in Project B, members of the agency in which these practices occurred acted to curtail them as quickly as possible, in order to prevent the loss of prestige or power which another agency's accusations might have brought about. If they were not successful in curtailing these practices quickly, other agencies were likely to do so by bringing them to public attention or by making formal complaints. Such complaints—and the threat that they might occur—increased the social distance, antagonism, and mutual surveillance between agents of the different agencies, especially where each agent's performance was dependent on the performance of the others. Finally, it was impossible to arrange special illicit advantages for agents' relatives, so there was little incentive—other than those of family solidarity—to encourage relatives to seek lots and business opportunities in Project B.

Interpersonal relations and the response to the existence of corrupt behavior in each project interacted in a circular fashion. Residence patterns in Project A fostered friendship, collaboration, and personal interdependence across agency boundaries and led to the tolerance and collusion necessary for corruption. Once corrupt practices were initiated and as they involved ever more of the functionaries of each agency, they reinforced the tolerance and discretion which had been necessary for their emergence. Residence patterns in Project B inhibited such solidarity, and early complaints between agencies fostered an attitude of antagonistic surveillance, which effectively prevented the emergence of corruption. This surveillance impelled each agency to guard continually against the malfeasance or omissions of the other.

Comparison of these two examples appears to support the proposition that the degree of antagonistic surveillance or collaborative exchange within and among bureaucratic agencies is a key determinant for the incidence of official corruption. But two cases can only be presented as possible bases for further research, although the theoretical argument behind them has clear implications for the effective control of corruption in interdependent bureaucratic agencies. Surveillance of *all* agencies is cumbersome, expensive, and subject to subversion. If the evidence I have gathered here is valid, however, it shows that effective resistance to corruption in only one agency may be sufficient to foster the competitive surveillance necessary to restrict corruption in other agencies. As soon as there are obstacles to individual gain through corruption in one agency, its agents may be forced to depend exclusively on performance for their own advancement. They may therefore tend to guard against all behaviors, including corruption, in other agencies and in their own which might reduce their own effective performance. Their surveillance would impede other agents' opportunities for corrupt gain and would thus force them also to depend on and secure their own performance potential.

Guaranteeing effective resistance to corruption in any one agency would require that local directors of that agency be recruited independently of any pressures (political or otherwise) which might compromise their capacity to control corruption in their own agency. It would also require that these directors be given sufficient support from the regional or national headquarters to resist the opposition to or sabotage of their programs by other agencies. While both of these requirements pose some difficulties, it would be clearly easier and less expensive to use vertical controls to keep a single agency free of corruption than it would be to control all of the interdependent agencies.

Such a solution, of course, requires that it is possible to establish and maintain at least one such agency corruption-free. It is not my intention to deny the significant organizational consequences of the "soft state" or of strong particularistic social norms. Both my theoretical proposition and policy suggestions, therefore, are only relevant where the state can control at least some of its own public agencies, and where agencies willing to complain can expect support from higher levels of the administration. The organizational perspective on corruption used here suggests that the modernization theories which focus on the relative strength of the state and its apparatus and on the attitudes and culture of bureaucrats do not provide an adequate explanation of why and how government functionaries violate the legal and procedual prescriptions for their positions. Rather, it suggests that specific modern bureaucratic forms superimposed on organizationally weak civil communities may engender numerous opportunities for corruption against which these communities themselves have no adequate defense. The very different incidence of corruption in these two projects in no way reflected the capacity of local or endogenous institutions to protect these communities. Rather, these differences are accounted for by organizational features within the exogenous bureaucracies. It may be the case that entire communities organized in and effectively integrated into functionally specific institutions do have effective alternative defenses against bureaucratic abuses of authority. We have seen in previous chapters, however, why these did not exist in the Amazon.

CHAPTER 8

The Failure of Cooperatives

We have now seen how the high costs of compliance with modern bureaucratic procedures led to severe distortion of the state's colonization and rural development programs in the Amazon. We have also seen that modern bureaucracies in the institutionally simple Amazon had such control over resources and local organization that the only effective check on corruption was from within the bureaucracy itself. The processes described in these cases could be explained without recourse to models of unbalanced energy flows from extractive to peripheral economics, if we simply departed from the affirmation that Amazonian rural communities were not adapted to dealing with complex modern bureaucracies. If we wish to explain why Amazonian communities were so weak in the first place, however, we must return to the history of extraction and its effects on social organization there. If we wish to understand why the bureaucracies concentrated so much control over the resources local communities needed, we must return to the social organizational results of intensified energy flows to productive centers.

Energy flows and their differential embodiment in complex social organization and infrastructure provide sociological complements to the ideas of labor value, prices, and profits, which economists use to distinguish articulated from disarticulated social formations. The disarticulated social formations of the periphery accumulate, concentrate, and direct much less human and nonhuman energy into the complex, highly differentiated, and institutionally integrated organizational and productive forms that characterize the articulated social formations of the core. The core society's capacity to concentrate and direct both human and nonhuman energy provide it with various forms of control—over markets, political organization, and productive resources—in or from the periphery.

The modern state and its bureaucracies constitute a particularly powerful instance of these energy-intensifying organizational forms. The individual agencies of the state, however, compete among themselves.

The separate bureaucratic agencies of the state can be described, following Adams (1982:16-19), as expansive dissipative structures which evolve toward increased energy consumption as long as adequate energy resources are available. This expansiveness and the associated competition between separate agencies enhance the distortions and the ultimate irrationalities of the modern state's attempts to direct and transform socioeconomic processes on its own periphery.

Various analyses of modern bureaucracies suggest that their agencies fit Adams's definition of expansive dissipative structures. Flannery's (1972) notions of hypercoherent complex institutions which become increasingly self-serving to the detriment of the organization from which they emerged to serve, Crozier's (1964) and Dalton's (1959) analyses of the competitive and expansive strategies of bureaucratic agencies and their departments, Block's (1977) view of the particular interests of state bureaucrats in the maintenance of their own positions and of the structures which define them, and Kraus, Maxwell, and Vanneman's (1979) analysis of the self-interests of bureaucrats all use different vocabularies, but they are consonant with an energetic model of the self-maintenance and expansiveness of separate dissipative structures within complex social structures.

Competition for resources between expansive agencies may be systemically rational within articulated social formations. These social formations are themselves expansive, and competition between agencies may actually mediate and rationalize both class conflict and competition for resources between dynamic sectors of the economy. Competition between agencies creates a mutual vigilance that makes compliance with state directives more likely. Finally, the existence of multiply differentiated, functionally specific, and interdependent self-serving organizations and agencies in the articulated social formation provides an extensive system of institutional checks on system-threatening or policy-distorting expansion strategies by particular agencies.

In the Amazon bureaucratic dissipative structures compete for resources within a statutory, budgetary, and policy environment defined almost exclusively by a central state capable of concentrating and directing far more energy than any set of local or endogenous organizations or institutions. Bureaucratic agencies of the central state, therefore, could expand, compete with each other, and strive to maintain themselves in system-destructive or policy-distorting ways, because there were no other local autonomous institutions which could call them to account. The bureaucratic agencies themselves controlled most of the resources relevant to their own competiton.

In order to maintain themselves, bureaucratic agencies must comply with and accomplish statutory, procedural, and policy goals and directives from the state, which delegates jurisdictional and budgetary power to them. The agencies want to accomplish these tasks at the least energy cost to themselves—so they can spend their energy in expanding and competing for more power—and the result may lead to formalistic and legalistic, rather than economically and socially viable, solutions to problems. In addition, the agencies that derive the greatest amounts of budgetary and jurisdictional power are the ones most adept at delegating the more onerous and politically least rewarding parts of their mandate to the weaker, dependent agencies, which are obliged to carry out these tasks in order to maintain or expand what limited functions and powers they have (Bunker, 1979).

Programs which aim at legitimating the state in disarticulated societies rather than at accelerating and facilitating nationally predominant modes of accumulation are especially likely to suffer these effects. Legitimacy-seeking social welfare programs typically aim to offset the effects of these modes of accumulation on classes or regions most excluded from their benefits (O'Donnell, 1978:19-20). Such attempts contradict the internal logic of the predominant mode of production in any social formation. Successful implementation is unlikely to gain significant political rewards and may provoke opposition from fractions of the dominant class. These programs are likely to be delegated to weaker agencies and are therefore susceptible to discontinuities, distortions, and interferences, as well as to insufficient funding and authority.

State programs to establish agricultural production cooperatives for small farmers in Pará constitute an extreme case of the contradictions between the predominant logic of accumulation and the legitimacy-seeking strategies of the state. In remote communities of agricultural producers in a disarticulated peripheral economy whose major exports were extractive, the populations affected by these programs had virtually no organized power base either to make claims against the agencies of the state or to reward them with effective political support.[1]

Cooperatives did, however, provide the state a potent set of legitimating symbols in the Amazon. Cooperative ideology invokes the reformist solutions to class conflict and exploitation which the Rochdale weavers originally devised to bypass intermediaries in the direct sale of their own product. It also invokes myths of upward mobility and prosperity which originated with the spectacular growth of the cooperatives of the American Midwest. Cooperatives provide an ideal vehicle for an income-concentrating capitalist regime's search for political legitimacy. With their emphasis on egalitarian participation, direct representation, member education, and collective solutions to commercial exploitation, they allow the regime which supports them to give the appearance of siding with the small, poor, direct producers against wealthier businessmen who benefit from their labor. The cooperative itself, however, implies no change in the regime of private property or in the distribution of land, and the intermediaries who are bypassed are generally small entrepreneurs. To the extent that the cooperative actually increases production and commerce of agricultural goods, it serves the state's interests at little political cost.

Agricultural cooperatives organized by small farmers achieved considerable economic success in various regions of the center-south of Brazil, where they played an important role in the rapid expansion of wheat and soy cultivation under an increased mechanization of agriculture and concentration of land tenure. Various agricultural colleges and universities there initiated special programs to train technicians in cooperative management and accounting, and the state governments ran special programs to promote cooperatives. The cooperatives themselves had in some cases formed special national and regional associations to promote their own interests and to diffuse their own ideology. The state could invoke these successes in its legitimacy-seeking programs to establish cooperatives in the poorer, noncapitalist agricultural regions.

The reformist ideology which cooperatives served to legitimate is evident in the land reform laws which govern INCRA. The Estatuto da Terra and later land legislation included a special type of cooperative, CIRA (Integral Cooperative for Agrarian Reform), as a required component of all nationally run colonization projects. INCRA, with legal authority and responsibility for both official colonization and for the registration and supervision of cooperatives, was thus legally required to establish a CIRA in each of its colonization projects in the Amazon. As with other aspects of the colonization projects, INCRA found it convenient to delegate this task to other, less powerful agencies without granting these agencies the autonomy or the secure budgets necessary to carry out the delegated tasks.

Earlier attempts to establish marketing cooperatives for small farmers in the Amazon foundered on a series of planning and administrative deficiencies, with disastrous consequences for both the farmers and the agencies involved. In 1962 the Banco de Crédito da Amazônia (BCA), the precursor of BASA, founded a series of agricultural cooperatives. In addition to providing technical assistance and bookkeeping, it made loans to the cooperatives for equipment, warehouses, and offices, and for crop financing. Accounting and control over application of individual credit were extraordinarily loose, and BASA ended this program in 1973 with heavy losses, leaving many badly indebted farmers unable to obtain credit from other banks.

Various government agencies in Pará were interested, for quite different reasons, in resuscitating some of the failed cooperatives which BASA had formerly supported. In addition to providing collectivist, democratically representative organizations in which small farmers could be presented as participating politically in an economic enterprise which they controlled themselves, cooperatives were seen variously as a means of stimulating agricultural exports, supplying staples to urban areas, breaking the stranglehold of the *aviamento* system in the riverine communities, enabling the members of failed cooperatives to pay off old debts and to assume new ones, and providing local organizations through which the various rural development agencies could do their work. They also presented an opportunity for the dependent agencies to bargain for resources from the more powerful agencies legally mandated to support and supervise cooperatives.

A task force with representatives from most of the agricultural and rural development agencies was assembled in 1974 to decide which of the failed BASA cooperatives could be revived. This group recommended six cooperatives from the BASA programs, and several more which had been established independently of BASA and which had continued to function, as worthy of salvaging. A multi-agency program, PICEP, was established for this purpose in 1975.

The problems which hindered effective planning and coordination between the various rural development agencies beset PICEP from its inception. The planning group could not make effective decisions because of the different levels of commitment and the different interests of the participating agencies. The hierarchical rank of each agency's representative to PICEP corresponded to the importance of PICEP for the agency itself. Thus, the representative from EMATER was empowered to make a number of decisions which significantly committed his agency, while the agents from the SUDAM, BASA, and to a lesser extent from INCRA were only able to report back to their superiors and await further orders before proceeding. As those superiors were generally involved in a number of other projects that they considered more important, these consultations caused considerable delay and frustration.

The original plans and enthusiasm for coordinated participation died a rapid and quiet death, never officially noted, and EMATER, with some material and logistic support from SAGRI (Pará's Secretariat of Agriculture) assumed more and more of the initiative. The complex legal, jurisdictional, and fiscal interests of the other agencies, EMATER's lack of independent funding, and the very different statutory, economic, and organizational condition of the various cooperatives weighed more in EMATER's programming than did the original plans drawn up by the multiagency task force. EMATER negotiated funding for three co-operatives from the SUDAM and for three more from POLAMAZONIA. It had to secure approval for all of its cooperative activities from INCRA, and it negotiated special arrangements and funding for each of the cooperatives that INCRA had founded along the Transamazon highway and was now requesting that EMATER supervise. It had to renegotiate bad debts with BASA and the other creditors for the failed cooperatives that the bank had lent money to, and it had to negotiate with the BNCC (National Cooperative Credit Bank) for crop purchase loans for various undercapitalized cooperatives. Most of these jobs were carried out under the supervision of two cooperative technicians, trained in the South, who had recently been hired by EMATER and who had to learn about the very different productive, commercial, political, and administrative systems they were confronting while carrying on these negotiations.

EMATER's program of cooperative development included orientation and technical assistance to two highly successful cooperatives which operated relatively close to Belém; one of these was run by local cattle raisers to supply Belém's beef market, the other was made up of a group of Japanese immigrants who were producing most of Pará's black pepper. Most of these cooperatives' members were quite prosperous, and the cooperatives were stable; EMATER's services consisted mostly of facilitating contacts and providing information. EMATER also worked with two other pepper growers' cooperatives, one in Santa Izabel in the outskirts of Belém, and another in Monte Alegre, about eight hours downriver from Santarém. The task force had recommended working with these cooperatives because, although they were quite stable, their profits and their growth had been slow. EMATER helped the members of Santa Izabel, 70 percent of whom were Japanese, in their search for credit and markets for the high quality melons they were starting to grow in order to diversify their pepper crop. It helped the much smaller Monte Alegre cooperative, all of whose forty-four members were Japanese, to secure credit to increase their pepper crops. In addition to some technical assistance to both cooperatives, it supplied a trained accountant to each of them.

All four of these cooperatives were already economically viable, had clear titles to their buildings and land, and could respond easily to the additional aid and opportunities which EMATER provided. The remaining four cooperatives in EMATER's program, two of which had participated in the BASA program and were seriously indebted and two of which had recently been founded on the Transamazon highway but had not yet started to sell crops, presented much greater difficulties.

Negotiating the Encumbrances of Past Failures

EMATER's work with the cooperatives that had received support from BASA illustrates the problems of collaboration between agencies with divergent mandates and interests, the extra costs which these divergencies impose on the weaker agencies, and the waste of resources which interagency negotiations often entailed. The first of the older cooperatives, COLASAL (Santarém Farmers' Cooperative) was founded in 1959 under the tutelage of Santarém's mayor and with the direct participation of various municipal politicians and the manager of the Santarém branch of a national bank, the Caixa Econômica Federal. Its twenty-three original members voted Cr$4,600 as membership capital, divided into forty-six shares to be bought equally by the original members. The cooperative grew slowly for four years, with little change in its membership. It realized a small, steady profit, and its basic capital almost tripled by 1963, by which time it had acquired a warehouse and a rice-processing machine.

After a visit and generous promises from representatives of the BCA in 1963, COLASAL changed its statutes to correspond to those required by that bank's cooperative credit department. In addition to limiting the area in which it operated, the most significant change was to increase by fifteen times the minimum membership share, to be financed by BCA loans to each member. After rewriting its statutes, COLASAL received a BCA loan of almost 100 times the value of its own capital to build a large warehouse and office complex, install a new large rice mill, and buy a truck for its members' rice crops. The BCA started to make individual crop loans to members, indicating COLASAL as the collecting agency; the value of the loan was to be deducted from payments for rice delivered. The cooperative also opened a consumer goods section and affiliated itself with the Central Cooperative of Belém to facilitate consumer goods purchases and crop sales.

The cooperative encountered serious problems of corruption and mismanagement soon after it initiated its relations with the BCA. A federal commission eventually placed the entire cooperative under the management of a Ministry of Agriculture functionary, but allegations of dishonesty and embezzlement continued. By 1970 the cooperative's total debt amounted to over Cr$141,000,000. It continued its operations until 1973, when BASA, the BCA's successor, discontinued its credits, leaving most of its members ineligible for individual loans from any bank.

EMATER initiated its efforts to resuscitate the cooperative in 1975. Using money from POLAMAZONIA, with salary supplements from INCRA, EMATER posted a manager, an accountant, and an extension agent to the cooperative. Before it could start to work with the co-operative, however, it had to reach an agreement with BASA for the restructuring and eventual payment of its debt. Despite EMATER's having initiated negotiations, and despite its own participation in PICEP, BASA attempted to foreclose on COLASAL in 1976. The cooperative program agents directed most of their efforts during the following months to convincing INCRA, SAGRI, and various state and local politicians to bring sufficient pressure on BASA to convince it to desist. By the end of 1976 BASA had accepted, in principle, a recomposition of the debt under the threat of further revelations of its own mis-management of the cooperative and of public accusations that BASA was thwarting a program financed by POLAMAZONIA and other development agencies. The actual bargaining, however, went on for another two years, during which time EMATER could not use the cooperative's patrimony to guarantee further credits with other banks. BASA, once free of the political pressure which its threat to foreclose had provoked, made demands in the restructuring of the debt that the agents felt would make it impossible for the cooperative to survive.

The net effect of the multiple negotiations, improvisations, and al-liances that were necessary simply to keep COLASAL from sinking completely was that EMATER was keeping three functionaries so busy running a marginal business and two of their supervisors so involved in bargaining with other agencies that they had very little time to work with the members who should, in principle, eventually run the co-operative themselves. EMATER's strategy was to free the cooperative's considerable patrimony from debt encumbrance so that it could be used both as a guarantee for credit and to process and sell members' rice, but the debt load they were carrying and the negotiations in which they had to engage made this impossible. INCRA's interference in the use to which its support was to be put and EMATER's need to secure INCRA approval for its operations in Santarém further complicated the situation. By 1980 EMATER was searching for ways to withdraw its direct management without forcing COLASAL to close down com-pletely.

The history and problems of the other cooperative from the BASA program were similar, though less dramatic than those of COLASAL. The Cooperative of Maracaná had less than half the members that COLASAL had, and its debt to BASA, though heavy, was considerably less. Unlike COLASAL, it had been started under direct BCA super-vision; it had used BCA and BASA money to construct a large warehouse and rice mill. Like COLASAL, it had suffered from mismanagement, faulty accounting, and possibly embezzlement. The EMATER agents were able to negotiate a restructuring of the debt with BASA and the

BNCC much more rapidly than they were in Santarém, but again they were forced to run the cooperative as a business under their direct supervision instead of as a cooperative. EMATER'S expenditures remained greater than the total value of rice purchased, so the entire endeavor remained dependent on year-to-year negotiations with the SUDAM.

EMATER worked less intensely, and without appointing managers and accountants, with several other of the BASA cooperatives whose members were themselves trying to deal with the debts they had accumulated, but their total efforts affected only a small portion of the more than sixty cooperatives into which BASA had poured credit, equipment, and personnel time. There were many cooperatives whose expensive warehouses and offices stood empty, whose crop-processing and transport equipment was rusting away, and whose deeply indebted members could no longer get bank credit for any purpose. These the task force, and EMATER, had considered too hopeless to rescue. Many of them were probably not viable in the first place, but BASA's recalcitrance so raised the costs of finding any use for this infrastructure that the buildings remained closed, despite the critical need for warehouse space that impeded rural development plans for crop commercialization throughout Pará. EMATER negotiated multiple *convênios* in order to resuscitate BASA's costly failures, but BASA's own insistence on controlling this process and its refusal to relax its normal default procedures enormously hampered these efforts. EMATER's interest in the program was part of its own expansion strategies, but as a dependent agency it could only follow these strategies by engaging in extensive interagency negotiations, which absorbed a great deal of its agents' energies and much of the budget EMATER derived from other agencies.

The Enduring Problems of Instant Organization

Though free of the encumbrances which the legacy of BASA support had left the other cooperatives, the cooperatives in the Transamazon colonization projects faced a series of difficult problems. In order to comply with the legal requirement that each colonization project have a CIRA, INCRA officials from the cooperative sector of the regional headquarters in Belém had made lightning visits in 1973 to Marabá, Altamira, and Itaituba to establish cooperatives in the PICs there. They did little more than call a meeting, explain what a cooperative was and what the legal procedures for registering one involved, and supervise an election for cooperative officials before leaving.

A major embezzlement and the flight of the embezzlers paralyzed the Marabá cooperative almost immediately, and that effort was abandoned. In Altamira and Itaituba, however, the men elected as presidents of the new cooperatives took on the task and the expense of fulfilling the complex legal and bureaucratic procedures for registering the cooperative. These chores were so onerous and hard to understand that the cooperative in Altamira contracted a local lawyer, who in turn hired an accountant to run the cooperative for them. This lawyer, who appears to have won the confidence of the members sufficiently to run the cooperative with little or no surveillance by the president or other elected officials, convinced a large landowner, a resident in Altamira before the Transamazon highway was built and engaged at the time in providing a number of services to INCRA, to give the cooperative a forty-hectare lot on the outskirts of the town. This extraordinary achievement, however, was all he managed to do for the cooperative. By 1975 the cooperative owed him Cr$53,000 for salary and expenses, but had not yet collected or sold a single grain of rice. He was dismissed in that year, when INCRA contracted with EMATER to assume the management of the cooperative. The EMATER technicians' salaries were to be paid from EMATER's *convênio* with POLAMAZONIA. Before the lawyer left though, he drew up, and the cooperative's elected officials approved, a contract which granted him the right to subdivide and sell the forty-hectare lot for a 20 percent commission on all sales, with all the expenses of sale, surveying, and registration to be assumed by the cooperative.

EMATER hired three southern-trained technicians, one to manage the crop sales, another to manage a consumer goods sector, and an accountant to run the cooperative, which was now called COOPER-FRON (Mixed Agricultural Cooperative of the New Frontier). Two extension agents already working in Altamira were assigned to promote cooperative membership. The three technicians, posted to Altamira early in 1976 after several months of work and orientation in Belém, were soon involved, with support from the cooperative supervisors in Belém, in a complex round of bargaining with various agencies and organizations. After extensive review of the COOPERFRON's books and meeting minutes, they had sufficient documentation to force a settlement with the lawyer and to extract partial control of the cooperative's remaining urban lots. INCRA officials had promised a large loan for capital expenses, assistance with the construction of office and warehouse buildings, and a lot to build them on while BASA had indicated that it would provide extensive credit which the cooperative could make available to members as soon as the cooperative had real property to guarantee the loan. The amount of direct assistance and loans from INCRA was not clearly specified, however, and the cession of the lot was delayed, in part because of objections from other departments within INCRA. EMATER's cooperative agents in Belém finally started bargaining directly with INCRA in Brasília. This required a considerable portion of their time and travel budget, but for over a year even these trips did not achieve the release of the promised money or access to their lot.

At this point the technicians in Altamira hit on a new bargaining strategy. They had discovered that one of BASA's failed cooperatives had been located in Altamira prior to the advent of the highway. This cooperative had acquired a large lot in the middle of what was then a small, quiet river town. When the highway crews and INCRA arrived in 1971, the cooperative was highly indebted and effectively moribund. As it had with numerous other landholdings which did not yet have the benefit of the new INCRA land titles in the colonization area, INCRA simply appropriated this lot, the size of a large city block. INCRA constructed its own offices there, as well as buildings which it later rented out to other agencies and organizations. When the members of the cooperative objected to this, INCRA declared that the cooperative had ceased to function and unilaterally revoked its operating license, thus violating its own requirements of due process.

EMATER's cooperative technicians recruited a number of the older cooperative's members and encouraged them, together with the elected officials of COOPERFRON, to denounce the illegality of this revocation to INCRA, the press, Altamira's representatives in the local state government, and Pará's representatives in the national senate. Representatives of the two, now informally merged, cooperatives traveled to Belém and to Brasília to present their demands for either the return of the old cooperative's land or a substantial settlement.

The EMATER agents and elected COOPERFRON representatives used this campaign in their negotiations with INCRA. They enlisted effective political support; one of Pará's senators gave a speech in the Senate detailing the cooperative's complaints against BASA and INCRA in May 1980, and papers in Belém and in Brasília gave the story some coverage. The cooperative agents claimed that they were subjected to pressures from the local EMATER supervisor to desist from this campaign and that their support from Belém had become questionable, but the enthusiastic support they were receiving from COOPERFRON's members and officers allowed them to continue these activities against the strongly implied, if not direct, opposition of their superiors. They made astute use of the divisions within INCRA to marshal support from some INCRA offices in their struggles with other INCRA offices.

COOPERFRON was still in a precarious state when I left the field in 1978. Both its members and its EMATER directors were becoming more enthusiastic and optimistic about the battles they were waging, but the cooperative was not yet selling any crops and therefore had no income. Its travel and administrative expenses were enormous. When I returned in 1980, however, it had received enough credit to build two large warehouses, was running a large and well-stocked consumer goods store, was building another warehouse, and had several vehicles, some of its own and some on loan from INCRA, to transport the pepper and cocoa it was buying from its members. It had not received all of the support and money which INCRA had originally offered, nor had it succeeded in getting the CIBRAZEM and CFP funding for its warehouses that at one point it had bargained for. The demands for the return of the old cooperative's land continued without resolution. The cooperative was, however, clearly a going concern and ready to start assuming a portion of the EMATER technicians' salaries. It would still be dependent on external support and administration for some time, but its members had become sufficiently well organized, vociferous, and experienced in political bargaining that it seemed improbable that they would lose their funding.

COOPERFRON's progress after 1978 was in large measure the result of the extraordinary and unorthodox negotiating tactics of its EMATER directors, but it also benefited from the increasing prosperity of its members as the cocoa and pepper they had planted started to produce and from the absence of an officially supported crop purchase system for anything but rice in the colonization area. Originally planned to serve the majority of the colonists, it ended up with slightly over 300 of the more prosperous colonists who had succeeded in making the transition from annual to perennial crops. Thus, its success was dependent on abandoning its initial goals and conforming to the increased inequality which the breakdown of the PIC's originally stated purposes had engendered (see Chapter 6).

The cooperative in the Itaituba colonization project suffered similar problems. In this case the elected president attempted to deal with the legal complexities of registering the cooperative himself. After two years of considerable expense and frustration, he awarded himself Cr$14,250 from the proceeds of the rice that the members had delivered to pay for their shares, saying that this amount would compensate him for his expenses and for the neglect of his crops which his frequent trips had entailed.

By 1977 the cooperative had not sold anything but the rice originally given as farmers' shares, but had incurred a small debt. INCRA assigned one of its own agents to supervise the cooperative and hired an accountant to work there. EMATER also assigned an agent, again on

POLAMAZONIA funds, to work with the cooperative, but provided neither housing at the cooperative's base nor a vehicle to carry the agent the 125 kilometers from his own post to the cooperative's headquarters. Eventually, over one-fourth of the project's colonists joined this cooperative, but the majority of members continued to sell most of their crops to the CFP or to private buyers, leaving the actual running of the cooperative to INCRA. INCRA's continued participation discouraged a major EMATER commitment to this project, and the EMATER agents and resources were in any event overextended.

Cooptation and False Statutory Compliance

INCRA's attempts to comply as cheaply as possible with its statutory obligation to establish CIRAs also led to peculiar policy distortions in various agencies' support programs for an already established cooperative. Its manipulation of the cooperative in Monte Alegre after 1977 greatly complicated EMATER's role there. In addition to including a small Japanese community, Monte Alegre was the site of one of the earliest national colonization projects. Started in 1938, this project had been alternately managed and abandoned by various of INCRA's predecessors. When the major push to promote colonization in Pará started in 1971, INCRA decided to revitalize and eventually emancipate the Monte Alegre colonization project. The lots granted here had been only about a fourth the size of the 100-hectare modules decreed in 1971. Most of them had by this time been seriously overexploited; the soils were depleted and in some cases severely eroded. INCRA contracted with EMATER for agricultural extension work in the area, however, and proceeded to title the colonists' lots to facilitate credit and to fulfill the requirements for emancipation.

After the problems they had encountered in their attempts to establish cooperatives in the much more prosperous Transamazon colonization projects, INCRA's cooperative development officers in Belém were reluctant to embark on a similar endeavor in Monte Alegre. They were obliged, however, to establish a CIRA before they could emancipate the project. INCRA's cooperative program director solved this dilemma by proposing that the small cooperative society run by the Japanese pepper growers change its statutes to correspond to those legislated for CIRAs and open its membership to the much greater number of colonists who grew rice, corn, and beans. In exchange he offered major INCRA financing for the construction of warehouses and office buildings and for the purchase of vehicles and machinery. He enlisted the aid of the director of EMATER's cooperative program to help him convince the directors of the cooperative to agree to these changes.

The Japanese farmers were apprehensive about losing contol of their small, steady organization to an influx of much less prosperous Brazilian farmers who grew quite different crops than they did. The EMATER cooperative director believed that INCRA's conditions were not as favorable to the cooperative as they could have been and was skeptical about the extent to which INCRA could or would keep its promises. He was in a difficult position, however, because much of his own program depended on the continued good will of the INCRA cooperative director. His position was particularly delicate because the cooperative's directorate had publicly credited him with their success in negotiating new loans and opening new marketing arrangements and had said that they would accept his advice. He was able, finally, to help them negotiate more favorable terms with INCRA, and the cooperative became a CIRA.

EMATER's role in these negotiations continued, however, as INCRA did not fulfill, either in time or in value, the various promises on which the transformation had been negotiated. EMATER continued to act as intermediary in order to get as much from INCRA as possible. The organizational needs of the new CIRA required extensive EMATER counsel and intervention. The greatly expanded resources of the cooperative inspired some of its younger members to push for diversification and expansion into new projects, including taking over CO-LASAL in order to secure a base in the large and growing Santarém market. This initiative was opposed by the older members of the directorate, who had managed the cooperative with a minimum of internal strife since its inception, and by the EMATER staff, who doubted the ability of the directorate to expand its operations so drastically without losing control of them.

Ironically, the greatly increased minimum shares which the new statutes specified had approximately the same effect as the previous formal limitation of cooperative membership to pepper growers. Even though membership had almost doubled by 1980, the new CIRA included only a small fraction of the Brazilian farmers in the area, and the new members appeared disposed to leave the running of the cooperative to the pepper-growing members. The new directorate included only one Brazilian farmer. INCRA's energy-saving solution to its own statutory requirement for the colonization program, at least initially, simply placed many more resources under the control of a relatively prosperous group of farmers without directly affecting the colonists for whom the CIRA was designed.

Authoritarian Bureaucrats in a Showcase Project

The most remarkable case of a government agency's establishing a cooperative to satisfy its own legal obligations and to solve its own internal problems rather than to facilitate farmers' commercialization of their crops occurred in the PIC Altamira. A great deal of INCRA's budget for this PIC was concentrated in a special project, PACAL, to grow sugar cane. Some of the PIC's best soils and flattest lands, starting about eighty-five kilometers west of the town of Altamira, were allocated to this project. INCRA attempted to use this grandiose and expensive project as a demonstration that colonization could both contribute to the regional economy and dramatically increase individual colonists' incomes.

The Amazon imported most of its sugar and cane alcohol from the Northeast. INCRA proposed that a sugar mill near Altamira would provide jobs and reduce imports from other regions. A team of experts from the Brazilian Institute of Sugar and Alcohol (IBAA) claimed that the site chosen was not appropriate, but INCRA went ahead with this project. INCRA also refused offers of assistance and advice from IBAA and other agencies with more experience in sugar-cane cultivation and milling. Instead, INCRA contracted a São Paulo company to build a huge mill. The mill theoretically had an annual capacity of 500,000 sacks of sugar. It was built at an exorbitant cost, and the capacity of its various components varied greatly. Only a few parts of the mill were capable of operating at the specified capacity; the rest of the mill had a much lower capacity. Total capacity, of course, equalled the capacity of the smallest component. One of INCRA's employees at the mill, a professional mill operator of long experience hired after INCRA had serious troubles in keeping the mill operating, told me that he believed the construction firm had taken advantage of INCRA personnel's ignorance of sugar milling to use components already available or particularly profitable without regard to how well they fit together.

These problems were compounded by INCRA's attempt to use PACAL as a showcase where the press and national and international political figures could be flown in to PACAL's special airstrip to see the great effort Brazil's government was making on behalf of the rural poor. In addition to building a fairly elaborate residential and administrative nucleus, INCRA insisted that the mill be located at the top of a large hill, where it could be seen from the highway and from much of the surrounding countryside. Sugar processing, however, requires vast amounts of water, so mills are best located where water can flow down to them, not where water must be pumped up to them. Access to sufficient water constituted a major problem.

INCRA agents did not discover this for several years, however, because only about 300 hectares of cane had been planted when the mill was inaugurated in 1974. In order to secure a return on an investment which after maintenance and modifications amounted to over US$7 million, INCRA applied various forms of pressure on the colonists in the designated area, which extended about forty kilometers along the highway, to plant sugar cane. EMATER agents told me that some colonists had accused INCRA agents of uprooting other crops in this area and of preventing the colonists from obtaining credit for other crops, especially cacao. There were, in fact, some successful cacao plantations in this area, but sugar clearly predominated.

The mill was still operating far under capacity in 1976, and INCRA started to bulldoze forests to motivate the farmers to plant more cane. Some colonists complained that their lots had been bulldozed without their authorization and protested INCRA's decision that the costs of the clearing were to be deducted from their crop payments.

The problems of the mill, and of the sugar area as a whole, were exacerbated by the fact that, because of its public relations importance, the entire project was run by a special office in Brasilia, bypassing the Belém office completely. EMATER agents were contracted through a special *convênio* to do extension work until 1977, but as the mill encountered more and more problems, INCRA agents assumed greater control over all aspects of the project. This meant that the project managers spent much of their time in Brasília and so did not have direct and continuous contact with the colonists and with their problems. It also meant that they could bypass normal bureaucratic channels once they had decided on a course of action. They had much larger budgets, and much more influence, than the local directors of INCRA and the other agencies. Indeed, by 1977, PACAL's budget, for a project which included less than 10 percent of the Altamira colonists, was greater than that of the rest of the PIC. The special powers of the project directors were an important factor in the extraordinarily high debt levels of many of the colonists. When they decided to mechanize clearing, for example, they were able to arrange that the Banco do Brasil finance the entire operation directly, but that the debt be charged to individual colonists. The colonists confronted a small group of bureaucrats who were frequently absent but who assumed more and more direct control not only over the mill but also over the management of their farms. The bureaucrats insisted that it would all work out to the colonists' great advantage; the colonists were repeatedly told that when everything was running right (always the next season) they would be far wealthier than the colonists in the rest of the PIC. EMATER agents who discovered extensive irregularities in the rural credit applications prepared by the INCRA directors of PACAL were warned off by their own supervisor.

A small number of colonists did very well with their sugar cane, but the vast majority encountered severe problems. Sugar is a difficult, unpleasant, and technically complex crop. It must be fired, at a carefully controlled heat, before it is cut; and cutting the fired cane, with its long, sharp, stiff leaves, is dirty, hot, painful work. The cane must be processed within three days of the burn, or it will spoil. If the distribution of trucks is not well managed, or if the roads, precarious throughout the project, are not passable, or if the mill, which was subject to frequent breakdown, cannot receive the harvest, the entire crop is lost.

INCRA contracted with a private company to run the mill in 1976. This company could not keep the mill running. After repeated breakdowns and badly snarled cane deliveries, the INCRA directors of the project decided to manage the mill themselves. INCRA, however, did not have the statutory powers or authorization to run a business. INCRA's directors sought to solve this problem by converting the entire project into a CIRA, which, as a cooperative, would be licensed to conduct business. In a single meeting convened in 1977, they explained what a CIRA was, convinced the assembled colonists that they wanted to found one, and supported the election of PACAL's most successful and wealthy cane grower, with whom they were already collaborating closely, as president. That this man had already bought up six lots in addition to the one to which he was legally entitled was in clear violation of INCRA rules, but this did not in any way impede his close collaboration with the project's managers. These agents were able to use their special influence in Brasília to expedite the registration of the new CIRA, to have themselves appointed as supervisors, and to arrange a three-year grant of Cr$80 million directly from INCRA and additional credits from the Banco do Brasil.

By coercion, huge, irregular loans, and extensive mechanized clearing, the INCRA directors finally achieved a sugar crop that would come close to using the full supposed capacity of the mill. It was only as they prepared for this harvest that they discovered that the real capacity of the mill was only about 60 percent of what they had believed. They attempted to convince INCRA's directorate in Brasília to provide emergency funds to amplify the mill so as not to lose a major share of the crop. They felt a special urgency, because this crop was already committed to payment for the first installments of the enormous debts they had arranged for the colonists. The directorate balked at this request, but was finally won over, as it had been in the past and would be again, by the threat that a calamity in the project which it was still using as a showpiece would be a disaster to the agency's credibility.

The funding was approved too late to incorporate the necessary modifications before the harvest began, and a major part of the crop was lost. INCRA did reimburse a portion of some farmers' losses and renegotiated the loans with the Banco do Brasil, but the farmers, already apprehensive about ever paying off their debts, were badly frightened. They were also acutely aware that the small group of colonists elected as cooperative officers but whose entire function was to approve without question the decisions of the INCRA directors had been among the small number whose entire crops were duly transported and processed.

Several of the new CIRA's members also belonged to COOPERFRON; one was COOPERFRON's president. These men, and several other members of the CIRA-PACAL, objected to the INCRA supervisors' making major decisions without consulting the members. The supervisors, in turn, defined their own situation as an emergency in which they needed to make a number of decisions and engage in negotiations in which they committed the cooperative, and its members, without the delays that participation and consultation would entail. As their major internal opposition came from the members and officers of COOPERFRON, and as these men invoked COOPERFRON's more participatory management style in their criticisms of the CIRA-PACAL supervisors, considerable antagonism developed between the supervisors of the two cooperatives. This was exacerbated by the growing tensions over EMATER's support of crops other than sugar in the PACAL area and by the enormous discrepancies in official funding for the two cooperatives.

As soon as it was licensed, CIRA-PACAL had received more than ten times the funding that COOPERFRON had been requesting without success. The EMATER supervisors of COOPERFRON then offered to combine their entire operation with PACAL. CIRA-PACAL's directors, however, refused to open their cooperative to general membership from the entire PIC. They argued that it made more sense to concentrate their efforts and budgets on the farmers who already were privileged by the better land and extensive services which PACAL provided. COOPERFRON's members and EMATER supervisors then accused INCRA of attempting to create a group of wealthy farmers in a project whose original intention and ideology had been egalitarian. EMATER agents subsequently learned in Brasília that the CIRA's directors were opposing and delaying INCRA compliance with the promises of money, credit, and land for COOPERFRON.

Simultaneously, the repeated requests for a large-scale emergency funding for PACAL were generating opposition within INCRA. PACAL appeared to be an enormous hole into which unending amounts of money were poured without any of its multiple problems being solved. Some of the opposition within INCRA came from high-level functionaries who supported the bid of a private company to buy the mill outright. The PACAL supervisors adopted a more threatening position within INCRA, attempting to overcome opposition by claiming that failures of planning and execution at the begining of PACAL's history, which they themselves knew well and which implicated many of INCRA's highest ranking officers, would all be revealed if PACAL failed, and that the past use of PACAL to garner public and political support for INCRA would make such revelations particularly damaging. These tactics brought more emergency funding in 1978, but by this time the directors were faced with the growing opposition from the CIRA members, from the increasingly vociferous and confident members of COOPERFRON, and from EMATER. INCRA supervisors in Belém were more critical of the anomalies of a major and highly funded special project over which they had no control operating in the middle of a PIC for which they were responsible.

The embattled PACAL supervisors became even more authoritarian in their management, outspoken in their threats, and extravagant in their promises. The 1978 funding came too late, however. The mill needed more work than the limited time and equipment available allowed. Once again, large portions of that year's sugar crop were lost due to machinery breakdowns and lack of coordination in the use of trucks and cane loaders. The CIRA members' protests and the failure of the emergency funding to achieve any positive results led to the removal of the INCRA supervisors in 1979. The CIRA was dissolved.

INCRA then put PACAL under the management of COTRIJUI, a large wheat-growers' cooperative in southern Brazil. This cooperative, one of the largest in the country, had been very successful in promoting the mechanization of many of its members' farms. One result of its prosperity was the rapid expansion of the farm size of some of its members and an increasing land and cost squeeeze on the rest. In order to solve the resulting land-tenure problems of both its large and small members, COTRIJUI negotiated with INCRA for 400,000 hectares of land behind the official colonization area near PACAL. It planned to colonize this land, providing infrastructure, credit, services, and orientation for 2,000 of its own members who were willing to sell their farms in the South. INCRA was enthusiastic about the project, as it hoped that COTRIJUI's experience and wealth would invigorate the region's economy and help to revitalize the PIC Altamira. COTRIJUI's legitimacy as a cooperative allowed INCRA to cede this large area without the criticisms it would have encountered if it had granted such extensive rights to a private company.

COTRIJUI established an office in space rented from INCRA and proceeded to survey and construct roads into the area. Surveying crews soon discovered that an indigenous group, the Arara, were occupying the area reserved for COTRIJUI. The Arara had maintained limited trading relations with Altamira until the violence of the road-building crews had made them retreat into the forest. After several attacks on and the surveyors, FUNAI interdicted the area while it attempted to contact and pacify members of the tribe. These efforts were stopped in 1979, when two FUNAI agents were seriously wounded.

COTRIJUI started negotiations with INCRA for land in Rondônia or Mato Grosso, but this prospect was less attractive to INCRA, as it did not offer any escape from its obligations to the PIC and as there were many more private colonization companies seeking land there (Schmink, 1981). In an effort to achieve some return from its investments in Altamira, and, according to some of its local agents, to do INCRA a favor which might expedite its bid for land elsewhere in the Amazon, COTRIJUI undertook to run PACAL in 1979.

PACAL's new directors stated publicly that the less-educated colonists from the poor Northeast did not know how to work. They decided not to hire the experienced cane harvesters from that region but recruited workers, at much greater expense, from their home area, Rio Grande do Sul. These workers, accustomed to the lower temperatures and relatively comfortable agricultural work of the temperate South, burned the cane badly and then refused to work in what they saw as appallingly difficult conditions. The leaders of the crews, who were predominantly colonists from the South, did not organize the harvesting and loading properly and were hampered by the defection of their crews, most of whom returned home after less than a week. New crews were finally recruited from the Northeast, but much of the harvest was lost due to delay.

COTRIJUI condemned a large portion of the cane which was delivered, claiming that its saccharose content was too low. Unlike INCRA, COTRIJUI was neither interested nor able to arrange debt renegotiations with the Banco do Brasil, and the bank started to withhold money from loans arranged with CEPLAC for cacao from farmers who grew both crops. COTRIJUI withdrew from the PACAL the following year, and a private company took over its management.

Placing the mill under the direction of a company whose only interests are to run it at a profit can only exacerbate the problems of the individual, impossibly indebted colonists. If the mill becomes viable, these colonists are likely to end up selling their valuable lots to entrepreneurs or successful colonists with sufficient capital to buy them out and manage the potentially profitable plantations. If the mill cannot be run at a profit, the entire undertaking must be abandoned at a huge loss to INCRA, to the bank, and to all of the colonists.

CIRA-PACAL was exceptional only in the size of its budget and in the enormity of the problems which such huge commitments of agency finances and prestige created. The establishment and the ultimate collapse of PACAL illustrate, in magnified, intensified, and dramatic form, the distortions of both state policy and bureaucratic rationality which the extension of overly complex, costly, and powerful agencies into the Amazon provoked. Once again, we have seen how contradictions between the imperatives of legitimacy and the imperatives of economic viability create severe ambivalence in the programs of state agencies. We have seen again how these contradictions are aggravated by the expansive and self-serving nature of agency organization, by the resulting competition between agencies and even between programs of the same agency, and by the combinations of concessions and threats that agencies use to maintain or enhance their own bureaucratic control. We have seen again how the great power imbalance between the center's complex modern bureaucratic agencies and the unstable rural communities left the agencies to operate with few effective external restraints on their own strategies for self-maintenance. We have also seen again how much of the costs of these distortions weigh on the rural populations.

Legitimation, Ideology, and Interagency Conflict

Except for the pepper-exporting and meat-selling cooperatives, which were founded independently of government support, and COOPER-FRON, whose title to valuable urban land, whether ultimately recognized or not, has provided it with a powerful bargaining lever over INCRA and BASA, the cooperatives absorbed large amounts of both government and farmers' funds with little or no return. Many of their problems resulted directly from their imposition of exogenous modern institutions on people and areas with little or no experience in the complex legal forms which they required. These problems were exacerbated because unequal knowledge of these forms provided opportunities for corruption and theft. The division of responsibility for and control over the fate of various agencies with different and frequently opposed interests hampered all attempts to overcome the inherent difficulties of establishing these exogenous institutions. The primacy of the goals of self-maintenance, protection, and expansion within each agency and the subordination of official policy goals were clear in the bargaining relations between the various rural development agencies in other programs, but this predominance of agency self-interest was especially visible in the cooperative program, where the tension between goals of political legitimacy often ran counter to any hope of economic return to either the state or the farmers.

Individual agents, especially those in supervisory positions, strove to maintain their own departments and special projects. The cooperative agents were able to fight effectively for their own projects because of the specific legitimating function of the cooperative program. The improvised business arrangements, the entrepreneurial initiatives, and the highly aggressive negotiations with their own agencies and with BASA and INCRA required a remarkable degree of autonomy and personal conviction. Many of the other agents believed in the importance of their jobs and worked hard at them, but the reformist ideology with which the entire cooperative program was imbued seemed to give the cooperative promotion agents an especially fervent feeling of mission. They saw their work as more disinterested, as having a deeper impact, and as freer from the political compromises which affected the other rural development programs. They tended as well to see themselves and their mission as superior to the agents and missions of the other programs and were particularly critical of the various forms of official corruption. Indeed, despite the extensive corruption which had contributed to the failure of previous cooperatives, they saw themselves, and the properly run cooperatives which they planned to establish, as both immune from and a bulwark against corruption.

Their missionary fervor and their belief in the special efficacy of cooperatives encouraged them to take far more public initiatives in their negotiations with the various agencies than was common in EMA-TER, especially for functionaries at their hierarchical level. These agents learned how to exploit the importance of the cooperatives as legitimating vehicles, and so would publicly criticize other agents and agencies who put obstacles in their way. They also became very effective at marshalling support from politicians at the local, state, and national levels. They were aware of the limits to the power which the legitimating function of their mission gave them, but became quite skillful at working within those limits.

Paradoxically, while the legitimating function of their mission allowed them to take initiatives and to criticize other agencies, immune from the sanctions that similar behavior would have provoked against other bureaucrats of similar rank, the anomalous position of cooperatives tended to create special obstacles for their program. Especially in the volatile and difficult conditions of the Transamazon, viable and dynamic cooperative organizations of colonists would constitute a potential threat to most of the government agencies and to their political interests. Such cooperatives would facilitate public airing of colonists' complaints against agency malfeasance and omission. They would also threaten various commercial interests, both legitimate and corrupt. Finally, they would in the long run take over some of the functions for which various development agencies were funded. While such a transition would technically be considered a sign of successful development, it would also undercut the importance of the agencies themselves. For all of these reasons, the cooperative program functionaries had to deal with even greater obstructions and restrictions than their fellow bureaucrats.

As Crozier (1964) and Block (1977) have shown, the bureaucracies and the bureaucrats of the state, once established, operate primarily to assure their own survival and, if possible, expansion. Other goals are subordinated to this central one. The self-interest of bureaucratic agencies poses an enormous problem for developmental states which govern heterogeneous and unequally developed economies and regions and whose control of their own bureaucracies is already compromised by extensive dominant class penetration of their various agencies. In the case of the Amazon, all of these difficulties were exacerbated by the extreme dispersion and disarticulation of rural communities which a history of extraction had brought about and by the extreme imbalances in the resources available to state bureaucracies and those available to peasant communities. Bureaucrats' decisions, taken to recover debts to their banks, to expand the operations of their own agencies, to comply with nationally mandated procedural requirements, or to maintain an economically unviable undertaking to which their agency was committed, were all played out in terms of relations between the agencies themselves; the rural communities thus became pawns in interagency power struggles.

NOTE

1. Data for this chapter are drawn from interviews with agency personnel and cooperative members and officers, from observation of intra- and inter-agency planning sessions and of meetings, organizing sessions, and cooperative education classes, and from extensive examination of each cooperative's books and records. I was assisted in the latter task by a team of research assistants, which included two accountants.

CHAPTER 9

Modernizing Land Tenure

Much of the modernization which rural development programs brought about was the haphazard result of the extension of different agencies and their normal operating procedures from the modern capitalist economy of the center-south to the noncapitalist economies of different parts of the Amazon. These effects were enhanced by the behaviors of individual bureaucrats imbued with the idea that the modern procedures and goals of their agencies, and the belief and action systems which they had learned in their lives, work, and training in the center-south or in the cities of the north, possessed an inherent value which Amazonian peasants and northeastern immigrants had to understand and accept to improve their living conditions and increase their production. The disjointed forms of modernization that agency procedures and bureaucrats' behaviors brought about often impeded the realization of economic and social welfare goals; increased program costs for both the bureaucratic agencies and the peasants; imposed exorbitant costs and inappropriate technologies; facilitated corruption; intensified power struggles between agencies; fostered new and greater forms of social inequality; and required a degree of coordination that was virtually impossible to achieve between the modern agencies assigned to work in the Amazon.

In addition to specific economic and social welfare goals, however, the state also aimed at modernization as a goal in itself and as a condition through which it could achieve legitimacy. Making men modern and providing them with modern social and economic systems was one way that the national state could claim that it was creating an integrated nation in which all citizens could participate. Establishing modern systems was also a way in which the state could extend and facilitate bureaucratic control over social and economic organization in all parts of the national territory. Modernization in the Amazon, then, resulted from the normal procedures of exogenous bureaucracies, from the behaviors of bureaucrats, and as a specific goal of the state.

Modernization and Political Predominance

Modernity as a specific goal of the state poses some difficult theoretical problems. We have already seen, in preceding chapters and in numerous other critical studies, enough evidence to reject the idea that modernity is naturally good, valuable, or useful in overcoming underdevelopment. We have also seen, however, that modernization has significant effects on national development programs and on the human groups they affect, so we cannot simply dismiss modernization as a conceptual error of earlier development theorists. We can look at the North American and the European experience and describe modernity there as the result of the economic, technological, political, and social changes which have accompanied the emergence and evolution of capitalist modes of production within articulated social formations, and we may be able to describe the modernization of Latin American industrial centers in the same way.

Modernization in peripheral areas appears to reverse this sequence, however; rather than following the development of a capitalist economy, modernization was imposed by the state in the Amazonian periphery prior to the emergence or evolution of capitalist relations of production there. Indeed, the high costs of administrative modernization in various development programs were due to the absence of correspondingly modern economic, social, political, and legal institutions. Marxist notions of the primacy of the economic (Foweraker, 1981) in explaining the actions of the state in the Amazon must therefore be qualified to include the motives of ideological consistency and bureaucratic facility within the state's political imperative to maintain itself and to expand its control.

Many of the state's economic programs were, of course, designed to favor and strengthen large-scale capitalist entrepreneurs. Even the programs designed to control them, or to favor other excluded groups, however, ended up facilitating the expansion of large-scale capitalist ventures. The theoretical problem in analyzing the state's initiatives in the Amazon is to separate effect from intent. The modern organizations, procedures, and ideologies that bureaucrats imposed effected and accelerated, often without intent, the predominance of the modern capitalist economic system which had shaped their own bureaucracies in the South. The modern forms established in the Amazon had quite different effects in the periphery's subordinate economy, however, than they did in the center's nationally dominant economy.

Modernization, as the adoption of new technologies, as the orientation of production to markets rather than to subsistence, as the inculcation of exchange values and profit motives, and as the restriction of consumption to enhance capital accumulation, was an important but implicit part of the ideology which informed EMATER's technical assistance and rural extension programs. These goals, if met, would increase small-scale agriculture's contributions to urban-industrial requirements for a cheap and steady food source. Because EMATER's primary dedication during the 1970s was to colonization projects located in economically marginal areas without easy connections to urban centers, however, the agency's definition of its own goals as centering on the well-being of the farmers themselves, rather than on enhancing the competitiveness of national industry by keeping food prices down, was essentially accurate. Modern agricultural systems established along the Transamazon highway could only serve to legitimate the state if the colonists who settled there did improve their standard of living. The failure of various agencies to achieve this goal for the intended population because of the multiple breakdowns of planning, coordination, and execution does not negate the basic consonance between EMATER's definition of its goals and the state's reasons for establishing the colonization projects.

EMATER also defined its activities in other areas, where increased agricultural production and sale would indeed facilitate urban-industrial development, as improving the life conditions of the farmer. In these areas, however, there was an inherent contradiction between the agency's definition of its own modernizing goals, the intentions of the state, and the interests of the commercial classes whose members bought the farmers' produce and sold them production inputs and consumer goods.

The results of EMATER's modernization were not those the agency intended in either the colonization projects or in the urban hinterlands. These results did, however, facilitate the expansion of modern capitalist forms and economies. EMATER's programs provided the services and administrative infrastructure necessary to the expansion of capitalist enterprise into the area, often at the cost of EMATER's original clients.

Procedural Violations of Use Rights and the Problem of State Intentions

INCRA's more diversified mandates make the question of official intent and actual effects of modernization more difficult. Unlike EMATER, INCRA plans and pronouncements officially stated modernization as one of the agency's goals (de Arruda, 1973). Within INCRA's multiple mandates, modernization of land tenure, in the form of surveying, titling, and registering land, was supposed to (1) ameliorate social tensions and conflicts over land ownership by subordinating the question of land rights to routinely adjudicable procedures, (2) assure social justice by treating all claimants as equal before the law, (3) facilitate economic development by making land an easily negotiable commodity, either in sale or lease and as collateral for agricultural credit, and (4) allow the state to regulate access to land according to its own development plans. Unlike EMATER, however, INCRA's modernizing mission obliged it to deal directly with, rather than pretend to ignore, nonmodern economic and legal forms. INCRA had to take into account the rights in land which, under Brazilian law, follow a specified period of uncontested occupation, and the rights of indemnification for the value of improvements made on occupied land (Sodero, 1968). It also had to deal with a series of prior state and municipal forms of conceding rights in land, either through lease, direct possession, or use rights (Campanhole, 1971). At the same time, INCRA had to deal with a series of changes in its own internal procedures and in the laws which regulated these procedures.

INCRA was legally bound to conduct a survey (*discriminatória*) of all existing titles, use, and occupation of land prior to surveying and titling any area. Technically, this meant that INCRA had to publish an official convocation—with sixty days advance notice—for all persons who believed they had legitimate claim to land within a specified area. Legally, INCRA was entitled to proceed as if this single convocation nullified the rights of anyone who did not present their claims then and there, but communication and transport difficulties forced most INCRA offices in the Amazon to extend the response period.

After the convocation of all claimants to land, INCRA lawyers were obliged to evaluate the validity of each claim. In cases where the claim was based on some previous title or cession from the local state or municipal governments, the lawyers had to request the appropriate *cartórios* or state land registries to verify the claims. This process required that *cartórios* examine the original land cession and then follow the chain (*cadeia dominial*) of all subsequent transfers by inheritance or sale. If the claim was based on effective and peaceful occupation, the lawyers had to await reports from INCRA agronomists and agricultural technicians to verify the occupation, the extent and history of use, and the value of the improvements or investment on the land.

If, as was often the case, there was a break in the chain of registered ownership, either because a buyer or heir had neglected to register the transfer or because the land transferred and registered had originally been claimed on the basis of effective use, the lawyers had several options. They could reject the claim, they could suspend the process pending further proof of ownership, or they could decide that the chain of registered ownership went back a sufficient time to allow its acceptance. Remarkably, there were no official criteria to guide the lawyers in these decisions. Even within the same office, and sometimes in the processing of the same lot by different lawyers, there was considerable difference in the criteria the lawyers themselves adopted. Judgments about the time of continuous registration necessary to validate an interrupted ownership chain showed an especially wide range. Nor were there any clear criteria to follow in the cases where the process was suspended pending further evidence.

INCRA lawyers knew well that both *cartório* and state land registries kept their books in fairly chaotic confusion and that their sending an incomplete record did not necessarily mean that the proper registrations had not occurred. The only recourse for the claimants, however, was to search through the records at their own expense. Large companies which had bought land from multiple previous owners were able to present thousands of pages of documentation; the poorer claimants to individual lots could not. As the amount of work to be done was vast, INCRA agents tended to settle the large claims, which were supported by massive, even if still incomplete, documentation, and to be impatient with the contrary claims of the actual occupants of some of this land.

The disposition of the claims based on effective occupation was even more arbitrary, as it depended on judgments by both lawyers and agronomists. The lawyers used the agronomists' judgment as evidence. These judgments varied with the individual agronomists' criteria of effective economic occupation. Some agronomists were willing to accept fallow land as being effectively used; others were not. In a few, extreme cases, I talked to agronomists who refused to consider certain crops as effective use of the land because they insisted that the soils were not appropriate to the crops planted on them. When I pointed out, in one case where I had visited the cultivated area with the agronomist, that these crops were obviously contributing to the family's diet, and that the family did not have access to the types of soils he said were appropriate for these crops, he replied that these considerations were irrelevant, that the plants would neither live as long or produce as much as they would on the proper soils, and that they should therefore not have been cultivated there in the first place. While this case is extreme—the man in question had had relatively little field experience and a fair amount of administrative experience—it does illustrate some of the problems that claimants to use rights encountered and the latitude of individual judgment on which they depended.

Use right claims were also complicated by several reductions in the maximum area that INCRA would accept for validation. Some lawyers were willing to proceed with claims for areas of the larger sizes if these had been initiated prior to the changes in the regulations; other insisted that the process be initiated again to conform to the newly specified maximum area.

Another problem that all claimants faced was the lack of trained INCRA personnel to comply with the complex legal processes that the land survey and titling regulations required. Some of the lands claimed through use rights were never visited at all; others were only inspected in the most cursory fashion. The INCRA agents made frequent mistakes and omissions in collecting the necessary information and in many instances had to send for additional information from the claimants. This often obliged claimants to travel to administrative centers, or to ad hoc second, third, and fourth convocations called by INCRA technicians.

In addition to the delays which these errors caused, the claimants lost considerable time and spent considerable money in collecting the necessary documents and making the necessary trips. I accompanied a work crew, which included the head of the local INCRA office, a lawyer, and three agricultural technicians on a journey they made to one such ad hoc convocation. The claimants, some of whom had traveled over sixty kilometers, had understood from the variety of informal means through which news of the meeting had been spread through this extensive rural area that their titles had finally been issued by INCRA and that they could now receive them. Most of the eighty-one men who appeared at the meeting were bitterly angry when they discovered that INCRA agents had forgotten to ask for all the necessary information from twenty-three of the claimants in the first convocation, and that the INCRA delegation had come to read off the names of these twenty-three and then to request the information required from those who had come. Some of the claimants, not knowing the purpose of the meeting, had not brought necessary documents such as identity card numbers or other legal records with them. The head of the local office gave a stirring harangue about the ways that INCRA served the small farmer, reproached those who had not brought the requisite documents, and asked those present to remind those who had not come that INCRA could not serve them unless they cooperated with its requests.

The tasks of the various *Projeto Fundiário* offices (administratively distinct from the colonization offices) varied greatly with the history of settlement and occupation of the areas for which the different offices were responsible. In the *terra firme* areas opened up by the new highways, previous settlement had been sparse and in some areas had become sparser as Indians fled from the road-building crews or were relocated. Portuguese-speaking forest dwellers there usually had little or no contact with markets except through the extraction of Brazil nuts or rubber. Because of their scattered and isolated settlement patterns, and because INCRA had access to vast extents of newly opened land, the *Projeto Fundiários* (PF) generally found it easy and convenient to force the relocation of forest inhabitants to new areas and to ignore the land rights claims of those who refused to move. As it was able to relocate most of the original inhabitants, these PFs were able to perform special surveys (*discriminatória branca*) in which they declared an area essentially free of effective occupation and therefore available for sale in large lots (up to 3,000 hectares).[1]

INCRA could then open these areas for bidding by individuals and companies. Successful bidders were given five years to complete investment projects, subject to INCRA approval and supervision. Through a special agreement with the Banco do Brasil, successful bidders could use the land as collateral for credit even though their title was not clear until their projects had been completed. By 1980 INCRA was routinely granting extensions of the five-year terms.

PF functions and procedures were considerably different, and more complex, in the hinterlands of established cities and towns in riverine areas. It was in these areas that conflicting claims to land and overlapping rights granted by various earlier land titling agencies were most likely to occur. Population densities were much greater. Land claimants had far more communication among themselves, far more knowledge of their legal rights, and much easier access to the offices of INCRA and of other government agencies.[2] Here, the tenure surveys were usually initiated in response to "social tensions"—INCRA's phrase for potential or actual conflict over land, caused by competing claims between long-term users of land and entrepreneurs who had recently purchased or acquired title to the land they occupied. In such cases up to 700 or more families might be threatened with expulsion by a single claimant to a large tract. In these areas INCRA procedures were often complicated by the fact that a single company might have bought up multiple titles, some of which comprised multiple previous purchases or acquisitions. As little of this land had ever been surveyed, actual boundaries were vague; even if area was specified, it was often ambiguous whether the lots adjoined, overlapped, or were separated by other holdings.[3]

INCRA tended to support the presumption that the large land claims were valid even before the titles had been investigated and attempted to arbitrate or negotiate resettlement and indemnification of the occupants who claimed use rights. In one case, near Santarém, INCRA authorities expressed impatient annoyance to a group of small holders who refused to relocate from an area claimed by a lumber company which had bought up over ninety titles. These INCRA functionaries were ready to promise the occupants other land even though none of the purchased titles had yet been validated, their location and size were open to question, and many of their ownership chains were clearly flawed. The proposed relocation would have required the occupants to move from riverine sites where they combined hunting, fishing, and a limited amount of horticulture and forest extraction to areas where they would have been much more dependent on agriculture. When I pointed this out to the agronomist who was handling the case, he replied that the people there were poor and lazy, didn't work because they could hunt and fish instead, and that it didn't make any sense to allow them to occupy land from which the lumber company could derive revenues and which would provide jobs. Several days later, the director of the Santarém PF told me of a meeting in which he and other local businessmen and landholders had complained to the local Catholic bishop that the priests in the contested area were agitating the inhabitants of that area to subversive political activity and requested him to take action to curb them. One of the businessmen present later told me they also told the bishop that further church activities in support of the occupants would likely reduce financial support for the church. In fact, the occupants and their clerical supporters were doing nothing more subversive than refusing to concede their use rights to the title buyers whose claims were still invalidated and largely untenable.

Schmink (1977, 1982, personal communication) has described similar confrontations and outcomes among small holders, claimants to legal title over large areas, and INCRA bureaucrats. Her analysis brilliantly shows the ways that the ideology of the bureaucrats, the procedures they are obliged to follow, their cultural and educational commonalities with the large landowners, their fear of collective political action by small holders, and a desire to reduce an excessive work load to terms that they can both understand and deal with all bias INCRA agents in favor of the large landowners and against the peasants. She also describes graphically the ways that these agents use the accusation of political subversion to cow the peasants who protest against expulsion from the lands they occupy, even when competing, entrepreneurial claimants cannot present legally acceptable titles.

Schmink's analysis strongly suggests that INCRA's, and other agencies', tendencies to favor large holders generally result, not from the specific policies of the state, but from the decisions of individual bureaucrats attempting to handle their own work situations at the least cost to themselves and consonant with their own beliefs and values. The general legal and economic direction of state policy does tend to favor the large landholders, but procedural bias and distortions undermine the state's attempts to control and reduce the political, social, and economic disruptions which accompany the capitalist expansion it promotes. Even where legislation and policy are designed to protect use rights, the logic of individual bureaucrats' decisions vitiates that intent. INCRA bureaucrats exercise considerable discretion; their own ideologies include the value of modern systems, and many have little patience with what they see as backward economic and social organization.

Local Politicians in Central State Bureaucracies

Since 1979 INCRA has appointed local political figures rather than technicians as directors of many of its PFs. While local knowledge and some degree of local political accountability may be important in discriminating between various uses and rights in land, this new policy, part of recent government relaxations of restrictions on political activity, has greatly strengthened the influence of local class interests in INCRA programs. In 1980 in a small river town I sat in on a meeting among a local rancher, who had requisitioned land from INCRA four years earlier, an INCRA lawyer, an INCRA agronomist, a local rancher and politician who also served as head of the local PF, and a peasant who had occupied and cleared part of the requisitioned land eighteen months earlier. The INCRA crew had traveled overnight by boat from the PF offices. The meeting was held in the office of the local head of the IBDF, who was also present and who was the brother of the man who had requisitioned the land and had lodged a complaint against the peasant. They were sons of a locally prominent merchant-ranching family.

Earlier in the day I had accompanied the INCRA agronomist and the rancher to the peasant's house. We had walked through several hectares of manioc and rice to reach the house and then waited until the peasant returned from fields we had not seen. The agronomist explained that he was there to inspect the peasant's improvements on the land (*benfeitorias*) and to request that he accompany us to the hearing. We did not see the rest of the cultivated area, though the peasant invited us to walk through it. The agronomist made disparaging comments about the quality of the house and surrounding buildings which were in fact, though made of logs and mud, immaculately maintained. The peasant accompanied us back to town and waited at the IBDF offices while the INCRA personnel had lunch in the home of a local rancher and businessman who was a friend of the rancher involved in the case.

Once the meeting started, it quickly became apparent that the INCRA director's strategy was to negotiate a settlement between the claimants, even though the rancher's requisition had not yet been processed and in fact had been made under regulations that had by this time been changed. The land the peasant had occupied was several kilometers away from the pastures which the rancher had cleared, but the rancher claimed he would use that area as part of the required forest reserve. The peasant then surprised everyone by producing a document showing that he had filed, and an INCRA technician had accepted, a request to validate and eventually title his lot during a recent INCRA *discrimina-tória*. Technically, this put him on an equal footing with the rancher, as both had filed requests for the land and both processes were still pending. The PF director said, however, that the second claim had been accepted in error and that the peasant, rather than INCRA, was to blame because he had settled in an area for which a requisition had already been filed. The question of how the peasant was to know what land had been requisitioned when the INCRA technician himself did not know was not raised. He was then told that the best solution would be for him to accept indemnification by the rancher for the value of his buildings and crops.

A long, tense bargaining session then began. The peasant stated what he thought his buildings and crops were worth, and the agronomist talked about how poor his crops and buildings really were. The rancher made a counter offer, and the PF director told the peasant that he was being unreasonable. The peasant, always deferential, refused to deal with the global figures but at each stage of the bargaining argued about the value of each separate crop or building. When his assembled adversaries shifted ground and started discussing with him the value of each crop, he responded with a question: How could he sell that particular crop if it had not yet been harvested? When the INCRA lawyer intervened, explaining that they were really talking about indemnification and not about sale and then continued on to explain what indemnification was, the peasant professed not to understand. He was then offered the right to harvest his crops if he took down his buildings, for which he would also be indemnified immediately. He responded only to the offer that he would be allowed to harvest his crops, and the INCRA personnel, relieved, turned the discussion back to the value of the indemnification. When the issue of taking down his buildings was raised again, the peasant asked them if they hadn't just agreed that he could harvest his crops and how could he possibly harvest his crops if he had nowhere to live and nowhere to store them? By this time everyone in the room appeared both frustrated and confused, except for the peasant, who gave every indication of not fully understanding what was being said to him but still appeared quite calm.

Eventually, as prices climbed up to several times the first amount offered by the rancher, but still less than a third of the peasant's original request, and after the peasant had been assured that he could stay on until his harvest, and that the rancher would send his truck to move materials from the house and other buildings to a new site, together with whatever fruit trees were small enough to transplant, the peasant and the rancher reached an agreement. While the INCRA lawyer drew up a contract for them to sign, the peasant sat and discussed local politics and likely trends in the urban markets for various crops with the PF director. He clearly understood, and discussed in detail, a wide range of issues of considerably greater complexity than the sale of crops which were still in the ground.

By feigning a stereotyped, and frustrating, lack of comprehension, the peasant had played a superb bargaining game against a rather formidable array of opponents, but he still ended up giving up his occupancy, and the considerable labor in clearing and building, for less than US$500. The next move itself would be onerous and difficult, and he would lose part of the next growing season. Most important, he would almost surely have to locate much farther from the town and so would be able to market his crops less easily.

The costs of the trip, including INCRA salaries and travel allowances, the salaries of the boat crew, and the fuel used, were somewhere between three to four times the indemnification the peasant finally accepted. The INCRA personnel had throughout the meeting consistently overlooked the agency's own responsibility in having filed the second request, which effectively gave occupation rights to the peasant, and had consistently intervened to lower the indemnification that the peasant was to receive.

Conflict, Legitimacy, and Land Title

Land-titling procedures and the investigations and interventions which precede them are costly for the government and enormously expensive for small holders who have to deal with a complex and inefficiently run bureaucracy whose procedures and presuppositions favor their wealthier competitors. Though INCRA's norms and regulations are designed to protect a wide range of anterior rights in land, actual bureaucratic procedures, interpreted with considerable individual discretion by INCRA functionaries, work against the interests of small holders and peasants.

These effects, however, simply exacerbate the long-range consequences of turning land held in various forms of use right into land which can be held as titled, negotiable property. The roots of the conflict over land, which INCRA's titling programs are designed to avoid, lie in the increased opportunities for profit that government subsidies and special credits for agriculture, together with the expanded urban markets of the Amazon, have created. The extreme imbalances between the political and economic resources of large landholders, investors, and speculators, on the one hand, and the subsistence cultivators and extractors who can only compete with them by submitting to complex and expensive modern bureaucratic procedures, on the other, become finally a routinized substitute for the violent expulsion of peasants from their land that INCRA was assigned to prevent. Because land titles are ideologically presented as equally accessible to all legitimate claimants, and because the titling laws make specific provision for anterior, premodern use rights, the state can hide the fact of violent expropriation and expulsion behind a facade of legal modernity. The ideological preferences, procedures, and class identification of individual bureaucrats make effective access to these institutions even more expensive than they would be anyway.

Remarkably, INCRA itself has no executive arm and no routine recourse to a court or police system to enforce its land regulations. In one particularly dramatic case, a rancher who had sold land in the south of Pará invested in clearing and planting pasture on several thousand acres of land under the jurisdiction of INCRA's Monte Alegre colonization project. Though the local INCRA agents made repeated complaints about this flagrant violation of restrictions on holding size, they were unable to effect his removal. INCRA can call in the army or police only when conflict over land erupts into violence, or when INCRA claims that the potential for violence is impeding its work.

Unless they specifically need an INCRA title for credit purposes, large landowners can ignore INCRA regulations with impunity. The occupant of a small plot may also ignore INCRA, but by doing so loses whatever recourse he has against expulsion. Obtaining INCRA validation remains an expensive and uncertain process, but many small holders continue to submit to the necessary procedures.

INCRA does not effectively prevent the illicit seizure and clearing of large areas by investors and speculators. Nor does it stop the purchase of old, lapsed, or fraudulent titles by large capitalist concerns and the subsequent expulsion of peasants who have neither the political, economic, or legal resources to defend their use rights in land. Even the idea that documenting land will provide recourse against future expulsion is illusory in most cases. INCRA's PFs have surveyed only a small fraction of the lands which *decreto-lei 1.164* put under its jurisdiction. Thus far, it has worked primarily in areas which capitalist investors wish to bid on or where land conflict has already emerged. In the latter case INCRA tends to favor the claimant to large holdings. Small holders who successfully seek INCRA documents tend to be those located near but not in areas of direct conflict between title and occupation.

INCRA does provide the state with a means of presenting itself as working to control violence and as protecting the rights of peasants by providing supposedly equal, supposedly rational, bureaucratic access to the land titles which guarantee ownership under the modern capitalist legal systems. By providing this access as the peasants' only recourse against violent expulsion, the state, and INCRA, effectively oblige them to abandon alternative, nonmodern forms of tenure and to use their land and their labor on it to pay the additional costs of complying with modern bureaucratic land survey, documentation, titling, and registry procedures. The refusal of many INCRA agents to appreciate or understand the nonmodern, noncapitalist ways in which peasants have used not just land, but also their total environment, enhances the ways that the state imposes modern systems and forces the abandonment of local subsistence strategies. The process is different than the violent expulsion of peasants by large landowners, because INCRA brings about these results in programs officially designed to regulate access to land by legal means, but the final result may be quite similar.

The great poverty of most of the small-holding occupants, their subjection to exploitative rates of exchange for both the goods they sell and for the informal credit they receive through the *aviamento* system, and their susceptibility to violent expulsion all serve to maintain the state's and INCRA's modernizing ideologies. INCRA and the state can plausibly defend their claims that the modernization of land tenure contributes to social justice, social welfare, and the control of violence. The economic and social systems which INCRA procedures disrupt provide only a precarious standard of living and precarious access to crucial resources. Their poverty appears especially great in comparison to the idealized notion of temperate zone small farms integrated into national markets and national social service systems. This notion provides the ideological basis for the U.S.-derived rural extension models. By perpetuating the myth of the modern small farm, through INCRA, through EMATER, and through small-farm credit programs and other support systems, the state provides INCRA, and INCRA's bureaucrats, a rationale to justify their procedural discrimination against noncapitalist uses of the natural environment and their bias toward modern economic and legal organization.

This is not to say that a modern land-tenure system based on individual ownership of surveyed, titled, and registered land would not serve to curb violent expulsion of small holders. Nor is it to say that bank credits and other supports available to small holders with titled land might not increase their production on the land. These results were not achieved, however, because (1) land titling has been limited and highly selective, both in INCRA's choice of areas to be surveyed and in INCRA's procedural bias toward certain modern types of land claim and land use, (2) the support systems which might provide a return, through access to credit, for example, on the high costs of land titling, are not effective for the small farmers in the Amazon, and (3) the uses to which successful claimants to large titled areas in the Amazon have put their land, primarily lumbering and ranching, have disrupted the physical environment, limited its future utility, and drastically reduced the number of people it will support. Ideally, modernized land tenure would form part of a modern agricultural system in which productive farmers were legally protected against expulsion and against exploitative rates of exchange or credit. In practice, land-tenure modernization legitimates and accelerates the Amazonian peasants' loss of land, their access to resources, and their livelihood, however impoverished.

The expansion into the Amazon of predatory forms of capitalism, based on wasteful and destructive use of natural resources, must be separated from the effects of particular bureaucratic decisions and procedures. These procedures and the ideologies which form bureaucratic decisions are consonant with the dominant ideology of the national capitalist center, so their effects tend to facilitate, and to amplify the effects of, the expansion of capitalist social relations and capitalist ownership of land into new areas. This consonance of bureaucratic procedures and ideologies with the expansion of capitalist relations does not, however, necessarily indicate intent on the part of the state.

Indeed, though they make for complex, tedious reading, the procedures outlined in INCRA's various manuals and in its sixteen-volume *Vade Mecum* appear to be a highly rational approach to protecting effective land tenure while transforming its legal basis. Unless one attributes extraordinary degrees of conspiratorial genius to the anonymous lawyers who devised these procedures to regulate and protect access to land, it is hard to see anything in these documents beyond a complete lack of information or imagination about economic and social systems different than those the modern lawyers already knew about; that is, these documents outline procedures for modernizing land tenure which would probably work reasonably well in a socio-economic system that was already modern. In the Amazon, however, these procedures actually impede the realization of one of their stated goals, to protect the legitimate occupants' rights in land. To the extent that the state seeks legitimacy and control by attempting to regulate capitalist expansion, as it has in some of its Amazonian development programs, the consonance of bureaucratic ideologies and procedures with the predominant national modern capitalist mode of production limits the power of the state by impeding effective implementation of its policies.

The state may attempt to impose modern forms on its own periphery in order to legitimate itself and to enhance its bureaucratic control, and in this it is possible to see the priority, if not the dominance, of political decisions over economic systems. The particular forms of modernity which Brazilian state policies, implemented by a modern, uncoordinated bureaucracy, have created, however, make it increasingly difficult for peasant communities to sustain themselves, because they are forced to comply with exogenous institutional requirements that cost them a great portion of their available money and do not enhance either the productive or commercial potential of their labor. At the same time that this imposed modernization makes peasant survival more difficult, the extension of routinely titled land will eventually facilitate land sales and the concentration of land tenure. Because government programs have had little success in developing alternative forms of productive employment, modernization is likely to depopulate rural areas without providing the emigrants with other means of subsistence. Development programs and bureaucracies initiated under the apparent political control of the state thus achieve unintended results, which facilitate eventual predominance of and control by private capital over the political organization of the state.

Analysts of the recently independent African nations have discussed the effects of the overdeveloped state that African politicians and bureaucrats took over as a legacy of colonially imposed administrative systems (Leys, 1976). The modern state, grounded in rapidly industrializing national centers, is equally overdeveloped in relation to the less industrialized, less modern regions of Brazil and of other regionally unequal or heterogeneous Latin American countries. The problem in Africa and in the less developed regions of Latin American nations is that the state and its bureaucracy are far more ponderous, powerful, and complex than the African national, or Latin American regional, economies which they govern. Such states simply could not have emerged from such economies, but the colonial experience, on the one hand, and the accidents of national boundaries, on the other, impose the superordinate state on these economies and facilitate the use of their natural and human environments by classes and economic systems that can appropriate their natural and labor values cheaply without directly suffering the consequences of their overexploitation.

Eisenstadt (1963), Shivji (1976), Mamdani (1976), and Kraus et al. (1979) have shown how bureaucrats and bureaucratic agencies tend to hypertrophy, to the nurturing and protection of their own interests, and to extensive impact on government policy in developing states. All of these effects are enhanced by the incongruence between the development of the state and the development of the economy and society it regulates.

Inappropriate, excessively expensive, and socially destructive modernization occurs in these circumstances because the overdeveloped modern state and the overpowerful bureaucrats it employs can impose institutions which regulate and control access to resources crucial to human life—e.g., land and agricultural production in the Amazon. Inhabitants of the region must either attempt to conform or risk losing access to these resources, but conformity is too expensive for their own economic systems to bear. Modern systems, even if not adaptive to these environments, thus overwhelm locally adaptive systems.

NOTES

1. INCRA's peremptory expropriation of land near the actual colonization areas did eventually cause it some difficulties. In addition to the suit brought by the member of the defunct Altamira cooperative, over 250 holders of titles granted by the state of Pará in 1959 initiated a complaint against INCRA in 1979 to recover lands around the town of Altamira, which INCRA had expropriated in 1971. INCRA eventually returned control over the area to the town of Altamira, which in turn had to issue a whole new set of titles.

2. When, for example, a large company claimed rights to extensive rubber plantations around Alter do Chão, a community on the Tapajós River, about forty kilometers from Santarém, small holders organized by a local leader rented trucks and demanded a meeting with the head of Santarém's PF. They got both the meeting and their titles. The high density of rubber planatations, their renewed prosperity from rising rubber prices, their common interest in a single crop, and their proximity to Santarém gave them an exceptional advantage even in comparison to the other communities in the densely settled *várzea* around Santarém (see Bunker, 1981a). It was more usual for individual claimants to take advantage of a trip to town to press their claim, but even this possibility was much greater in the riverine communities than it was on the *terra firme*.

3. In many cases title-buying entrepreneurs took advantage of these ambiguities to expel occupants and extract resources from a much larger area than their combined titles specified (Pinto, 1977).

Conclusion

In this book I have shown that the processes which led to and still maintain the underdevelopment of the Amazon can only be understood if we account for the succession of modes of extraction as they emerged from the interaction of regional and global constraints, pressures, and opportunities and as they affected both natural and human environments. None of the prevailing models of development adequately explains these processes. None of the conventional prescriptions for development can be expected to reverse their effects.

Massive state intervention in the Amazon has accelerated the environmental and social disruptions which extractive export economies have visited on the region for over 350 years. The organizational complexity of modern bureaucratic agencies, which the state has directed to carry out its capital accumulation and social welfare programs, impeded and distorted the implementation of development policies and compromised the state's own legitimacy, autonomy, and bureaucractic authority. Exogenous institutional forms imposed on a social formation devoid of their necessary organizational complements greatly increased program costs to the state and to the Amazon's inhabitants, provided opportunities for corruption, and weakened the state's control of its own apparatus. They also led to expensive and wasteful self-maintenance and expansion strategies in individual agencies.

Early chapters showed how local dominant classes' responses to world market opportunities ultimately impoverished the resource base on which their own wealth and profits depended. They also showed that modern state policies which accelerated accumulation of capital by large companies through fiscal subsidies, tax holidays, and physical access to resources further impoverished the region without solving national balance-of-payments problems. Indeed, there is strong evidence that the Manaus free trade zone and the massive investments in Carajás have aggravated trade balance deficits. In all of these projects the state reinforced the capacity of the dominant classes to penetrate the state apparatus and reduced its own administrative efficiency. The state's programs also intensified the ecological and demographic disruptions which had limited the capacity of Amazonian social formations

238

to respond in sustainable and progressive ways to changing world-system opportunities and pressures. The resulting socioeconomic simplification and destablization prevented the emergence of enduring or effective local organization. The absence of effective civil organization at the local level reduced the state's capacity to implement policy in the Amazon. Its complex bureaucracies were obligated to act in an institutional vacuum, because the correspondingly complex institutional forms on which they were designed to act could not emerge in this impoverished region.

Each of the last five chapters focused on specific types of programs and bureaucratic procedures that exemplify the processes by which complex social forms imposed on an environment simplified by sustained energy loss caused unintended and systemically irrational results. These examples could have been extended into a veritable catalog of bureaucratic horrors, but further exemplification is unnecessary to this analysis.

These diverse case studies of policy distortion and program failure were intended to examine the propositions of an ecological model which explains uneven development, unequal exchange, and regional subordination as the consequences of (1) the physically necessary relations between extraction and production, (2) the resulting imbalance of energy flows between regional ecosystems, and (3) the differential incorporation of energy in different regional social and economic formations. By proposing that our calculus of value must include not just the labor and capital incorporated into commodities but all forms of energy and matter potentially or presently, directly or indirectly, useful to the maintenance and reproduction of human society, I have expanded the notion of uneven development to include the differential rates and amounts of energy embodied in learned human experience, in social organization, and in enduring infrastructure. This has allowed me to show that unequal exchange and uneven development between regions occur not simply in terms of more labor for less labor, or in the channeling of surplus value from one region to another, or in the differential rates of exploitation by different dominant classes. Rather, we have seen that the differential capacity to direct human and nonhuman energy and to conserve part of energy flow-through in subsequently useful forms distinguishes the core from peripheral social formations more profoundly than the terms of trade for their respective commodities or their different processes of accumulation. The embodiment of energy in economic and social organization encompasses far more of the essential differences and relations between core and periphery than measures limited to commodity production and exchange can.

Energy-intensive social complexity is the fundamental and necessary condition for the national center's exploitation of its own periphery, but this same complexity limits central ability to administer and direct peripheral social processes. The energy-intensivity of the center allows it to subordinate the periphery, but the incongruence of energy-intensive and energy-dispersed social forms prevents the central state from rationally achieving its own purposes there.

This discrepancy between the power to repress and the power to direct and coordinate is seen most clearly in the actions of the developmental state in a nation of unevenly developed regions with heterogeneous social formations comprised of different modes of production and extraction. The "functional dualism" of industrial capitalism and semiproletarian agriculture (de Janvry, 1981) or the transfer of surplus value between articulated modes of production (Bettelheim, 1972; Long, 1975; Foster-Carter, 1978) may enhance accumulation by nationally dominant classes who control the predominant mode of production in a disarticulated economy. Thus, there may be an economic logic in the persistence of quite heterogeneous modes of production and social relations within the same nation. However, because of the expansive nature of the agencies which comprise it and because of its own imperatives of uniform control and nationally validated subjective legitimacy, the national state seeks to homogenize its own administrative and regulatory systems across these heterogeneous social formations.

These imperatives lead to distortion and irrationality in both policy and implementation. The state evolves in correspondence with the nationally predominant modes of production and in response to the problems and contradictions of accelerated economic processes and complex social relations. It responds to, interacts with, is shaped by, and shapes the organizational and institutional forms of its own economic center and base. Its operating procedures and ideological assumptions are more or less compatible with the central social formation. The procedural rationality of bureaucratic organization reflects this compatibility, and the separate agencies depend on it to carry out their own specific functions. Even though some of the state's bureaucratic forms may be imported and not initially congruent, they are at least partially adapted to the nationally predominant social formations or they are eventually discarded.

The state is maintained by the appropriation of tax and other revenues from production and circulation within this dominant mode and between it and the subordinate modes. To the extent that subordinate social formations channel surplus to the dominant social formations, the state's taxation of these subordinate social formations also occurs as a function of its relation with the dominant social formations.

When the state attempts to homogenize its control and bureaucratic procedures across diverse or heterogeneous social formations, it both incurs and imposes extra costs which far outweigh its acceleration of production and accumulation in the national periphery. These costs contribute to its failure to achieve its stated goals. They also aggravate the socioeconomic disruptions which result from imposing these procedures on social formations that have different, and simpler, institutional and organizational bases.

The state's pact with national and international capital and its own control of force, revenues, and jurisdiction, together with the developing technologies of transport and communication, allow it to present the image of homogenizing the political and administrative structures of the nation. The institutional disjunctures between the state's own complex organizational forms and the organizational and institutional forms of the subordinate peripheries, however, impede the state's power to realize its own projects. The state's power to realize both economic and social welfare projects at its own center depends in very large measure on its consonance with the overall directions and logic of the predominant economic and social processes which it regulates. The state does not dominate or transform autonomously; it can only facilitate and regulate what the economy and society are carrying forward.

This is not to deny that a political regime can fundamentally alter political and economic relations. Those who capture the state, however, capture only repressive and allocative powers. Repression may restrict both social and economic development. It may favor some classes and sectors over others, but it is these sectors and their interaction with the politically subordinated sectors and classes that will bring about whatever socioeconomic transformations that occur under such a regime. Evans (1979) clearly shows that even when the state assumes entrepreneurial functions, it must complement and depend on civil sectors of the economy. Only the complete transformation of class relations in a socialist revolution would eliminate this dependence of the state on the organizations of civil society, and even socialist states are affected by prior social and economic formations.

Its association with the nationally predominant social formations gives the state the power to repress, to allocate budgets, and to assign jurisdiction on the periphery. Its power to direct, to regulate, and to facilitate, however, are all seriously compromised there. Its subsequent organizational weakness undermines that part of its subjective legitimacy which is derived from its own projected image of efficacy. Its apparatus becomes susceptible to dominant class penetration. It fails to achieve its stated goals, but even in its failure it disrupts extant social, political, and economic organization and institutions. To the extent that the state, either to increase subjective legitimacy or to facilitate and enhance accumulation, decides to transform social organizations and economic systems in these peripheral areas, its failure increases its vulnerability and loss of prestige. The state's self-legitimating claims that it can transform the underdeveloped society (Cardoso, 1973; O'Donnell, 1978; Evans, 1979) are revealed as an illusion which can be maintained only when there is fundamental consonance of state policy with the evolutionary directions of the central social formation.

It is in this regard that problems of regionally uneven development force us to rethink notions of the predominance of the political (Foweraker, 1981), of the relative autonomy of the state, and of the efficacy of the bureaucratic-authoritatian state (O'Donnell, 1973). The failure of social welfare programs designed to achieve subjective legitimacy by appearing to include subordinate classes and regions in the predominant forms of expanded reproduction is but one of many symptoms of the complex, modern, energy-intensive national state's inability to function rationally across heterogeneous social formations. When the state extends its own apparatus and policies into a socially simplified, energy-poor region devoid of organizations and institutions which can compete against the state's agencies and for the resources they control, the state enhances both its own, and the peripheral societies', permeability to dominant classes at the national center.

The energy imbalances which mark the difference between the articulated economy and complex differentiated social organization, on the one hand, and the disarticulated, simplified economy, on the other, allow the first to subordinate the second, but the national state's attempts to coordinate, regulate, and transform socioeconomic processes in the disarticulated economy are profoundly wasteful. I have explained these failures in terms of the energy flows which structure both articulated and disarticulated social formations and which underlie the necessary relations between extractive and productive economies. This explanation incorporates concepts of differentiation, integration, and functional specificity derived from modernization theories. I believe that these concepts still provide the richest and most precise characterization of the institutional forms of complex, energy-intensive societies. The case studies I have presented, however, show that the imposition of these forms on subordinate, energy-poor systems inverts the outcomes predicted by modernizationists such as Smelser and Eisenstadt. We can explain this inversion by analyzing the ways that modern organizational forms consume, concentrate, incorporate, and redirect both human and nonhuman energy and the ways that these forms interact with others which consume and incorporate far less energy. Analysis of the organizational and ideological characteristics of state bureaucracies, which reproduce the defining charcteristics of modernity, complements the energetics explanation of this inversion.

By comparing the energy costs and benefits of different organizational forms and by elaborating on the simple ecological dictum that any organism that consumes more energy than can be directed or transformed within its environment will reduce that environment's productive potential and thus undermine its own reproduction, we can understand how the extension of energy-expensive organizational complexity into simplified, energy-losing social formations inevitably fails to promote development there. By considering modern bureaucratic agencies as separate dissipative structures (Adams, 1982), we have seen how their own expansive strategies and competition create and maintain systemically irrational results. Finally, by considering the unbalanced energy flows from periphery to center and the resulting accumulation and concentration of energy-consuming structures in the center, we can understand how the state, and the predominant social formation, can continue and increase these destructive actions.[1]

Energy Measures and Development Theory

This is not to say that energy measures themselves explain class relations or regional inequalities, or why the administrative forms of the modern national state are so complex and so costly that they distort policy and reduce productive potential in noncapitalist social formations. Energy measures provide just that—measures. I have argued, however, that understanding uneven development and interregional exploitation requires that we attribute values to natural energy transformations and that we consider the effects of any economic activity on the long-term capacity of society to reproduce itself. Energy measures provide a means of assessing these effects. Our explanations, however, must still include the economic and political relations between classes, the social organization of different regional formations, the imperatives and policies of national states and their bureaucracies, the relations between unequally powerful national states, the effects of capital flows and commodity exchange between regions, and the structuring of demand within the world economy.

The incorporation of energy values and energy measures into these explanations and the insistence that our analysis take account of how energy uses in all of these processes affect the long-term potential for social reproduction and development allow us to see the errors and the partialities of the various theories of development and underdevelopment. All of these theories have assumed variants of labor theories of value; all have extended economic models based on the false notion

that production systems in some sense are self-enclosed and can reproduce themselves; none has taken into account that production systems require extraction systems; that extraction systems subservient to
present forms of industrial production inevitably deplete their own
resource bases; and that this process is as finite as the limited stock of
matter and energy which is or will become convertible to human uses.

It is still impossible to specify the actual energy values involved in
these flows, partly because we do not yet have all the appropriate
measures or understand all of the biotic interrelations necessary to
gauge present energy flows and uses, and partly because future energy
values to human society are impossible to predict. All we can do is to
compare grossly the energy requirements and capabilities of complex
and simpler social forms and to outline abstractly the necessary relations
and dynamics between productive and extractive economies. Nor is it
yet possible to specify the various extractive-productive mixes of different economies, or the different ecological and energetic consequences
of different extractive economies in different ecosystems. Rather, we
can only elaborate the logic of these relations within the framework
and limitations of the laws of thermodynamics and of what we know
about social and economic evolution. This does, however, allow us to
offer more complete and coherent explanations of the multiple, visible
forms of productive development and extractive underdevelopment,
of their necessary physical relations, and of the consequences of these
relations.

I have argued here that understanding regional development requires
integrating two different levels of analysis. I borrowed selectively from
theories of modernization and of modes of production to explain the
consequences of certain uses of both the natural and the social environment within a particular region. Modernization theories provide
a useful vocabulary for the social forms and the special knowledge
and ideologies that have emerged with energy-intensive economies.
The concept of mode of production allows us to consider the economic,
the social, the political, the commercial, the infrastructural, and the
demographic—not only as a complex, highly interrelated whole system
but also as a system evolved out of the sequence of all prior systems.
The vocabularies of neither modernization nor the modes of production
are sufficient, however, until we inform them with an understanding
of the energy transformation processes which sustain any society.

I have also borrowed from world-systems and dependency perspectives at the global level of analysis. World market as systemic and
comprising multiple regional economies, world system as dominated
by core economies, and world system as accelerating accumulation in
a small part of the world all provide important concepts for under-

standing the impact of the global on the regional. But because these theories also draw too much on labor theories of value, because they ignore important elements of the highly distinct developmental or evolutionary sequences in different regions, and because they are themselves too oriented to flows of capital and goods, they cannot account for the multiple effects of unbalanced energy flows between different regions.

I have argued throughout that uneven development between regions and the capacity of one region to subordinate another reflect not only the unequal exchange of labor values but also the very different embodiment of energy flow-through in social organization and infrastructure. All social organization, technology, and information are the results of previous human uses of energy and matter. This is not to say that energy and matter cause, or that the laws of thermodynamics explain, organization, technology, and information, only that none of these can occur without the conversion of matter and energy. The social organization, technology, and specialized information and knowledge systems of complex industrial societies have all emerged from and correspond to the vastly accelerated flow-through of energy and matter. Simultaneously, they enhance both the social capacity to transform energy and matter and the efficiency of human energies in directing nonhuman energies. To the extent that extractive economies lose energy and suffer disruptions of social and physical organization which might enhance the efficiency of their human energies, the corresponding simplification of technologies, information, and community makes them more vulnerable to encroachments and environmental disruption by social formations which have become complex and therefore capable of directing and controlling a wide range of different energy forms. The ability of the Brazilian state to extend expensively disruptive bureaucratic forms into the Amazon is only one manifestation of uneven sociological development; the Brazilian state is itself subject to parallel unevenness in its relations with the world core, and its own haste to exploit the Amazon results from its need to offset the inequality of its own exchanges, and those of the dominant classes on which it depends in various ways.

Accelerated energy flow-through does not itself create social complexity or enhance the scale of human and nonhuman energies which can be effectively subordinated and directed toward unitary sets of goals by particular states, corporations, or allied class factions, but social complexity does evolve with accelerated energy flow-through, and the specialized knowledge and functional specificities of coordinated systems are requisites for and also enhance this acceleration of energy flow-through. Focusing on energy and energy flows does not explain these processes, but it does give us a measure of some of their essential components, and this measure in turn allows us to compare the results of different energy flow-throughs in different societies in terms of one society's dominance over another, especially as some regions lose energy to other regions whose social formations do embody this energy in different social and economic forms.

This approach to uneven development allows us to describe more fully than other approaches have the relations between economic, demographic, social, and ecological processes over time. It allows us to see how, in terms of economic and social growth, uneven development occurs and is maintained. At the same time, however, this approach raises a whole series of questions about the long-term maintenance of industrial modes of production, their effects on extractive regions, and their ultimate vulnerability to resource depletion.

Energy Flows and Social Reproduction

Because extraction is necessarily anterior to any process of production or transformation, economic models which consider modes of production as bounded, as reproducing themselves, or as indefinitely expansible are fundamentally wrong. Any economic model which considers that value is created only by human labor is fundamentally wrong. Any theory of international exchange which measures commodity flows between regions only in terms of capital, prices, or the labor incorporated into each is therefore also wrong.

Instead, our economic models and our theories of development must take account of the physical requirement that the continuation of any social formation, and of the modes of production which we may discern within it, depends either on the reproduction or regeneration of natural energy transformation systems or on the depletion of a limited stock of energy sources. An industrial mode of production can sustain itself only by drawing energy and matter from modes of extraction.

In the short term the idea that such modes of production can reproduce themselves, or can themselves create value, is negated by the physical dependence of production on extraction. In the long run the logic of maximizing profits or returns to labor accelerates the depletion of different, and eventually of all, natural resources. The acceleration of modes of production precipitates the exhaustion of modes of extraction and thus hastens the eventual collapse of all modes of industrial production.

The short-term acceleration of industrial production requires a relatively high valuation of human energy in the articulated industrial social formation and a corresponding undervaluation of natural resources and extractive labor. These discrepancies exacerbate the social and ecological despoliation of extractive regions which must ultimately limit the reproductive potential, not only of the extractive modes, but also of the productive modes which depend on them. In the meantime, however, energy flows from the first to the second increase the capacity of the productive modes to engender the market demands or opportunities, the technology, and the powerful social organizational forms which stimulate and allow locally dominant groups to disrupt essential energy transformation processes and human organization in extractive regions. This leaves the social formations of extractive regions progressively less able to defend their own social and physical environments.

The industrial modes of production have experienced what some Marxists incorrectly have called expanded reproduction by accelerating the flow-through of energy and matter, but this process is clearly finite. The progressive impoverishment of single extractive regions must finally impoverish the entire global system. Technological innovations which allow substitution of depleted natural resources by more abundant ones simply shift the process of depletion from one peripheral area to another. Decisions to arrest this process, however, can only be made at the local or regional level, which is precisely the level at which extractive sequences undermine the social power necessary to implement effective decisions to resist continued depredation. I return to this dilemma in the next section.

Energy and Power

The sociological literature on energy flows and on resulting differences in the complexity of social organization is limited, but control of energy flows can be shown to generate social power (Adams, 1975), about which there is an extensive sociological literature. The issue of power is central to questions of unequal exchange: those who suffer unfavorable rates of exchange are likely to have less power to begin with, and the unfavorable rates of exchange tend to enhance these power differentials over time. Finally, it is clear that social power depends on and is generated out of social organization. I have argued throughout this book that energy loss from particular extractive economies leads to both environmental and organizational simplification. Organizational simplicity limits the amount of human energy which can be directed and coordinated, and this limits the total amount of power which can be generated in a social formation. These limitations may enhance relative power differentials between different classes in the same region, but because they lessen total social power in the entire formation, they also reduce the power of regionally dominant classes relative to those of other regions. The absolute power of any dominant class is finally dependent on the total social and physical environment which its members can exploit. The weakness of locally dominant classes becomes a factor in the continued exploitation of the peripheral region by stronger, more energy-intensive social formations.

The sequence of modes of extraction in the Amazon clearly illustrates this principle. Each mode of extraction was organized in adaptation to the environment, physical and social, left by previous modes; each has further impoverished both of these environments. Because the rates of exchange between these modes of extraction, whose costs included the destruction of the natural and human resources, and the rest of the world system were extremely unbalanced, successive dominant groups in the region have themselves been impoverished. Those fragments of contemporary dominant groups tied to transnational corporations may be an exception only because of their ability to leave the region and transfer their operations elsewhere, but their options will also be progressively limited.

If social organization is adaptation to the relevant total environment, and if power is achieved through control over the environments of others (Adams, 1970, 1975), social organization and social power are both reduced as the environment itself is impoverished. The reduction of social organization reduces the effective use of social power. Flannery (1972) argues that the evolutionary tendency of human civilization is toward more complex, hypercoherent, and ecologically expensive forms of dominance. The costs of such organization may finally become so great that they undermine the environment and the resources on which they depend, but the organizations themselves do generate increased social power and complexity, at least until severe ecological disruption leads to collapse. The sequence of extractive economies in the Amazon, however, has impoverished the natural environment without developing social organization, useful infrastructure, or significant social power. The Amazon thus remains susceptible to new and destructive forms of predation by energy-intensive social formations. The final quesion for this study, then, is, are there any means by which local social organization can so adapt to its environment as to achieve power systems capable of defending themselves?

Given the economic and political power and the interests of the Brazilian state and of its domestic and international capitalist allies, the immediately apparent answer is no. The cartels which national states of primarily extractive economies may organize are not likely to emerge where extractive regions are subordinated to productive centers within the same nation. The increasing investments of foreign equity capital, of foreign credits, and of national capital in the Cerra dos Carajás and other mineral extractive projects seem likely to impel the Brazilian state to intensify its control over the exploitation of the Amazon. In its attempts to solve balance-of-payments problems by exporting minerals, the state has paradoxically committed itself to spending the equivalent of its foreign debt on the infrastructure for mineral extraction and transport (Pinto, 1982). Pressures to service new and old debts will increase environmental pressures on the Amazon and its inhabitants. Though state plans for Carajás include processing and agricultural projects integrated with the extractive enterprise, neither the history of other mining endeavors, nor the location of the Carajás reserves themselves, nor current endeavors to implement those plans offer much promise that such projects, even if established, will last longer than the mineral reserves themselves. In fact, Brazil's current debt problems are likely to curtail investment in the linked industrial projects and to stimulate predatory extraction aimed at the quickest possible returns.

Regional Developmental Potential and Global Constraints

Revenues from mining, if not completely consumed in extractive costs and debt services, could be directed back into the Amazon instead of to other areas in or out of Brazil. It is not impossible to imagine that it will finally be understood that the despoliation of more than half of the national territory impoverishes the nation as a whole. Nor is it impossible to imagine that some international solution to the staggering debt levels, which are distorting development for many countries, not just Brazil, will be found and enforced. These outcomes, however, would require changes in both regional and international power differentials which would allow peripheral regions to develop durable infrastructures, politically effective social organization, and self-sustaining economic systems. Present relations between extraction and production make it highly unlikely that these changes will occur, but we can nonetheless speculate about what they might entail in the Amazon.

First, it would be necessary that social organization in the Amazon adapt to its own physical and social environments rather than follow social organizational forms transferred from another environment. The species diversity of the forest, the disasters which have befallen monocropping systems in the Amazon, and the successful, highly diversified, and relatively stable swidden systems of some Amazonian indigenous groups all indicate that the intercropping of numerous humanly useful plants is essential to any strategy for sustaining human life in the

Amazon without destroying the physical environment. Denevan (1970, 1971) has recorded ways in which some indigenous groups manipulate the physical environment to enhance the productivity of natural interactions between soil, plants, water, and animals. Erickson (1979) has extended some of these ideas, suggesting that the raised fields which increased and prolonged agricultural yields by reproducing the levees that the river's meanders built up may also have been used for pisiculture. Smith (1980) has documented the numerous known locations of the *terra preta do índio,* deep black soils of considerable fertility built up by the accumulation of wastes from indigenous groups. Lathrap (1974) has shown that highly productive, dense societies were able to develop from an agriculture which emerged from and was maintained by the rich aquatic protein resources of the *várzeas.* These resources permitted the settlement size and permanence necessary to develop agriculture and then complemented the agricultural diet. Denevan (1982) extends Lathrap's analysis by showing how crops specifically adapted to different ecological zones may complement each other to fill human needs.

The ecological devastation of the Amazon started when the modes of extraction organized in response to world-system exchange opportunities focused on the single natural products for which there was greatest global demand. Human organization originally exploited a wide range of energy sources, from a wide range of species, because it had to satisfy the wide range of human nutritional needs. Each need was limited, however, so that no particular species and no particular ecological zones were less likely to be exploited past the point of regeneration or self-sustenance.

Human organization in the Amazon is no longer bounded by its own ecosystem, however, and it is highly unlikely that this large resource-rich area will be withdrawn from the world system of exchange. Indeed, given the continuing world demand for raw materials that can be extracted from the Amazon, it is likely that a large share of its participation in the world system will be based on extractive economies. The problem, then, is to determine how social and economic organizations adaptive to the Amazon's environment can emerge from or in proximity to these extractive economies.

One solution, already suggested, is to assure that more of the extractive revenues stay in the Amazon. This, however, can only occur if there are viable economic and social communities that can both demand certain concessions from the state and participate in and with extractive enterprise by providing some of the infrastructure, labor, provisioning, and technologies which they require. The random location of extractive enterprise, determined by the physical distribution of natural resources, makes such participation difficult, but a reversal of the long-term tendency of the Amazon's extractive economies to concentrate population in a few large cities would make such participation far more feasible than it is at present.

Much of the critical discussion of state highway programs among Amazonian planners and intellectuals has focused on the greater cost effectiveness and reduced ecological disruption of revitalizing river traffic. The debate over whether the extra time involved in moving goods by water would impose costs equal to those of highway development has been inconclusive. There are other, more important reasons than the cost of transport to focus on the developmental potential of the river itself. Most of the Amazon's population, even in cities, is still concentrated along river banks. Lathrap's analysis of the symbiotic, though unequal, relations between different groups occupying different ecological zones suggest that a return to *várzea*-based systems would not only permit a greater dispersion of population out of the cities but also would also provide a much more effective social organization for exploiting the upper reaches of tributaries and their associated *terra firme*. To the extent that *terra firme* was primarily accessible via the *várzea*-based communities, and the upland settlements which would depend on them for the trade necessary to complement what they could derive from their own ecological zones, these communities could exert some control over and demand participation in *terra firme* extractive enterprise. Symbiotic relations between *terra firme* and *várzea* populations could provide infrastructure, labor, food, and other support systems necessary to extractive enterprise. More important, however, such symbiotic systems could develop alternative economies which would allow them autonomy from the extractive enterprise and provide them with the political and economic bases to control the impact of extractive industries on their own physical environment.

The dilemma, of course, is that self-sustaining, symbiotic economies adapted to and exchanging across different ecological zones can only be maintained in a system that permits ecosystem maintenance and long-term conservation to prevail over short-term profit maximization. It seems plausible that human groups take much more care to conserve the environment they inhabit than do human groups which can exploit these environments from a distance, but environmental conservation may preclude energy-intensive organization and therefore leave ecologically adapted systems vulnerable to economic and social domination by energy-intensive social formations. The problem, then, is how local groups can achieve adequate power within their own environment to protect it against outside predation. We know that such local control is no guarantee against overexploitation and depredation of the environment, but it is probably a necessary condition.

Regional Power and Class Struggle

I argued in Chapter 1 that Bettelheim's and Palloix's attempts to reduce international inequalities to internal inequalities overlooked essential systemic processes of global exchange. An inversion of their position, i.e., that a particular country is less likely to suffer unequal international exchange to the degree that its inhabitants and direct producers achieve more favorable internal exchange rates, seems more plausible, however, as long as we remember that we are talking about a particular country and not attempting to explain the entire global system of exchange. The negotiation of exchange rates is ultimately a matter of the relative power of the exchanging groups and their relative control over their own environments.

In this more general sense Emmanuel was right to seek the sources of underdevelopment in measures of inequality between classes. His mistake was to tie this idea of inequality to wages, even in profoundly noncapitalist societies. If we amplify his notion about wages to include all measures of unequal exchange, then we can say that countries where labor values and natural values are seriously undercompensated will tend indeed to be underdeveloped. The need, then, is to revalue both labor and nature so that human communities which extract, produce, and exchange goods can develop infrastructure and organization that conserve energy and that become an integral part of and contribution to the ecosystems in which humans participate.

Dominant classes depend on their societies' total environment; in this sense they depend on the organization of other classes' adaptation to the environment. The clearest lesson of class relations in the Amazon is that dominant groups which impoverish the rest of society ultimately impoverish themselves. Only when human communities with balanced exchange relations exist is it possible for social organization to adapt to its total environment in ways which sustain both human community and the ecosystem itself. It is, however, most unlikely that dominant classes will perceive that their long-term interests lie in revaluing human labor and natural resources unless other classes oblige them to understand this.

The point is not that the only solution for a resource rich region is exit from the world system of exchange. Rather it is that different regions participate in the world economy according to exchange opportunities perceived as advantageous by particular classes. These advantages vary enormously between classes. Hence, a change in power, and in exchange rates, between classes within a particular region would imply a very different participation by that region in the world economy. In this sense Bettelheim and Palloix are correct when they say that internal class relations determine the mode of a particular country's insertion in the world economy, but again, only with regard to the particular region. The world exchange system, because it is global and contains many regions, possesses its own dynamic, but it responds to changes in single peripheral areas. More balanced internal exchange rates in many or most peripheral regions would have profound effects on the world system, primarily by raising the relative monetary costs of extracted commodities and thus slowing their consumption in the core.

Ultimately, the need is to slow the flow of energy to the world center. As long as natural values in living and fossilized plants which have transformed solar energy into humanly useful forms are transferred predominantly to a small part of the world's total area, the world industrial core will continue to dominate markets in ways which limit the development potential of the rest of the world. The capacity to direct and use natural or nonhuman energies is closely associated with the expanded scope of social organization and with the increased complexity and inequality within the hierarchies which dominate social organizations (Adams, 1975). Flannery (1972) points out, though, that the increased concentration of control over both human and nonhuman energies eventually means socially costly hypercoherence and ecologically costly overexploitation of natural resources. Hypercoherence ultimately leads to ecological and social collapse as increasingly stratified systems undermine their own resource base. The present undervaluation of both natural and labor values in peripheral societies speeds up the evolution toward collapse by reducing the monetary costs of exploitation.

The exchange relations which bind this system together depend on locally dominant groups to reorganize local modes of production and extraction in response to world demand, but the ultimate collapse will be global, not local. The continued impoverishment of peripheral regions finally damages the entire system. While it is conceivable that resource shortages on a world-wide scale will ultimately stimulate a global revaluation of natural resources, the power to force such revaluation lies in the extractive regions themselves, but this can only occur if social inequalities between classes and between regions are sharply reduced.

I have proposed elsewhere (Bunker, 1979) changes in Brazilian rural development strategy which might foster local organization capable of demanding more favorable rates of internal exchange. I have also

shown (Bunker, 1981a, 1982b) that under the present excessively centralized bureaucratic organization and policy formulation even the agricultural communities most favorably situated in local markets remain
extraordinarily vulnerable to disruption by new extractive economies.
Local economies effectively integrated into favorable markets and sufficiently powerful to resist predatory incursions into their own environments cannot emerge in the Amazon unless the state protects them
so that their social organizations and economies can to develop autonomously.

Neither the current interests of the state, nor the class and regional
structure of Brazilian society, nor the present organization of the state's
regulatory apparatus is compatible with these goals. The decentraliza-
tion of political power and the drastic reductions of social inequality
which would be needed as the minimal first steps toward such goals
would require radical revaluation of both nature and community. The
final question confronting us is whether regional and global social and
economic organizations can achieve such revaluations before the in-
eluctable crises of the constantly accelerated human exploitation of a
limited stock of resources remove any other options.

Rappaport (1971) describes a mature ecosystem as one in which all
species enhance the survival and reproduction potential of the rest even
while maintaining themselves. Following Geertz, he shows how successful swidden systems achieve this by reproducing the symbiotic
coevolved relations of mature tropical forest ecosystems. The history
of capitalist development, the history of noncapitalist countries' responses to world markets, and the history of complex precapitalist
civilizations do not provide much hope that societies not bounded by
regionally limited ecosystems can achieve this maturity. Humans in
complex societies have thus far used their prescience to increase their
control over natural energy flows and over the social organization of
human energies in ways which undermine the ecosystems that sustain
them. Human groups could, however, use their prescience to enrich,
rather than impoverish, the ecosystems in which they participate, both
by striving to assure and strengthen natural regeneration and energy
transformation processes and by enhancing the effectiveness of their
own social organization. Systemic undervalution of either nature or of
human labor, and the unequal exchange which enforces such undervaluation, can only distort and impede human enhancement of the
natural environment and of the socially created infrastructure and
organization that are finally their contribution to the ecosystem. Rappaport's mature ecosystem, then, requires not only an egalitarian human society, but also an egalitarian human society which sees itself as
part of, rather than master of, the natural environment. The population

of extractive regions may learn this from their own experience long before it becomes apparent to the populations of productive regions, but their capacity to enforce this understanding and to resist the continued depradation of their own environments would require forms of social organization, coordination, and power that the internal dynamics and the external relations of extractive economies currently make impossible.

NOTE

1. The Amazon itself accounted for only 4 percent of gross national product under the conventional accounting calculus for 1972. This calculus reflects the economic and political value criteria employed by the state and nationally dominant classes. Environmentally and socially destructive programs can continue because of the accumulation of these values at the center and because, over the short term, these programs enhance the flow of these values to dominant classes at the energy-intensive national center and international core.

Bibliography

Adams, Dale W., Harlan Davis, and Lee Bettis
    1972   "Is Inexpensive Credit a Bargain for Small Farmers? The Recent Brazilian Experience." *Inter-American Economic Affairs* 26 (1):47-58.

Adams, Richard
    1970   *Crucifixion by Power.* Austin: University of Texas Press.
    1975   *Energy and Structure, a Theory of Social Power.* Austin: University of Texas Press.
    1982   *Paradoxical Harvest: Energy and Explanation in British History, 1870-1914.* New York: Cambridge University Press.

Alden, Dauril
    1976   "The Significance of Cacao Production in the Amazon Region during the Late Colonial Period: An Essay in Comparative Economic History." *Proceedings of the American Philosophical Society* 120 (Apr.):103-35.

Amin, Samir
    1970   *L'Accumulation a l'Echelle Mondiale.* Paris: Anthropos.
    1974   *Accumulation on a World Scale.* New York: Monthly Review Press.
    1976   *Unequal Development.* New York: Monthly Review Press.
    1977   *Imperialism and Unequal Development.* New York: Monthly Review Press.
    1978   *The Law of Value and Historical Materialism.* New York: Monthly Review Press.

Anderson, Charles W.
    1966   "Political Factors in Latin American Economic Development." *Journal of International Affairs* 20 (2):235-53.

Anderson, Perry
    1974   *Lineages of the Absolutist State.* New York: Monthly Review Press.

Anderson, Robin
    1976   "Following Curupira: Colonization and Migration in Pará (1758-1930)." Ph.D. diss., University of California, Davis.

Aragon, Luis
    1979   "Migration to Northern Goiás: Geographical and Occupational Mobility in Southeastern Amazonia, Brazil." Ph.D. diss., Michigan State University.

ARC (Anthropology Resource Center), Boston
    1980   "Massive Gold Rush in Yanomani Territory." *Bulletin* 4 (Jan. 5):3-4.

256

1981a   "The Yanomani Indian Park: The Next Carajás?" *Bulletin* 6 (May 10):5-8.

1981b   "The Carajás Project: A 'National Sacrifice Area'. . . ." *Bulletin* 6 (May 10):3-5.

1982   "The Continuing Struggle for Land Rights in Brazil." *Bulletin* 10 (Feb. 25):3-14.

Aspelin, Paul, and Silvia Coelho dos Santos
1981   *Indian Areas Threatened by Hydroelectric Projects in Brazil.* Copenhagen: IWGIA (International Work Group for Indigenous Affairs) Document 44.

Baer, Werner
1979   *The Brazilian Economy: Its Growth and Development.* Columbus, Ohio: Grid Publishing Co.

Banfield, Edward C.
1975   "Corruption as a Feature of Governmental Organization." *Journal of Law and Economics* 18 (1):587-605.

Baran, Paul
1957   *The Political Economy of Growth.* New York: Monthly Review Press.

Barnard, Charles I.
1938   *The Functions of the Executive.* Cambridge, Mass.: Harvard University Press.

Barraclough, Solon
1970   "Agricultural Policy and Strategies of Land Reform." In Irving L. Horowitz, ed. *Masses in Latin America,* pp. 95-171. New York: Oxford University Press.

BASA
1966   *Desenvolvimento Econômico da Amazônia.* Belém: BASA.

Bastos, A. C. Tavares
1975   *O Vale do Amazonas.* São Paulo: Companhia Editora Nacional.
[1866]

Bath, C. Richard, and Dilmus D. James
1976   "Dependency Analysis of Latin America: Some Criticisms, Some Suggestions." *Latin American Research Review* 25 (3):3-54.

Batista, Djalma
1976   *O Complexo da Amazônia.* Rio de Janeiro: Conquista.

Bayley, David H.
1966   "The Effects of Corruption in a Developing Nation." *Western Political Quarterly* 19 (Dec.):719-32.

Becker, Gary S., and George J. Stigler
1974   "Law Enforcement, Malfeasance, and Compensation of Enforcers." *Journal of Legal Studies* 3 (1):1-18.

Beckerman, Stephen
1978   "Comment on Ross' Article 'Food, Diet, and Hunting Strategy. . . .'" *Current Anthropology* 19 (1):17-19.

1979   "The Abundance of Protein in Amazonia: A Reply to Gross." *American Anthropologist* 81 (3):553-60.

Bettelheim, Charles
1972   "Theoretical Comments." In A. Emmanuel. *Unequal Exchange: A Study of the Imperialism of Trade,* Appendix I, pp. 271-322. New York: Monthly Review Press.

Blair, John
    1976   *The Control of Oil.* New York: Random House.
Blau, Peter
    1954   "Cooperation and Competition in a Bureaucracy." *American Journal of Sociology* 59 (May):530-36.
    1964   *Exchange and Power in Social Life.* New York: John Wiley and Sons.
Block, Fred
    1977   "The Ruling Class Does Not Rule." *Socialist Review* 7 (May-June):6-28.
Booth, David
    1975   "Andre Gunder Frank: An Introduction and Appreciation." In Ivar Oxaal, Tony Barnett, and David Booth, eds. *Beyond the Sociology of Development: Economy and Society in Latin America and Africa,* pp. 50-85. London: Routledge and Kegan Paul.
Bornschier, Volker, Christopher Chase-Dunn, and Richard Rubinson
    1978   "Cross-national Evidence on the Effects of Foreign Investment and Aid on Economic Growth and Inequality: A Survey of Findings and a Reanalysis." *American Journal of Sociology* 84 (Nov.):651-83.
Bottomore, T. B.
    1965   *Classes in Modern Society.* London: George Allen and Unwin.
Bradby, Barbara
    1975   "The Destruction of Natural Economy." *Economy and Society* 4 (May):127-61.
Brasil, República Federativa do
    1971   *I Plano Nacional de Desenvolvimento (1972-1974).* Guanabara: IBGE.
    1972   *I Plano de Desenvolvimento da Amazônia.* Belém: SUDAM.
    1974   *II Plano Nacional de Desenvolvimento (1975-1979).* Guanabara: IBGE.
    1975   *II Plano de Desenvolvimento da Amazônia.* Belém: SUDAM.
    1976   *Projeto RADAM: Levantamento de Recursos Naturais.* Vol. 6. Brasília: DNPM.
Brenner, Robert
    1977   "The Origins of Capitalist Development: A Critique of Neo-Smithian Marxism." *New Left Review* 104 :27-59.
Bretton, Henry L.
    1962   *The Politics of Decolonization.* New York: Praeger.
Brockway, Lucile H.
    1979   *Science and Colonial Expansion: The Role of the British Royal Botanic Gardens.* New York: Academic Press.
Brokensha, David, and Charles Erasmus
    1969   "African Peasants and Community Development." In David Brokensha and Marion Pearsall, eds. *The Anthropology of Development in Sub-Saharan Africa,* pp. 85-100. Lexington: University Press of Kentucky.
Brookfield, H.
    1975   *Interdependent Development.* London: Methuen and Co.
Bukharin, N.
    1972   *Imperialism and World Economy.* London: Merlin Press.

Bunker, Stephen G.
 1978   "Institutional Interdependence and the Failure of Rural Devel-
         opment Programs in Pará, Brazil." Paper presented at the annual
         meeting of the American Sociological Association, San Francisco.
 1979   "Power Structures and Exchange between Government Agencies
         in the Expansion of the Agricultural Sector." *Studies in Com-
         parative International Development* 14 (1):56-76.
 1980a   "Forces of Destruction in Amazonia." *Environment* 22 (Sept.):14-
         20, 34-43.
 1980b   "Barreiras Burocráticas e Institucionais a Modernização: O Caso
         da Amazônia." *Pesquisa e Planejamento Econômico* 10 (Aug.):555-
         600.
 1981a   "The Impact of Deforestation on Peasant Communities in the
         Médio Amazonas of Brazil." *Studies in Third World Societies* 13:45-
         60.
 1981b   "Class, Status, and the Small Farmer: Rural Development Pro-
         grams and the Advance of Capitalism in Uganda and Brazil."
         Latin American Perspectives 28 (Winter):89-107.
 1982a   "The Cost of Modernity: Inappropriate Bureaucracy, Inequality,
         and Development Program Failure in the Brazilian Amazon."
         Journal of Developing Areas 16 (July):573-96.
 1982b   "Os Programas de Crédito e a Desintegração Nao-Intencional
         das Economias Extrativas de Exportação no Médio Amazonas
         do Pará." *Pesquisa e Planejamento Econômico* 12 (Apr.):231-60.
 1983   "Policy Implementation in an Authoritarian State: A Case from
         Brazil." *Latin American Research Review* 18 (1):33-58.
 1984   "Modes of Extraction, Unequal Exchange, and the Progressive
         Underdevelopment of an Extreme Periphery: The Brazilian Am-
         azon, 1600-1980." *American Journal of Sociology* 89(5):1017-64.
Bunker, Stephen G., and Lawrence E. Cohen
 1983   "Collaboration and Competition in Two Colonization Projects:
         Toward a General Theory of Official Corruption." *Human Or-
         ganization* 42 (Summer):106-14.
Campanhole, Adriano
 1971   *Estatuto da Terra e Legislação Complementar.* São Paulo: Editora
         Atlas.
Cardoso, Fernando Henrique
 1972   "Dependency and Development in Latin America." *New Left
         Review* 74 (July-Aug.):83-95.
 1973   "Associated Dependent Development: Theoretical and Practical
         Implications." In A. Stepan, ed. *Authoritarian Brazil*, pp. 142-78.
         New Haven: Yale University Press.
 1975   *Autoritarismo e Democratização.* Rio de Janeiro: Paz e Terra.
 1977   "The Consumption of Dependency Theory in the United States."
         Latin American Research Review 13 (3):7-24.
Cardoso, Fernando Henrique, and Enzo Faletto
 1969   *Dependencia y Desarrollo en America Latina.* Mexico City: Siglo
         XXI Editores.
Cardoso, Fernando Henrique, and Geraldo Müller
 1977   *Amazônia, Expansão do Capitalismo.* São Paulo: Brasiliense.

Carvajal, Gaspar de
   1934   *The Discovery of the Amazon,* translated and edited by H. C.
          Heaton and Bertram Lee. New York: National Geographical So-
          ciety.
Carvalho, J. A. M. de, and M. de M. Moreira
   1976   *Migrações Internas da Região Norte,* 2 vols. Belém: SUDAM.
Casement, Sir Roger
   1912   *Correspondence Respecting the Treatment of British Colonial Sub-
          jects and Natives Employed in the Collection of Rubber in the
          Putumayo District.* London: His Majesty's Stationery Office.
Castro, Josué de
   1952   *The Geography of Hunger.* Boston: Little, Brown and Co.
Cehelsky, Marta
   1979   *Land Reform in Brazil: The Management of Social Change.* Boulder:
          Westview Press.
Chilcote, Ronald H.
   1974   "A Critical Synthesis of Dependency Theory." *Latin American
          Perspectives* 1 (1):4-29.
   1978   "A Question of Dependency." *Latin American Research Review*
          13 (2):55-68.
Cobbe, James H.
   1979   *Governments and Mining Companies in Developing Countries.*
          Boulder: Westview Press.
Collier, David (ed.)
   1979   *The New Authoritarianism in Latin America.* Princeton: Princeton
          University Press.
Collier, Richard
   1968   *The River That God Forgot.* London: Collins.
CONDEPA
   1975   *Pará, Desenvolvimento* 1 (Dec.).
Contini, Emilio
   1976   "A Colonização na Transamazônica." M. A. thesis, Fundação
          Getúlio Vargas, Rio de Janeiro.
Coquery-Vidrovitch, Catherine
   1976   "The Political Economy of the African Peasantry and Modes of
          Production." In Peter C. W. Gutkind and Immanuel Wallerstein,
          eds. *The Political Economy of Contemporary Africa,* pp. 90-111.
          Beverly Hills: Sage.
Coser, Lewis A.
   1956   *The Functions of Social Conflict.* Glencoe: The Free Press.
Cotler, Julio
   1972   "Las Bases del Corporatismo en el Peru." *Sociedad y Política* 2
          (Oct.):3-11.
Crozier, Michel
   1964   *The Bureaucratic Phenomenon.* Chicago: University of Chicago
          Press.
Cruz, Ernesto
   1958   *A Colonização do Pará.* Belém: INPA/CNPq.
da Cunha, Euclydes
   1913   *A Margem da História.* Porto: Livraria Chardron de Lelo e Irmão.

Dahrendorf, Ralf
    1958   "Out of Utopia: Toward a Reorientation of Sociological Analysis." *American Journal of Sociology* 64 (Sept.):115-27.
    1959   *Class and Class Conflict in Industrial Society.* Stanford: Stanford University Press.
Dalton, Melville
    1959   *Men Who Manage.* New York: Wiley.
Daly, Herman E.
    1977   *Steady-State Economics.* San Francisco: W. H. Freeman and Co.
Davis, Shelton
    1977   *Victims of the Miracle: Development and the Indians of Brazil.* New York: Cambridge University Press.
Dayton, Stan
    1975   "Brazil '75: For Mining, the Best Is Yet to Come." *Engineering and Mining Journal* 176 (Nov.):89-104.
de Arruda, H. P.
    1973   *Colonização na Amazônia Brasileira.* Brasília: INCRA.
de Janvry, Alain
    1981   *The Agrarian Question and Reformism in Latin America.* Baltimore: Johns Hopkins University Press.
Delacroix, Jacques, and Charles Ragin
    1978   "Modernizing Institutions, Mobilization, and Third World Development: A Cross National Survey." *American Journal of Sociology* 84 (July):123-50.
Denevan, William M.
    1970   "Aboriginal Drained-Field Cultivation in the Americas." *Science* 169 (August):647-54.
    1971   "Campa Subsistence in the Gran Pajanal, Eastern Peru." *Geographical Review* 61:496-518.
    1973   "Development and the Imminent Demise of the Amazon Rain Forest." *The Professional Geographer* 25 (2):130-37.
    1976   "The Aboriginal Population of Amazonia." In W. M. Denevan, ed. *The Native Population of the Americas in 1492,* pp. 205-34. Madison: University of Wisconsin Press.
    1982   "Ecological Heterogeneity and Horizontal Zonation of Agriculture in the Amazon Floodplain." Paper presented at the 31st Annual Latin American Conference, Gainesville, Fla.
Dias, Manuel Nunes
    1970   *A Companhia Geral do Grão Pará e Maranhão.* Belém: Universidade Federal do Pará.
Domar, E. O.
    1970   "The Causes of Slavery or Serfdom: A Hypothesis." *Journal of Economic History* 30 (Mar.):18-32.
dos Santos, Theotonio
    1970   "The Structure of Dependence." *American Economic Review* 60:231-36.
    1973   "The Crisis of Development Theory and the Problem of Dependence in Latin America." In H. Bernstein, ed. *Underdevelopment and Development,* pp. 57-80. Harmondsworth: Penguin.

Dube, S. C.
    1958   *India's Changing Villages: Human Factors in Community Development*. London: Routledge and Kegan Paul.
Eisenstadt, S. N.
    1963   "Problems of Emerging Bureaucracies in Developing Areas and New States." In B. F. Hoselitz and W. E. Moore, eds. *Industrialization and Society*, pp. 159-74. The Hague: Mouton.
    1964   "Social Change, Differentiation, and Evolution." *American Sociological Review* 29:375-86.
    1966a   "Breakdowns of Modernization." In J. L. Finkle and R. W. Gable, eds. *Political Development and Social Change*, pp. 371-92. New York: Wiley.
    1966b   *Modernization: Protest and Change*. Englewood Cliffs, N.J.: Prentice Hall.
    1970   "Social Change and Development." In S. N. Eisenstadt, ed. *Readings in Social Evolution and Development*, pp. 3-27. Oxford: Pergamon Press.
Emmanuel, Arghiri
    1972   *Unequal Exchange: A Study in the Imperialism of Trade*. New York: Monthly Review Press.
Epstein, T. S.
    1973   *South India: Yesterday, Today and Tomorrow*. London: Macmillan.
Erickson, Clark L.
    1979   "Indigenous Models for Alternative Development." Unpublished paper, Urbana, Ill.
Evans, Peter
    1979   *Dependent Development: The Alliance of Multinational, State, and Local Capital in Brazil*. Princeton: Princeton University Press.
Fals Borda, Orlando
    1970   *Estudio de la Realidad Campesina: Cooperación y Cambio*. Geneva: UNRISD.
    1971   *Cooperatives and Rural Development in Latin America*. Geneva: UNRISD.
Fearnside, Philip
    1981   *Carrying Capacity for Human Populations: Colonization in the Brasilian Rainforest*. Manuscript, Manaus, Amazonas.
Feder, Ernest
    1970   "La 'Función Social de la Tierra' y la Pobreza Rural en la América Latina." *El Trimestre Económico* 37 1, 145:3-38.
    1973   "Poverty and Unemployment in Latin America: A Challenge for Socio-Economic Research." In *The Rural Society of Latin America Today*, pp. 29-67. Institute of Latin American Studies. Stockholm: Almquist and Wiksell.
    1976   "The New World Bank Programme for the Self-Liquidation of the Third World Peasantry." *Journal of Peasant Studies* 3 (3):342-54.
Fesharaki, Fereidun
    1976   *Development of the Iranian Oil Industry: International and Domestic Aspects*. New York: Praeger.

Findley, Roger W.
  1973   "Problems Faced by Colombia's Agrarian Reform Institute in
          Acquiring and Distributing Land." In R. E. Scott, ed. *Latin Amer-
          ican Modernization Problems: Case Studies in the Crisis of Change,*
          pp. 122-92. Urbana: University of Illinois Press.
Fittkau, Ernst Josef
  1970   "Role of Caimans in the Nutrient Regime of Mouth-Lakes of
          Amazon Affluents." *Biotropica* 2 (2):138-42.
  1973   "Crocodiles and the Nutrient Metabolism of Amazonian Waters."
          Amazoniana 4 (Mar.):103-33.
Flannery, Kent V.
  1972   "The Cultural Evolution of Civilizations." *Annual Review of Ecol-
          ogy and Systematics* 3:399-426.
Foster-Carter, Aidan
  1976   "From Rostow to Gunder Frank: Conflicting Paradigms in the
          Analysis of Underdevelopment." *World Development* 4 (Mar.):167-
          80.
  1978   "The Modes of Production Controversy." *New Left Review* 107:47-
          78.
Foweraker, Joe W.
  1981   *The Struggle for Land.* New York: Cambridge University Press.
Frank, Andre Gunder
  1967   *Capitalism and Underdevelopment in Latin America: Historical
          Studies of Chile and Brazil.* New York: Monthly Review Press.
  1969   "Sociology of Development and Underdevelopment of Sociol-
          ogy." In Andre Gunder Frank, ed. *Latin America: Underdevel-
          opment or Revolution,* pp. 21-94. New York: Monthly Review
          Press.
  1979   *Dependent Accumulation and Underdevelopment.* New York:
          Monthly Review Press.
Furtado, Celso
  1963   *The Economic Growth of Brazil.* Berkeley: University of California
          Press.
  1965   "Political Obstacles to the Economic Development of Brazil." In
          Claudio Veliz, ed. *Obstacles to Change in Latin America,* pp. 145-
          61. London: Oxford University Press.
  1970   *Economic Development of Latin America: A Survey from Colonial
          Times to the Cuban Revolution.* London: Cambridge University
          Press.
Galtung, J.
  1971   "A Structural Theory of Imperialism." *Journal of Peace Research*
          8 (2):81-117.
Gaventa, John
  1980   *Power and Powerlessness: Quiescence and Rebellion in an Appa-
          lachian Valley.* Urbana: University of Illinois Press.
Georgescu-Roegen, Nicholas
  1970   "The Entropy Law and the Economic Problem." Paper presented
          in the Distinguished Lectures Series, the University of Alabama,
          reprinted in *The Ecologist* 2 (July):347-81.
  1971   *The Entropy Law and the Economic Process.* Cambridge, Mass.:
          Harvard University Press.

1975   "Energy and Economic Myths." *Southern Economic Journal* 41 (Jan.):347-81.

Gillette, Cynthia, and Norman Uphoff
1973   "The Credit Connection: Cultural and Social Factors Affecting Small Farmer Participation in Credit Programs." *AID Spring Review of Small Farmer Credit* 19, paper 7.

Goodland, R. J. A., and H. S. Irwin
1975   *Amazon Jungle: Green Hell to Red Desert?* Amsterdam: Elsevier.

Goodland, R. J. A., H. S. Irwin, and G. Tillman
1978   "Ecological Development for Amazonia." *Ciencia e Cultura* 30 (3):275-89.

Goodland, Robert J. A.
1980   "Environmental Ranking of Amazonian Development Projects in Brazil." *Environmental Conservation* 7 (1):9-26.

Goulding, Michael
1980   *The Fishes and the Forest.* Berkeley: University of California Press.

Gutkind, Peter C. W., and Immanuel Wallerstein
1976   "Editor's Introduction." In P. C. W. Gutkind and Immanuel Wallerstein, eds. *The Political Economy of Contemporary Africa*, pp. 7-29. Beverly Hills: Sage.

Harris, Marvin
1979   *Cultural Materialism.* New York: Random House.

Hébette, Jean, and Rosa Acevedo
1979   "Colonização Espontánea, Política Agrária, e Grupos Sociais." In José Marcelino Monteira da Costa, ed. *Amazônia: Desenvolvimento e Ocupação*, pp. 141-92. Rio de Janeiro: IPEA/INPES Serie Monografica No. 29.

Hecht, Susanna B.
1979   "Spontaneous Legumes of Developed Pastures of the Amazon and their Forage Potential." In Pedro A. Sanchez and Luis A. Tergas, eds. *Pasture Production in Acid Soils of the Tropics*, pp. 65-80. Cali: CIAT.

1981   "Deforestation in the Amazon Basin: Magnitude, Dynamics and Soil Resource Effects." *Studies in Third World Societies* 13:61-110.

Hechter, Michael
1971   "Towards a Theory of Ethnic Change." *Politics and Society* 2:21-45.

1972   "Industrialization and National Development in the British Isles." *Journal of Development Studies* 8:155-82.

1975   "Review of I. Wallerstein's 'The Modern World System.' " *Contemporary Sociology* 4:217-22.

1976   "Ethnicity and Industrialization: The Proliferation of the Cultural Division of Labor." *Ethnicity* 3:214-36.

Hemming, John
1978   *Red Gold: The Conquest of the Brazilian Indians.* Cambridge, Mass.: Harvard University Press.

Heriarte, Maurício de
1874   *Descrição do Estado do Maranhão, Pará, Corupá, e Rio das Amazonas* (excerpts in Nimuendaju, 1952, and in Palmatary, 1960).

Herndon, William
1853   *Exploration of the Valley of the Amazon.* Washington, D.C.: U.S. Navy Department.
Herrera, Felipe
1965   "Disunity as an Obstacle to Change." In Claudio Veliz, ed. *Obstacles to Change in Latin America*, pp. 230-52. London: Oxford University Press.
Higgott, Richard A.
1980   "From Modernization Theory to Pubilc Policy: Continuity and Change in the Political Science of Political Development." *Studies in Comparative International Development* 15 (4):26-58.
Hindess, Barry, and Paul C. Hirst.
1975   *Pre-Capitalist Modes of Production.* London: Routledge and Kegan Paul.
Hobsbawm, E. J.
1964   "Introduction." In Karl Marx, *Pre-Capitalist Economic Formations,* pp. 9-66. New York: International Publishers.
Homans, George C.
1950   *The Human Group.* New York: Harcourt, Brace, Jovanovich.
1974   *Social Behavior: Its Elementary Forms.* New York: Harcourt, Brace, Jovanovich.
Horowitz, Irving Louis
1972   *Three Worlds of Development: The Theory and Practice of International Stratification.* 2d ed. New York: Oxford University Press.
Huizer, Gerritt
1969   "Community Development, Land Reform, and Political Participation." *American Journal of Economics and Sociology* 28 (2):159-78.
Hunt, C. L.
1966   *Social Aspects of Economic Development.* New York: McGraw-Hill.
Huntington, Samuel P.
1968   "Modernization and Corruption." In Samuel P. Huntington, ed. *Political Order in Changing Societies*, pp. 59-71. New Haven: Yale University Press.
Hyden, Goran
1980   *Beyond Ujamaa in Tanzania.* Berkeley: University of California Press.
Ianni, Octávio
1979   *A Luta pela Terra.* Petrópolis: Vozes.
IBGE
1977   *Geografia do Brasil: Região Norte.* Rio de Janeiro: IBGE.
1978-79-80 *Anuário Estatístico.* Rio de Janiero: IBGE.
INCRA
1972   *PIN, Colonização da Amazônia.* Brasilia: INCRA.
Inkeles, Alex
1969   "Making Men Modern: On the Causes and Consequences of Individual Change in Six Countries." *American Journal of Sociology* 75:208-25.
1971   "Continuity and Change in the Interaction of the Personal and the Sociocultural Systems." In B. Barber and A. Inkeles, eds. *Stability and Social Change*, pp. 265-81. Boston: Little, Brown.

Inkeles A., and D. Smith
    1974   *Becoming Modern: Individual Change in Six Developing Countries.*
            Cambridge, Mass.: Harvard University Press.
Isaacson, John
    1981   "The Amazon at the Time of Contact, a View from the Rio
            Tapajós." Manuscript, Urbana, Ill.
Janzen, Daniel H.
    1973   "Tropical Agroecosystems." *Science* 182 (21 Dec.):1212-19.
Kahl, Joseph A.
    1968   *The Measurement of Modernism.* Austin: University of Texas Press.
Katzman, Marvin
    1976   "Paradoxes of Amazonian Development in a 'Resource Starved'
            World." *Journal of Developing Areas* 10 (July):445-60.
Kiemen, Mathias C.
    1954   *The Indian Policy of Portugal in the Amazon Region, 1614-1693.*
            Washington, D.C.: Catholic University Press.
Killick, Tony
    1980   "Trends in Development Economics and Their Relevance to
            Africa." *Journal of Modern African Studies* 18 (3):367-86.
Kleinpenning, J. M. G.
    1977   "An Evaluation of the Brazilian Policy for the Integration of the
            Amazon Region." *Tijdschrift voor Economie en Social Geografie*
            68 (5):297-311.
Kraus, Richard, William E. Maxwell, and Reeve D. Vanneman
    1979   "The Interests of Bureaucrats: Implications of the Asian Expe-
            rience for Recent Theories of Development." *American Journal
            of Sociology* 85 (1):135-55.
Laclau, Ernesto
    1971   "Feudalism and Capitalism in Latin America." *New Left Review*
            67 (May-June):19-38.
Lambert, Jacques
    1969   *Latin America: Social Structures and Political Institutions.* Berkeley:
            University of California Press.
Landsberger, Henry, and Cynthia N. Hewitt
    1968   "Ten Sources of Weakness in Latin American Peasant Move-
            ments." Paper presented at the Second International Congress
            of Rural Sociology, Eschede, Holland, Aug.
Lathrap, Donald W.
    1968a   "Aboriginal Occupations and Changes in the River Channel on
            the Central Ucayali, Peru." *American Antiquity* 33 (Jan.):62-79.
    1968b   "The Hunting Economies of the Tropical Forest Zone of South
            America: An Attempt at Historical Perspectives." In R. B. Lee
            and I. De Vore, eds. *Man the Hunter,* pp. 23-29. Chicago: Aldine
            Publishing Co.
    1974   "The Moist Tropics, the Arid Lands, and the Appearance of
            Great Art Styles in the New World." In Mary Elizabeth King
            and Idris R. Traylor, Jr., eds. *Special Publications, Museum of Texas
            Tech.*, pp. 115-58. Austin: University of Texas Press.
    1977   "Our Father the Cayman, Our Mother the Gourd: Spinden Re-
            visited, or a Unitary Model for the Emergence of Agriculture in
            the New World." In C. A. Reed, ed. *Origins of Agriculture,* pp.
            713-31. The Hague, Paris: Mouton Publishers.

Leacock, Seth
    1964   "Economic Life of the Maué Indians." *Boletim do Museu Paraense Emílio Goeldi* 19 (Apr.):1-31.
Leff, Nathaniel H.
    1964   "Economic Development through Bureaucratic Corruption." *American Behavioral Scientist* 8 (Nov.):8-14.
Leite, Serafim
    1943   *Historia da Companhia de Jesus no Brasil*. Rio de Janeiro: Imprensa Nacional.
Lenin, V. I.
    1939   *Imperialism, the Highest Stage of Capitalism*. New York: International Publishers.
Lenski, Gerhard
    1966   *Power and Privilege: A Theory of Social Stratification*. New York: McGraw-Hill.
Lerner, Daniel
    1968   "Modernization: Social Aspects." In D. L. Sills, ed. *International Encyclopedia of the Social Sciences* 10:38-95. New York: Macmillan and Free Press.
Levin, Jonathan
    1960   *Export Economies*. Cambridge, Mass.: Harvard University Press.
Leys, Colin
    1975   *Underdevelopment in Kenya*. London: Heinemann.
    1976   "The 'Over-developed' Post-Colonial State: A Reevaluation." *Review of African Political Economy* 5:39-48.
Linz, Juan J.
    1973   "The Future of an Authoritarian Situation or the Institutionalization of an Authoritarian Regime: The Case of Brazil." In Alfred Stepan, ed. *Authoritarian Brazil: Origins, Policies, and Future*, pp. 233-54. New Haven: Yale University Press.
Long, Norman
    1975   "Structural Dependency, Modes of Production, and Economic Brokerage in Rural Peru." In Ivar Oxaal, Tony Barnett, and David Booth, eds. *Beyond the Sociology of Development: Economy and Development in Latin America and Africa*, pp. 253-82. London: Routledge and Kegan Paul.
    1977   *An Introduction to the Sociology of Rural Development*. Boulder: Westview Press.
Looney, Robert E.
    1973   *The Economic Development of Iran: A Recent Survey with Projections to 1981*. New York: Praeger.
Love, Joseph L.
    1980   *São Paulo in the Brazilian Federation*. Stanford: Stanford University Press.
Luxemburg, Rosa
    1951   *The Accumulation of Capital*. London: Routledge and Kegan Paul.
McCoy, Alfred W., and Edilberto de Jesus, eds.
    1982   *Philippine Social History: Global Trade and Local Transformations*. Honolulu: University of Hawaii Press.
McCrary, Ernest
    1972   "The Amazon Basin: New Mineral Province for the 70's." *Engineering and Mining Journal* 173 (Feb.):80-83.

1975a   *"Exploration at a High Level but Badly Snarled in Red Tape."*
Engineering and Mining Journal 176 (Nov.):163-64.
1975b   "Foreign Investment Starts Pouring into Brazil." *Engineering and Mining Journal* 176 (Nov.):162.
Macdonald, Regina
1972   "The Order of Things: An Analysis of the Ceramics from Santarém, Brazil." *Journal of the Stewart Anthropological Society* 4 (Fall):39-57.
Macdonald, Theodore, Jr.
1981   "Indigenous Response to an Expanding Frontier: Jungle Quichua Economic Conversion to Cattle Ranching." In Norman E. Whitten, Jr., ed. *Cultural Transformations and Ethnicity in Modern Ecuador,* pp. 356-81. Urbana: University of Illinois Press.
McEwen, William J.
1975   *Changing Rural Society: A Study of Communities in Bolivia.* New York: Oxford University Press.
Maclachlan, Colin
1973   "The Indian Labor Structure in the Portuguese Amazon, 1700-1800." In D. Alden, ed. *Colonial Roots of Modern Brazil,* pp. 199-230. Berkeley: University of California Press.
McMullan, M.
1961   "A Theory of Corruption." *Sociological Review* 19 (June):184-200.
Mahar, Dennis J.
1979   *Frontier Development Policy in Brazil: A Study of Amazonia.* New York: Praeger Publishers.
Malloy, James M., ed.
1977   "Authoritarianism and Corporatism in Latin America: The Modal Pattern." In James A. Malloy, ed. *Authoritarianism and Corporatism in Latin America,* pp. 3-22. Pittsburgh: University of Pittsburgh Press.
Mamdani, Mahmood
1976   *Politics and Class Formation in Uganda.* New York: Monthly Review Press.
Mandel, Ernest
1975   *Late Capitalism.* London: New Left Review Editions.
Martins, Carlos Estevam
1977   *Capitalismo do Estado e Modelo Político no Brasil.* Rio de Janeiro: Graal.
Martins, Jose de Souza
1975   *Capitalismo e Tradição.* São Paulo: Livraria Pioneira Editora.
1980   *Expropriação e Violência.* São Paulo: Hucitec.
1981   *Os Camponeses e a Política no Brasil.* Petropolis: Vozes.
1982   "O Estado e a Militarização da Questão Agrária na Amazônia." Paper presented at the 31st Annual Latin American Conference, Gainesville, Fla.
Martinez Alier, J., and J. M. Naredo
1982   "A Marxist Precursor of Energy Economics: Podolinsky." *Journal of Peasant Studies* 8 (Jan.):207-24.

Marx, Karl
    1964   *Pre-Capitalist Economic Formations.* New York: International Publisher.
Medina, J. T., ed.
    1934   *The Discovery of the Amazon According to the Account of Friar Gaspar de Carvajal and Other Documents.* New York: American Geographical Society.
Meggers, Betty
    1971   *Amazonia: Man and Culture in a Counterfeit Paradise.* Chicago: Aldine.
Meillassoux, Claude
    1973   "The Social Organization of the Peasantry." *Journal of Peasant Studies* 1 (1):81-90.
Melby, John
    1942   "Rubber River." *Hispanic American Historic Review* 22 (3):452-69.
Mendonça, Otávio
    1977   "Prefacio." In Paul Lamarão, ed. *Legislação de Terras do Estado do Pará.* Vol. I, 1890-1963. Belém: Grafisa.
Merton, Robert K.
    1940   "Bureaucratic Personality and Authority." *Social Forces* 17:560-68.
    1957   *Social Theory and Social Structure.* 2d ed. New York: Free Press.
Molano Campuzano, Joaquim
    1979   "As Multinacionais na Amazônia." *Encontros com a Civilização Brasileira* 11 (May):21-34.
Moran, Emilio F.
    1975   "Pioneer Farmers of the Transamazon Highway: Adaptation and Agricultural Production in the Lowland Region." Ph.D. diss., University of Florida, Gainesville.
    1979   "Strategies for Survival: Resource Use Along the Transamazon Highway." *Studies in Third World Societies* 7:49-75.
    1981   *Developing the Amazon.* Bloomington: Indiana University Press.
Muniz, Palma
    1916   *Imigração e Colonização, 1616-1916, Estado do Grão Pará.* Belém: Imprensa Oficial do Estado do Pará.
Munoz, Heraldo
    1981   "The Strategic Dependency of the Centers and the Economic Importance of the Latin American Periphery." *Latin American Research Review* 16 (3):3-29.
Murphy, Robert F.
    1960   *Headhunters' Heritage: Social and Economic Change among the Mundurucu Indians.* Berkeley: University of California Press.
Muzegar, Jahargir A.
    1977   *Iran: An Economic Profile.* Chicago: University of Chicago Press.
Myrdal, Gunnar
    1968   *Asian Drama: An Inquiry into the Poverty of Nations.* New York: Random House.
    1970   "The 'Soft State' in Underdeveloped Countries." In Paul Streeten, ed. *Unfashionable Economics: Essays in Honour of Lord Balogh,* pp. 227-42. London: Woedenfeld and Nicolson.

Nelson, Michael
   1973   *The Development of Tropical Lands: Policy Issues in Latin America.*
           Baltimore: Johns Hopkins University Press.
Nimuendaju, Curt
   1946   *The Eastern Timbira*, translated and edited by Robert Lowie.
           Berkeley: University of California Press.
   1952   "The Tapajó." *Kroeber Anthropological Society Papers* 6:1-12.
   1967   *The Apinaye.* Oosterhont: Anthropological Publications.
Nisbet, Charles
   1967   "Supervised Credit Programmes for Small Farmers in Chile."
           Inter-American Economic Affairs 21 (2):49-54.
Nye, J. S.
   1967   "Corruption and Political Development: A Cost-benefit Anal-
           ysis." *American Political Science Review* 61 (June):417-27.
O'Brien, Philip J.
   1975   "A Critique of Latin American Theories of Dependency." In Ivar
           Oxaal, Tony Barnett, and David Booth, eds. *Beyond the Sociology
           of Development: Economy and Society in Latin America and Africa,*
           pp. 7-27. London: Routledge and Kegan Paul.
O'Donnell, Guillermo
   1973   *Modernization and Bureaucratic-Authoritarianism.* Berkeley: Uni-
           versity of California Institute of International Studies.
   1975   "Reflexiones sobre las Tendencias Generales de Cambio en el
           Estado Burocrático-Autoritario." *Revista Paraguaya de Sociología*
           33 (May-Aug.):111-58.
   1977   "Corporatism and the Question of State." In James Malloy, ed.
           Authoritarianism and Corporatism in Latin America, pp. 47-87.
           Pittsburgh: University of Pittsburgh Press.
   1978   "Reflections on the Patterns of Change in the Bureaucratic-Au-
           thoritarian State." *Latin American Research Review* 13 (1):3-39.
Olson, Mancur, Jr.
   1965   *The Logic of Collective Action.* Cambridge, Mass.: Harvard Uni-
           versity Press.
Palloix, Christian
   1969   *Problemes de la Croissance en Economie Ouverte.* Paris: Maspero.
Palmatary, Helen Constance
   1960   *The Archaeology of the Lower Tapajós Valley, Brazil.* Philadelphia:
           Transactions of the American Philosophical Society, New Series,
           Volume 50, Part 3.
Palmer, Robin, and Neil Parsons, eds.
   1977   *The Roots of Rural Poverty in Central and South Africa.* Berkeley:
           University of California Press.
Pará, Estado do
   1976   *Diário Official do Estado.* Belém: Imprensa do Estado do Pará,
           November 9.
Pereira, L. C. Bresser
   1977   *Estado e Subdesenvolvimento Industrializado.* São Paulo: Brasi-
           liense.
Pereira, Osny Duarte
   1971   *A Transamazônica-Pros e Contras.* Rio de Janeiro: Editora Civil-
           ização Brasileira, S.A.

Pereira, Potyara A. P.
  1978   "Burocracia e Planejamento Regional na Amazônia." *Revista Brasileira de Estudos Políticos* 46 (Jan.):127-58.
Petras, James F., and Robert LaPorte, Jr.
  1971   *Cultivating Revolution: The United States and Agrarian Reform in Latin America.* New York: Random House.
Pinto, Lucio Flavio
  1977   *Amazônia, o Anteato da Destruição.* Belém: Grafisa.
  1980   *No Rastro do Saque.* São Paulo: Hucitec.
  1982   "Amazônia: A Fronteira do Saque." Paper presented at the 31st Annual Latin American Conference, University of Florida, Gainesville.
Pompermayer, Malori J.
  1979   "The State and the Frontier in Brazil." Ph.D. diss., Stanford University.
  1980   "Agrarian Structure and State Policies in Brazil." Paper presented at the meetings of the Latin American Studies Association, Bloomington, Ind.
Portes, Alejandro
  1973a   "The Factorial Structure of Modernity: Empirical Replications and a Critique." *American Journal of Sociology* 79 (July):15-44.
  1973b   "Modernity and Development: A Critique." *Studies in Comparative International Development* 8 (3):247-79.
  1976   "On the Sociology of National Development: Theories and Issues." *American Journal of Sociology* 82 (July):55-85.
  1979   "Housing Policy, Urban Poverty, and the State: The Favelas of Rio de Janeiro, 1972-1976." *Latin American Research Review* 14 (Summer):3-24.
  1980   "Convergencies between Conflicting Theoretical Perspectives in National Development." In H. M. Blalock, Jr., ed. *Sociological Theory and Research: A Critical Appraisal*, pp. 220-27. New York: The Free Press.
Prebisch, Raul
  1963   *Toward a Dynamic Development Policy for Latin America.* New York: United Nations E/CN. 12/680/Rev. 1.
Preobazhensky, E.
  1965   *The New Economics.* Oxford: Claredon.
Ragin, Charles, and Jacques Delacroix.
  1979   "Comparative Advantage, the World Division of Labor, and Underdevelopment." In R. F. Tomasson, ed. *Comparative Social Research*, 2:181-214. Greenwich, Conn.: JAI Press.
Raiol, Domingos Antonio
  1970   *Motins Políticos.* Belém: Universidade Federal do Pará.
Rappaport, Roy A.
  1971   "The Flow of Energy in an Agricultural Society." *Scientific American* 225 (Sept.):69-82.
Reichel-Dolmatoff, G.
  1976   "Cosmology as Ecological Analysis: A View from the Rain Forest." *Man*, n. s. 2:307-18.
Reis, Arthur C. F.
  1945   *O Processo Histórico da Economia Amazonense.* Rio de Janeiro: Imprensa Nacional.

1949   *Monte Alegre—Aspectos de sua Formação Histórica.* Belém: Grafica.
1968   *A Amazônia e a Cobiça Internacional.* Rio de Janeiro: Grafisa Record Editora.
Reis, Mauricio Rangel
1975   *Brasil: 35 Anos de Desenvolvimento.* Brasília: Ministério do Interior.
Rey, Pierre-Philippe
1973   *Les Alliances de Classes.* Paris: Maspero.
Roett, Riordan
1978   *Brazil: Politics in a Patrimonial Society.* New York: Praeger.
Ross, Eric
1978   "The Evolution of the Amazon Peasantry." *Journal of Latin American Studies* 10 (Nov.):193-218.
Russell, Joseph A.
1942   "Fordlandia and Belterra, Rubber Plantations on the Tapajós River, Brazil." *Economic Geography* 18:125-45.
Santos, Roberto
1968   "O Equilíbrio da Firma Aviadora e a Significação Econômica Institutional do Aviamento." *Pará Desenvolvimento* 3 (June):7-30.
1977   "História Econômica da Amazônia (1800-1920)." Master's thesis, Faculdade de Economia e Administração da Universidade de São Paulo.
1979   "Sistema de Propriedade e Relações de Trabalho no Meio Rural Paraense." In J. M. Monteiro da Costa, ed. *Amazônia: Desenvolvimento e Ocupação,* pp. 130-40. Rio de Janeiro: IPEA/INPES.
1980   *História da Amazônia (1800-1920).* São Paulo: TAO.
Sawyer, Donald
1977   "Peasants and Capitalism in the Amazon Frontier." Paper presented at the meeting of the Latin American Association, Houston.
Schmink, Marianne.
1977   "Frontier Expansion and Land Conflicts in the Brazilian Amazon: Contradictions in Policy and Process." Paper presented at the meetings of the American Anthropological Association, Houston.
1981   "A Case Study of the Closing Frontier in Brazil." Amazon Research Paper No. 1. Gainesville, Fla.: Amazon Research and Training Program.
1982   "Land Conflicts in Amazonia." *American Ethnologist* 9 (May):341-57.
Schnaiberg, Allan
1970   "Measuring Modernism: Theoretical and Empirical Explorations." *American Journal of Sociology* 76 (Nov.):399-425.
1980   *The Environment: From Surplus to Scarcity.* New York: Oxford University Press.
Schuh, G. Edward
1971   *O Desenvolvimento da Agricultura no Brasil.* Rio de Janeiro: APEC Editora, S.A.

Schumacher, Ernest F.
1973   *Small Is Beautiful: Economics as if People Mattered.* New York: Harper and Row.
Schwartzman, Simon
1977   "Back to Weber: Corporatism and Patrimonialism in the 70's." In James M. Malloy, ed. *Authoritarianism and Corporatism in Latin America,* pp. 89-108. Pittsburgh: University of Pittsburgh Press.
Scott, James C.
1969   "Corruption, Machine Politics, and Social Change." *American Political Science Review* 63 (4):1142-59.
Selznick, Philip
1949   *TVA and the Grassroots.* Berkeley: University of California Press.
1955   *Conflict and the Web of Group Affiliations.* New York: Free Press.
Shaw, R. Paul
1976   *Land Tenure and the Rural Exodus in Chile, Colombia, Costa Rica, and Peru.* Gainesville: University of Florida Press.
Shivji, Issa
1976   *Class Struggles in Tanzania.* New York: Monthly Review Press.
Silva, Graziano da
1978   *Estrutura Agrária e Produção de Subsistência na Agricultura Brasileira.* São Paulo: Editora Hucitec.
Simmel, George
1950   *The Sociology of George Simmel,* ed. and trans. by Kurt Wolff. New York: Free Press.
Sioli, H.
1973   "Recent Human Activities in the Amazon Basin." In B. J. Meggers, ed. *Tropical Forest Ecosystems in Africa and South America,* pp. 321-24. Washington, D.C.: Smithsonian Institution.
1975   "Tropical River: The Amazon." In B. A. Whitten, ed. *River Ecology,* pp. 461-88. Oxford: Blackwell Scientific Publications.
Skillings, Robert F., and Nils O. Tcheyan
1979   "Economic Development Prospects of the Amazon Region of Brazil." School of Advanced Occasional Papers Series, No. 9, Washington, D.C.
Smelser, N. J.
1963   "Mechanisms of Change and Adjustment to Change." In B. F. Hoselitz and W. E. Moore, eds. *Industrialisation and Society,* pp. 32-54. The Hague: Mouton in collaboration with UNESCO.
Smith, Nigel J. H.
1974   "Destructive Exploitation of the South American River Turtle." *Association of Pacific Coast Geographers* 36:85-101.
1976   "Transamazon Highway: A Cultural-Ecological Analysis of Colonization in the Humid Tropics." Ph.D. diss., University of California, Berkeley.
1980   "Anthrosols and Human Carrying Capacity in Amazonia." *Annals of the Association of American Geographers* 70 (Dec.):553-66.
1982   *Rainforest Corridors.* Berkeley: University of California Press.
Sodero, Fernando Pereira
1968   *Direito Agrário e Reforma Agrária.* São Paulo: Livraria Legislação Brasileira, Ltda.

Solberg, Carl
   1976   *Oil Power: The Rise and Imminent Fall of an American Empire.*
           New York: New American Library.
Stavenhagen, Rodolfo
   1964   "Changing Functions of the Community in Underdeveloped
           Countries." *Sociologia Ruralis* 4 (3-4):315-31.
   1966-67 "Seven Erroneous Theses about Latin America." *New York Uni-
           versity Thought* 4 (Winter):25-37.
Sternberg, Hilgard O'Reilly
   1973   "Development and Conservation." *Erdkunde* 23:253-65.
   1975   *The Amazon River of Brazil.* Weisbaden: Springer-Verlag.
Steward, Julian
   1967   "Perspectives on Modernization: Introduction to the Studies."
           In Julian Steward, ed. *Contemporary Change in Traditional So-
           cieties,* pp. 1-52. Urbana: University of Illinois Press.
Sweet, David
   1974   "A Rich Realm of Nature Destroyed: The Middle Amazon Valley
           (1640-1750)." Ph.D. diss., University of Wisconsin, Madison.
Tambs, Lewis A.
   1974   "Geopolitics of the Amazon." In Charles Wagley, ed. *Man in the
           Amazon,* pp. 45-90. Gainesville: University of Florida Press.
Tamer, Alberto
   1970   *Transamazônica, Solução para 2001.* Rio de Janeiro: APEC Editora,
           S.A.
Tavares, Vania Porto, Claudio Monteiro Considera, and Maria Thereza L.L. de
Castro e Silva
   1972   *Colonização Dirigida no Brasil, Suas Possibilidades na Região Ama-
           zônica.* Rio de Janeiro: IPEA/INPES.
Tendler, Judith
   1973   "The Trouble with Goals of Small Farmer Credit Programs."
           AID Spring Review of Small Farmer Credit 19, paper 6.
Terray, Emmanuel
   1972   *Marxism and Primitive Societies.* New York: Monthly Review
           Press.
Thiesenhusen, William C.
   1971   "Colonization: Alternative or Supplement to Agrarian Reform
           in Latin America." In Peter Dorner, ed. *Land Reform in Latin
           America: Issues and Causes,* pp. 207-26. Madison: Land Tenure
           Center, University of Wisconsin.
Thome, Joseph R.
   1971   "Improving Land Tenure Security." In Peter Dorner, ed. *Land
           Reform in Latin America: Issues and Cases,* pp. 227-40. Madison:
           Land Tenure Center, University of Wisconsin.
Throgmorton, David
   1983   "Meeting the Energy Crisis: A Case Study of Wyoming Resource
           Producers." Ph.D. diss., University of Illinois at Urbana-Cham-
           paign.
Torres-Rivas, Edelberto
   1969   *Processos y Estructuras de una Sociedad Dependiente: Centro-
           america.* Santiago: Ediciones Prensa Latinoamericana.

U.S. Census
    1949   "Historical Statistics of the United States." Washington, D.C.:
            U.S. Bureau of the Census.
Varma, Baidya Nath
    1980   *The Sociology and Politics of Development: A Theoretical Study.*
            London: Routledge and Kegan Paul.
Velho, Otavio Guilherme
    1972   *Frentes de Expansão e Estrutura Agrária.* Rio de Janeiro: Zahar
            Editores.
    1976   *Capitalismo Autoritário e Campesinato.* São Paulo: Difel.
    1979   "The State and the Frontier." In Neuma Aguiar, ed. *The Structure
            of Brazilian Development,* pp. 17-36. New Brunswick: Transaction
            Books.
Veliz, Claudio, ed.
    1965   *Obstacles to Change in Latin America.* London: Oxford University
            Press.
    1967   *The Politics of Conformity in Latin America.* New York: Oxford
            University Press.
Villela, Anibal, and Jose Almeida
    1966   "Obstáculos ao Desenvolvimento da Amazônia." *Revista Brasi-
            leira de Economia* 20 (June/Sept.):177-99.
Wallerstein, Immanuel
    1974a   "The Rise and Future Demise of the World Capitalist System."
            Comparative Studies in History and Society 16 (4):387-415.
    1974b   *The Modern World System: Capitalist Agriculture and the Origin
            of the European World Economy in the Sixteenth Century.* New
            York: Academic Press.
    1975   "Modernization: Requiestat in Pace." Paper presented in The-
            matic Panel for the Concept of Modernization at the annual
            meeting of the American Sociological Association, San Francisco.
    1976   "The Three Stages of African Involvement in the World Econ-
            omy." In P. C. W. Gutkind and I. Wallerstein, eds. *The Political
            Economy of Contemporary Africa,* pp. 30-57. Beverly Hills: Sage.
    1981   "On How Accumulation Works." *Contemporary Sociology* 10
            (Jan.):41-3.
Weber, Max
    1947   *The Theory of Social and Economic Organization,* ed. Talcott Par-
            sons. New York: Oxford University Press.
Weeks, John, and Elizabeth Dore
    1979   "International Exchange and the Causes of Backwardness." *Latin
            American Perspectives* 6 (Spring):62-87.
Weinstein, Barbara
    1980   "Prosperity without Development: The Paraense Elite and the
            Amazon Rubber Boom (1850-1920)." Ph.D. diss., Yale University.
    1982   "Capital Penetration and Problems of Labor Control in the Am-
            azon Rubber Trade." *Radical History Review* 27:121-40.
Weinstein, Jay, and John Weinstein
    1982   "The Soft State and Development Administration." In Jay Wein-
            stein. *Sociology/Technology: Foundations of Post-Academic Social
            Science,* pp. 210-30. New Brunswick: Transaction Books.

Wertheim, W. F.
    1971   "The Way towards Modernity." In A. R. Desai, ed. *Essays on Modernization of Underdeveloped Societies* 1:76-94. Bombay: Thacker and Co.
Whitten, Norman E., Jr.
    1978   "Ecological Imagery and Cultural Adaptability: The Canelos Quichua of Eastern Ecuador." *American Ethnologist* 80 (Dec.):836-59.
Wolf, Eric R.
    1967   "Levels of Communal Relations." In Robert Wauchope, ed. *Handbook of Middle American Indians* 6:299-316. Austin: University of Texas Press.
Wolf, Howard, and Ralph Wolf
    1936   *Rubber, a Story of Glory and Greed.* New York: Covici Friede Publishers.
Wood, Charles H.
    1980   "Peasant and Capitalist Production in the Brazilian Amazon: A Conceptual Framework for the Study of Frontier Expansion." Paper presented at the meeting of the Latin American Studies Association, Bloomington, Ind.
Wood, Charles, and John Wilson
    1982   "The Role of the Amazon Frontier in the Demography of Rural Brazil." Paper presented at the 31st Annual Latin American Conference, Gainesville, Fla.
Wood, Charles, and Marianne Schmink
    1979   "Blaming the Victim: Small Farmer Production in an Amazon Colonization Project." *Studies in Third World Societies* 7:77-93.

Index

Accelerator (economic), 28, 34; lack of in extractive economies, 26-27, 29

Adams, R., 13, 14, 15, 18n1, 32, 46, 56n2, 145, 200, 248, 253

Amin, S., 43, 48

Articulation, social, 32. *See also* Accelerator; Linkage

Aviador, defined, xiii, 67

Aviamento, defined, xiii, 6, 67; in rubber trade, 67-68; after rubber collapse, 73, 157, 234

Balance of payments, 81, 158

Banco do Brasil, xi; rural development, 129-31, 132; credit norms, 138

BASA, xi, 131-33; founded, 84; and cooperations, 202-7

Bettelheim, C., 42, 43-45, 54, 60, 252-53

Blau, P., 183, 184, 185-86, 190

BNCC, xi, 131, 132

Bornschier, V., 71, 152

Brenner, R., 38, 41

Brockway, L., 23, 24, 26, 68

Bureaucracy: costs of complexity, 9, 17, 124-25, 176, 199, 200, 240-43; expansiveness of, 52, 200, 240; power of, 98; central control of, 126; operating procedures of, 126; energy and, 145; ideologies of, 145, 242-43; competition within, 199-201, 219-21

Cardoso, F., 40, 41, 42, 51, 52, 79, 84, 99, 104, 111, 115, 152, 242

Cartório, defined, xiii, 166-69, 225-26

Cattle: on *várzea*, colonial, 64; state support for ranching, 81; environmental effects of, 89, 91-94

Caymans, 74

CEPLAC, 134, 136

CFP, xi, 169

CIBRAZEM, xi, 131-34; limits EMATER effectiveness, 133; costs of inefficiency passed to farmer, 169-70; corruption in, 181, 193, 195-96; and cooperatives, 210

Coevolution, 21, 28, 74

Colonists, 10; costs of programs to, 106; settlement patterns, 188

Colonization programs: to abate pressures for land reform, 101, 107, 128; Transamazon, 111, 155-56; budget reductions, 112-15

Conflict: violent, over land, 90-91, 96-97, 121-22

Convênio, xiii

Cooperatives, 5-7; ideology of, 201-2

Corruption, 180-98; in cooperatives, 206-8

Credit: in rural development programs, 125, 139, 160-61, 214-15; costs of, 155, 164-66; concentration of benefits, 173, 174

Crops: plantation, transfer from extractive mode, 25-26; perennial, 166, 174

Dams, 88

Decreto-lei 1.164, 109, 150, 162

Deforestation, 92, 93, 100nn1-3

de Janvry, A., 21, 32, 33, 39, 44-46, 53, 101

Denevan, W., 18n1, 58, 92, 250

Dependency perspective, 244; as critique of modernization, 20, 38-39; dependent development, 52

Depopulation: of indigenous groups, 62-63, 77; of peasant communities, 91-92

277

Note on the Author

Stephen G. Bunker is a member of the department of sociology at the University of Illinois at Urbana-Champaign. He attended Harvard University (B.A.) and Duke University (M.A. and Ph.D.). He has previously taught at the Universidade Federal do Pará (Brazil) and at the Universidad del Valle (Guatemala), and he has been a research associate at the Makerere Institute of Social Research (Uganda). His publications include articles in the *American Journal of Sociology*, the *British Journal of Sociology*, *Studies in Comparative International Development*, *Environment*, *Latin American Perspectives*, *Latin American Research Review*, and *American Ethnologist*.